PHASES OF CAPITALIST DEVELOPMENT

ANGUS MADDISON

Oxford   New York

OXFORD UNIVERSITY PRESS

1982

Oxford University Press, Walton Street, Oxford OX2 6DP

London Glasgow New York Toronto
Delhi Bombay Calcutta Madras Karachi
Kuala Lumpur Singapore Hong Kong Tokyo
Nairobi Dar es Salaam Cape Town
Melbourne Auckland
and associates in
Beirut Berlin Ibadan Mexico City Nicosia

Published in the United States by
Oxford University Press, New York

British Library Cataloguing in Publication Data

Maddison, Angus
Phases of capitalist development.
1. Capitalism—History
I. Title
330.12' 2' 09 HB501
ISBN 0-19-828450-0
ISBN 0-19-828451-9 Pbk

Library of Congress Cataloging in Publication Data

Maddison, Angus
Phases of capitalist development.
Includes bibliographical references and index.
1. Economic history. 2. Business cycles–
History. 3. Economic policy–History. 4. Capitalism–
History. I. Title
HC51. M26 330.9172' 2 82.3558
ISBN 0.19-828450-0 AACR2
ISBN 0-19-828451-9 (pbk.)

Set by DMB (Typesetting) Oxford
and printed in Hong Kong

ACKNOWLEDGEMENTS

I am grateful for critical comments on various drafts from Moses Abramovitz, J. W. Drukker, Roland Granier, Jan Kregel, Simon Kuipers, Sir Arthur Lewis, John Martin, Jan Pen, J. C. Riley, C. G. M. Sterks, A. Thirlwall, Jan de Vries, and Robert Wuliger.

I have had considerable help in checking estimates from statisticians in many countries as well as from those in international organizations. I am particularly grateful to Derek Blades, John Evans, Leila Pathirane, Constantin Poulakis, and Rita Varley of OECD, to Jerry Mark and Constance Sorrentino of the US Bureau of Labor Statistics, to Tom Griffin of the CSO in London, and to Anton Kausel and Riita Hjerppe for help with Austrian and Finnish estimates.

Some of the ideas developed here have already been published in an earlier form. I am grateful to Luigi Ceriani, who published four articles in the *Banca Nazionale del Lavoro Quarterly Review* in September 1972, June 1977, March 1979, and September 1980. Other parts of the argument have previously appeared in *Kyklos*, 1979; in W. Beckerman (ed.), *Slow Growth in Britain*, Clarendon Press, Oxford, 1979, and R. C. O. Matthews (ed.), *Economic Growth and Resources*, Macmillan, London, 1980.

I was fortunate in having the research assistance of Harry van Ooststroom, Dirk Stelder, and Rita Varley in the preparation of the study, and the help of my wife Penny Maddison, who typed the manuscript in all its drafts.

CONTENTS

TABLES

LIST OF GRAPHS

INTRODUCTION

In an earlier study, in 1964, I tried to explain why the advanced capitalist countries had progressed so rapidly in the postwar period.[1] This time, I set out to find the reasons for the sharp deterioration in performance since 1973. The analysis was again historical and comparative; the evidence quantitative and mainly macroeconomic. In fact, it proved difficult to diagnose the latest phase satisfactorily without trying to identify and reinterpret earlier phases as well. I was, therefore, led to survey the capitalist epoch as a whole—i.e., the performance of sixteen countries over the sixteen decades since 1820—and to make rough comparisons of these achievements with those of earlier epochs.

The first chapter presents my interpretation of the dynamic forces in capitalist development, compares them with conditions in preceding epochs, and includes a critical commentary on the theories of Ricardo, Marx, and Schumpeter, who also took a broad view of the capitalist process. Chapter 3 provides more detailed quantitative evidence to back up the diagnosis.

The dichotomy between leader and follower countries is fundamental to an understanding of the nature of technical progress and its diffusion. The underlying economic potential of these countries as a group is very strongly associated with the productivity achievements of the lead country. Chapter 2, therefore, analyses the characteristics of the three successive lead countries since 1700: the Netherlands, the UK and the USA. The USA has been a more dynamic leader than the UK was and has pushed out the technical frontier at a faster pace. Several European countries have now come very close to US productivity levels, and a historical change in the nature of technical leadership seems imminent. With collective leadership, there may well be some acceleration in the pace of technical change in future.

In fact, the average performance of these countries has not been a simple replication of that in the lead countries. Otherwise, there would have been only two phases, with the other countries following a British pace to 1890, and the faster one of the USA thereafter. In effect, there have been four major phases of performance since 1820, because growth has been both hindered and spurred by political events and changes in economic policy. Chapter 4 presents my analysis of these phases, together with the alternative explanation of other authors who have attempted to identify long swings in the tempo of capitalist development. In my explanation of the phase phenomenon, historical accidents—'system shocks'—are important, and the role of policy is also emphasized. I reject the notion of a regular Kondratieff rhythm and Schumpeter's arguments about the causal role of waves or clusters of innovation.

Chapter 5 is a detailed interpretation of the underlying factors determining productivity growth of the lead country and of the rather big fluctuations in the productivity performance of the follower countries.

Chapter 6 illustrates the impact of policy on economic performance. It concentrates on diagnosis rather than prescription, for the optimal policy mix is not simply a technocratic problem. There are inevitable conflicts between social groups and policy objectives, particularly in periods like the 1970s, when key institutions, attitudes, and the balance of economic power were changing.

The present survey is intended both to illuminate current economic issues in advanced capitalist countries and to contribute to their collective economic history. As far as economic history is concerned it makes the following points:

1. It generally rejects interpretations that stress natural limits to growth rather than the circumstances that inhibit innovation. In particular, it attacks the Malthusian approach of Leroy Ladurie and Abel to European performance in the sixteenth and seventeenth centuries.

2. It rejects the Rostow hypothesis that there was a long series of staggered take-offs in the economic development of these countries in the course of the nineteenth century. With the exception of Japan, and possibly Italy, the acceleration of growth after 1820 was quite general in these countries.

3. It advocates greater use of macroeconomic measures of economic performance and cyclical volatility, crude though these may be, rather than the traditional heavy reliance on partial indicators of movements in the industrial sector or in prices.

The appendices provide the quantitative evidence for my own analysis. I have tried wherever possible to provide comparable estimates for the sixteen countries, and have described the procedures and sources in some detail so that they may also serve as a working tool for those who wish to develop alternative measures or periodization. I have tried to use the best and latest sources available in constructing these estimates, which depend very heavily on the work of other scholars, government and international agencies. However, quantitative economic history is still in its bloom of youth, and many of the estimates, particularly for the period before 1870, will inevitably be subject to revision. One of the virtues of the comparative approach is that it both illuminates and provokes. It helps demonstrate where the significant data gaps are, and shows how they were filled in other countries.

1

ECONOMIC EPOCHS AND THEIR INTERPRETATION

THIS study is mainly concerned with the economic performance of the advanced capitalist countries since 1820. In the past 160 years, the total product of the sixteen countries considered here has increased sixty-fold, their population more than four-fold, and their per capita product thirteen-fold. Annual working hours were cut from around 3,000 to less than 1,700, which means that labour productivity increased about twenty-fold. Life expectation doubled, from about thirty-five to over seventy years. I call this the 'capitalist epoch' because its main engine of growth has been the acceleration of technical progress, with capital formation as the major instrument by which it was exploited to increase output.

The nature of capitalist performance and the reasons for its vigour can be more clearly apprehended if we contrast its driving forces with those of proceding epochs.

The rough schema of Table 1.1 divides past economic experience into six historical epochs and shows the major determinants of economic performance in each of these. In this evolutionary sequence the three factors of production (natural resources, labour, and capital) have been augmented by technical progress and education, and the efficiency of resource allocation has been improved through division of labour. From time to time, some countries have increased their income by plundering others, and this beggar-your-neighbour process has been subject to varying degrees of sophistication.

With the exception of Japan, all the advanced industrial countries are European or (like Australia, Canada, and the USA) are off-shoots of Europe, so the present review of economic epochs is confined to European conditions. In the past 1,500 years, European countries have been through four epochs: 'agrarianism' (500-1500), 'advancing agrarianism' (1500-1700), 'merchant capitalism' (1700-1820), and 'capitalism' (1820-1980).

This categorization of epochs is meant to be a rough description of the progressive evolution of the major material forces determining production potential. It is not intended to describe specific

Table 1.1
Determinants of Production Potential in Six Economic Epochs

	Epochs	Output a function of
(1)	Pre-agrarian (hunting, fishing, finding)	(N, L)
(2)	Agrarianism	(N', L', K)
(3)	Ancient imperialism	$(N', L'', K^*) + p$
	Reversion to agrarianism	(N', L', K)
(4)	Advancing agrarianism	(N', L', K')
(5)	Merchant capitalism	$(N', L'', K'')^s + p'$
(6)	Capitalism	$(N'', L''', K''')^s + p''$

N = natural resources
N' = natural resources appropriated and maintained
N'' = natural resources developed and augmented
L = raw labour
L' = labour force with bare modicum of skills, defensively oriented elite unlikely to generate or absorb new technology
L'' = ordinary labour with a modicum of skills plus an efficient bureaucratic military elite
L''' = labour force with formal education and the on-the-job training, scientific-technical and military-bureaucratic elite
K = moderate stock of working capital, investment sufficient to take care of replacement and widening (provision of stock for additional workers)
K^* = as for K, but with greater investment in roads and urban facilities
K' = as for K, with very gradual expansion of fixed capital per head (deepening)
K'' = as for K', except that capital deepening more important
K''' = moderate stock of working capital supplemented by much bigger stock of fixed capital. Investment in all types of capital (replacement, widening, and deepening) is a major vehicle for transmitting technical progress. Technical progress tangible and perceived as compared with K' and K'' where it was present but imperceptible
s = economies of scale and specialization
p = plunder (unrequited levies on products and manpower of colonized areas)
p' = plunder augmented or replaced by monopolistic trade
p'' = residual or negative plunder

forms of property, class relationships, or modes of exploitation which figure so largely in Marxist presentations of growth stages.[1] It is set out in broadly chronological order of the evolution of production potential, but all countries have not moved in steady succession through all these stages. Some have skipped an epoch; there have been cases of relapse; and there has sometimes been coexistence of countries whose economies were operating in different modes.

Finally, it should be noted that by calling the fourth epoch 'advancing agrarianism', it is not implied that it was exclusively rural and concerned only with agriculture, but only that this was predominantly the case.

In terms of characteristic amplitudes, the long-term trends of economic performance in the last four epochs are compared in Table 1.2.

TABLE 1.2

Performance Characteristics of Four Epochs

| | Average annual compound growth rates | | |
	Population	GDP per head	GDP
Agrarianism, 500-1500	0.1	0.0	0.1
Advancing agrarianism, 1500-1700	0.2	0.1	0.3
Merchant capitalism, 1700-1820	0.4	0.2	0.6
Capitalism, 1820-1980	0.9	1.6	2.5

Source: Population 500-1500 from J. C. Russell, 'Population in Europe 500-1500', *Fontana Economic History of Europe*, vol. 1, Collins, London, 1972, p. 36, other epochs from Appendix B below; per capita income 500-1700 by inference as described in text; 1700-1980 from Appendix A below.

ADVANCING AGRARIANISM

After the collapse of the Roman Empire and its communications system, Europe relapsed into agrarianism. For a millenium there was little net progress in population and none in per capita income. Within this generally stagnant situation there were sizeable fluctuations. There were two major declines in population with subsequent recoveries. The first population drop came after the fall of the Empire in a wave of epidemic disease in the sixth and seventh centuries, and the other in the fourteenth century after the bubonic plague epidemic known as the Black Death. There is some evidence that when population fell after these demographic catastrophes, the standard of living rose temporarily because there were several decades during which there was more land available per capita. Hence the demographic and living standard fluctuations were of an inverse character, meaning that the output trend was probably smoother than either of its components.[2]

For 1500-1700 the rate of progress was also very poor by present standards, but clearly better than in the previous millenium. There

TABLE 1.3
Population, 1500-1979

	1500	1700	1820	1979	Coefficient of multiplication, 1820-1979
	('000)	('000)	('000)	('000)	
Australia	0	0	33	14,417	437
Austria	1,420	2,100	3,189	7,506	2
Belgium	1,500	2,000	3,518	9,849	3
Canada	0	15	640	23,691	37
Denmark	600	700	1,097	5,117	5
Finland	150	250	1,169	4,764	4
France	16,400	21,120	30,698	53,478	2
Germany	12,000	15,000	24,905	61,359	2
Italy	10,500	13,300	19,000	56,518	3
Japan	15,800	26,800	28,900	115,880	4
Netherlands	950	1,900	2,344	14,030	6
Norway	300	500	970	4,074	4
Sweden	550	1,260	2,574	8,296	3
Switzerland	800	1,200	1,829	6,348	3
UK	4,400	9,273	20,686	55,952	3
USA	0	251	9,618	220,584	23
Total	65,370	95,669	151,170	661,863	4

Source: Appendix B; 1500-1820 figures for Australia, Canada, and USA exclude indigenous populations.

were no further demographic setbacks on the scale of the Black Death, though the peace of population growth was a meagre crawl in spite of high fertility. Per capita output grew at too slow a pace to be perceptible to contemporaries. Nevertheless Europe's population grew by a third in these two centuries, per capita output may have risen by a quarter, and total output by around two thirds (this implies an average per capita income of around $215 in 1500 and $265 in 1700). Productivity rose less than income per head because the increased output required longer working hours.

The above interpretation of the situation under advanced agrarianism is somewhat more cautious than that of analysts such as Kuznets and Landes, who have deduced that the long run trend of European living standards and productivity was positive from 1500 to 1700, and perhaps for several earlier centuries.[3] But it represents a more dynamic view than that of historians such as Le Roy Ladurie and Abel, who take a grimmer view of performance in this period, because they are disciples of Malthus.

TABLE 1.4

*Gross Domestic Product per head of Population
at 1970 US Prices, 1700-1979*

	1700	1820	1870	1950	1979	Coefficient of multiplication, 1820-1979
	($)	($)	($)	($)	($)	
Australia		(n.a.)	1,393	2,368	4,466	(n.a.)
Austria		400	573	1,140	4,255	11
Belgium		354	925	1,874	4,986	14
Canada		(n.a.)	619	2,401	5,361	(n.a.)
Denmark		363	572	1,922	4,483	12
Finland		(n.a.)	384	1,469	4,287	(n.a.)
France	275[a]	377	627	1,693	4,981	13
Germany		310	535	1,374	4,946	16
Italy		(n.a.)	593	1,085	3,577	(n.a.)
Japan		251	251	585	4,419	18
Netherlands	440	400	831	1,773	4,396	11
Norway		294	489	1,868	4,760	16
Sweden		307	415	2,219	4,908	16
Switzerland		333	786	2,262	4,491	13
UK	288	454	972	2,094	3,981	9
USA		372	764	3,211	6,055	16
Arithmetic average		351	671	1,834	4,647	13

[a] 1701-10.

Source: Appendix A and B. Figures represent US dollars at 1970 prices with exchange rates adjusted for differences in purchasing power of national currencies.

Thomas Malthus (1766-1834) first published his views on factors determining economic performance in 1798. He portrayed the general situation of humanity as one where population pressure put such strains on the ability of natural resources to produce subsistence that equilibrium was attained only by various catastrophes—such as famine, disease, and wars—which brought premature death on a large scale and which he described as 'positive' checks. Later he advocated introduction of 'preventive' checks, such as sexual abstinence, as the only way to avoid such calamities.

Malthus's influence has been strong and persistent, in part because of the forceful rhetoric in which he first couched his simple argument. Thus, while no one would consider his theory as valid for the capitalist epoch, many respectable historians consider his argument applicable to earlier periods. Here is a sample of his style of argument:

The power of population is so superior to the power in the earth to produce subsistence for man, that premature death must in some shape or other visit the human race. The vices of mankind are active and able ministers of depopulation. They are the precursors in the great army of destruction; and often finish the dreadful work themselves. But should they fail in this war of extermination, sickly seasons, epidemics, pestilence, and plague advance in terrific array, and sweep off their thousands and ten thousands. Should success be still incomplete, gigantic inevitable famine stalks in the rear, and with one mighty blow levels the population with the food of the world.[4]

In fact, the situation in 1500-1700 was not as Malthus suggested, even though most economies were operating under a low-income ceiling because of slow technological progress. The population was indeed subject to mini-famines when bad weather occurred, but not to endemic food shortages lasting over periods of many decades or longer, as some of his disciples suggest.

There are several reasons for disagreeing with Malthus, which are worth stating in view of the persistent popularity of his ideas.

1. European fertility in 1500-1700 was not at a biological maximum, but already reflected the operation of preventive checks on a significant scale. Unlike Asian countries, Europeans generally lived in conjugal rather than extended families, and in order to sustain living standards marriage did not take place at puberty but in the mid-twenties. Sexual restraint before marriage was enforced with reasonable success by a priesthood who set an example of celibacy, so that a substantial fraction of the population was celibate. These habits changed later in cases where Europeans emigrated to countries with abundant land, but their existence in pre-capitalist Europe has been firmly established by recent French and British demographic research.[5]

2. 'Average' living standards in 1500-1700 were well above subsistence. In all countries there was a substantial hierarchy of rulers, upper, and middle classes. The size of this group varied between countries for institutional and political reasons. For England in 1688 we have Gregory King's estimates which show average income per head of almost £8 but the poorest quarter of the population (cottagers and paupers) survived on a consumption level only 28 per cent of this.[6]

3. There was still a margin of unused land in western Europe, and it is clear from existing demographic studies that there was migration within Europe. There were much bigger reserves in America, Australia, Siberia, and Africa, which were to offer possibilities for international migration at a later period.

4. The intensity with which land was cultivated could be expanded considerably in most cases by greater per capita labour inputs.[7] In the Middle Ages there were very long off-seasons in which little work was done, and a great deal of land lay fallow. Later generations worked harder, reduced the fallow area and increased land productivity by pushing agricultural practice closer to that in horticulture.

5. Some of the major demographic setbacks cited by Malthusian pundits for this period (e.g. in the seventeenth century) were not due demonstrably to pressure of population on land but to different causes, such as disease or war. A fundamental weakness of the Malthusian argument is that its central thesis is based on the land-labour dichotomy, but death from disease and war are often used as evidence as if these catastrophes were ultimately due to food shortage.

6. Finally, the advancing agrarian economy was not one of complete technological stagnation. Medieval innovations had included windmills, horseshoes, horse harness, heavy ploughs, the haystack, the scythe, marling, fertilization, and the three-field rotation system. These innovations spread rather gradually, but they were certainly helping to increase agricultural output in northern Europe by 1500-1700.[8] Innovation was much slower in this epoch than it is now because the main locus of production was in agriculture, where innovation was too risky for most of the participants and often inhibited by tenure institutions. In urban handicrafts, guild restrictions also limited possibilities for change. Entry to skilled occupations was carefully controlled and technical knowledge was regarded as a mystery not to be shared with those outside the recognized confraternity. But the literate group of the population was no longer confined to a priesthood trained to conform with tradition rather than to innovate. After the introduction of printing around 1500, diffusion of knowledge was speeded up, and written communication took place in the vernacular rather than in Latin.

For these reasons, I conclude that the basically agrarian civilization of Europe in 1500-1700 was an advancing one, in which technical progress and a modicum of capital formation played some role. Nevertheless, there is an alternative Malthusian interpretation of this period in western European history which is advanced by some very respectable historians.

The most distinguished Malthusian interpreter of this period is Emmanuel Le Roy Ladurie, the most versatile and imaginative of the French economic historians of the 'Annales' school. This group practises a form of 'total history' which tries to give a vivid representation of 'material' (everyday) life in the past, and the natural conditions that determined it. It discards the conventional political, diplomatic, military, and dynastic coverage, and generally ignores countries in favour of regional or global characterizations. Their approach is cross-disciplinary, and the analysis is constructed around themes rather than chronology. It tries to produce an evocative picture of the structural unity of an epoch, interpreted in several dimensions. The school makes considerable use of quantitative material and long time series (histoire sérielle). These include estimates of prices and wages as well as the fascinating reconstruction of regional population history made possible by modern French demographic techniques. Ladurie himself has also explored climatic history by using records of wine harvests.

Ladurie strongly emphasizes the long-term stability of the French economy from 1300 to 1700, both in demographic and per capita terms. The immobile trend was interrupted by major catastrophes, but once recovery took place the ceiling on performance reasserted itself. He first put forward the thesis of stagnant income (for 1500-1700) in a regional study of Languedoc peasants (written in 1960) which explicitly espoused a Malthusian interpretation in which there was a tension between the dynamism of population and the rigidity of agricultural production which produced recurrent and prolonged population setbacks.[9] A second major study (in 1977) maintains the same conclusions in a survey drawing on a new generation of regional studies and using better data drawn from ecclesiastical tax records to infer, from the proportion taken in tithes, a rough estimate of total crop production.[10] Ladurie's statistical material on income levels is used illustratively rather than analytically, and virtually always for regions rather than for France as a whole. There is little discussion of the problem of adding up data for regions to get a cohesive picture for France as a whole, there is no discussion of the role of capital formation and technical change, or of the possible dimensions of inter-regional migration.

In both the major Ladurie studies·on long-term stagnation it is clear that disease and war were more important agents of demographic catastrophe than hunger. It emerges in the second study that Ladurie is somewhat embarrassed by the Malthusian label he had earlier used. He has vaguely sketched a general systems theory of demographic controls in men and animals which suggests somewhat unconvincingly that suicide and infanticide were more important means of population control than late marriage before the eighteenth century.[11] He now characterizes his approach differently, with almost no reference to Malthus but to a broader ecosystem and the trauma of war. He has also written at length on microbic migration, which has had devastating effects on population independent of hunger.[12] It is clear that he considers the real ceiling on per capita income growth to be a stagnant technology rather than shortage of land. He now tends to describe his approach as Ricardian rather than Malthusian.

Wilhelm Abel, the German agrarian historian, carries pessimism further than Ladurie, and suggests that real living standards in Germany and England actually fell from the first half of the fourteenth to the first half of the eighteenth century.[13] Abel's analytical framework is 'Malthusian' in the sense used by Ladurie in 1960. His conclusions on the long-term trends in living standards in Germany and England are derived by dividing some very long-term series on what are purportedly representative wages by the prices of wheat or rye. To cap the Malthusian argument and show the inverse relation of real wages to population à la Malthus, he juxtaposes an index of building wages in the South of England with the movement of population in 'central Europe' (England, France, and Germany). It is very odd that he should take an index for a small group of British artisans as representative of European per capita income levels, and his population estimates are also suspect. He shows a decline of 4 million in French population from 1620 to 1740, whereas most other estimators record a similar move in the opposite direction.

At one point it appeared that the Annales school had deviated from the Ladurie to the Abel position on real incomes, when Braudel and Spooner concluded an obscure argument by the assertion that 'from the late fifteenth century until well into the beginning of the eighteenth century, the standard of living in Europe progressively declined'.[14] Since then both Braudel and Spooner have retreated to the Ladurie position.[15]

MERCHANT CAPITALISM

The merchant capitalist epoch was one in which the leading European countries exploited their superior technology in navigation, shipbuilding and armaments to develop international trade through monopolistic trading companies. In the earlier case of Spain, mercantile aims and colonial policy were not merchant capitalist but more akin to those of ancient imperialism. Having squeezed out the plunder, Spain declined. But in the Netherlands, France, and the UK, the overseas empire of the merchant capitalist period had a more beneficial effect on the productive capacity of the domestic economy, because it not only augmented capital resources but helped considerably to enlarge the size of markets.

In the merchant capitalist period there was also an improvement in internal transportation, which helped break down the isolation of the self-sufficient village economies and created the possibility of economies of scale and specialization.

For the UK economy, the merchant capitalist epoch was a necessary launching pad for sparking off an acceleration of technical progress in textiles because it provided a particularly large market area.

The driving forces of the merchant capitalist epoch were brilliantly analysed by Adam Smith in 1776 in his book *The Wealth of Nations*. Smith (1723-90) emphasized the role of capital deepening in economic growth, the opportunities for economies of scale and specialization, and the role that policy could play in accelerating growth. He greatly broadened the significance of the historical approach for growth analysis by using it comparatively. He arrayed countries in an order that corresponds basically with the modern idea of real income per head and built an analytical scheme which gave a rough explanation of why they were thus located. There were some drawbacks in his approach; e.g., he did not really distinguish between the benefits accruing from technical progress and economies of scale, he overstressed natural harmony of interest between nations, and he largely ignored the plunder element in the success of merchant capitalism.

In fact, it is not surprising that Smith gave much less stress to technical progress than to economies of scale. He was contemplating a group of countries whose level of economic performance varied from perhaps $180 average per capita income to $440 using our unit of account. His ordering was roughly as follows (excluding what he calls 'naked savages' in pre-agrarian societies):

Netherlands
England
France
North American colonies
Scotland
China
Bengal (depressed by the East India company's plundering)

Smith was more concerned with policy action that would help push a country nearer to the high-income frontier (located in the Netherlands) available with given technology than he was with the opportunities offered by further progress. He gave greater stress to the opportunities arising from removing economic backwardness than to those from new technology.

Hence he treats capital mainly as a stock which can be increased in per capita terms to make it possible to use more complex methods of production rather than new techniques. In fact, in his definition, capital consisited of a fund to meet the cost of workers' subsistence, as well as provision of tools and equipment. The former element of circulating capital was bigger than the element of fixed capital. It is interesting that his most famous example of the potential gain from exploiting more complex processes relates to the pinmaking industry, which was by no means a new one. He was not of course unaware of technical change, but seemed to regard it as a matter of improvement engineering rather than creation of new products or inventing new processes.

In the course of breaking out from the crawling pace of advancing technology in the agrarian epoch, some of the most significant innovations involved navigation techniques and shipbuilding, and thus technical change itself was biased in favour of better communication and breaking down the isolation of the agrarian world.

In discussing policy, Smith stressed the natural harmony of interests of all parties from allocation of resources in free markets, and like his French contemporaries, the Physiocrats, he advocated the case for *laissez-faire* policies of non-intervention. In this he was a very successful advocate because his argument gradually won over British official opinion, and British influence diffused his policy message world-wide.

It should be added that Smith had in mind a rough dichotomy between advanced merchant capitalist countries like England and France, where policy changes were regarded as a completely effective way of moving from where they were on the income scale to the frontier position of the Dutch, and the situation in China and India. In the latter group, there were of course more institutional constraints on the adoption of sensible policies, but Smith also had in mind a more moderate view of the Malthus position; i.e., they were, because of more ancient settlement, in a situation where there was greater pressure on natural resources, and less scope for saving. Similarly, he considered North America to be in a different situation, where much faster output growth was feasible because of the existence of empty land, but where conditions for per capita growth performance were not necessarily better than in the advanced nations of Europe.

There is clearly some element of arbitrariness in dating the merchant capitalist epoch from 1700. The Dutch republic (which was the paradigm of merchant capitalism) had very substantial growth in the seventeenth century, but that century was fairly stagnant for several big countries as trade and shipping activity shifted from the Mediterranean to north-west Europe.[16]

CAPITALISM

The main difference between the capitalist and the merchant capitalist epoch is the enormous acceleration in the pace of technical progress, which has required a major increase in the rate of fixed capital formation. The growth of capital stock per worker has greatly increased, and all types of capital (replacement, widening, and deepening) have been rendered more productive because new vintages embody a sustained and substantial growth in technical knowledge. A significant difference from merchant capitalism is that the economic performance of the leading capitalist countries has not generally depended on beggar-your-neighbour exploitation (plunder) of other countries. This does not mean that such practices disappeared, but they were much less significant, except in the case of the UK when its capitalist growth started. Another important characteristic of the capitalist epoch has been the steadily increasing general level of education of the labour force. In 1820 the average member of the labour force probably had less than two years' education; by 1980 the average had risen to ten years. This has been necessary to adapt successfully to rapid economic change, and has also been of help in developing the stock of economically useful knowledge. Economies of scale and specialization have continued to be a source of productivity growth in the capitalist epoch, but their relative contribution to economic progress has been smaller than in the merchant capitalist period when technical progress was so much slower.

The above characterization of the capitalist epoch is an assertion that I will attempt to substantiate by the argument and evidence in subsequent chapters. It is, of course, impossible to identify the precise role of particular causes of growth in a survey of sixteen countries over 160 years. The output functions in Table 1.1 are intended to be indicative rather than operational, and the most basic question about capitalist development (what determines the rate of technical progress?) still remains a mystery.

In order to clarify the present characterization of the driving forces in capitalist development, it may be helpful to comment on the approach adopted by the three major economists who advanced their own schema of the capitalist production process: Ricardo (1772-1823), Marx (1818-83), and Schumpeter (1883-1950).

Marx and Schumpeter both had an extremely ambitious approach to capitalist development, involving a socio-political theory, historical and comparative perspective, and vast erudition in the history of economic thought.[17] Ricardo, by contrast, had a minimum of formal education, a narrower perspective, and a greater taste for abstract ideas. Nevertheless, he applied his luminous mind to production of a rigorous schema, which has had an enormous influence on subsequent analysis. He was also more concerned with pragmatic policy questions than Marx and Schumpeter.

Ricardo

Ricardo recognized the augmentation in productive power that machinery had brought and that held out perspectives of substantial economic growth in the non-agricultural sector. However, being strongly influenced by Malthus, he judged that productivity growth was likely to be much slower in agriculture than in industry. This was likely to be the case because the supply of land was fixed, population was growing, and the increased demand for food would lead to use of less fertile land. As population grew the relative price of food would therefore rise, and this would impact unfavourably on industrial costs. Ricardo assumed that wages tend to be at a subsistence level, and thus, when food prices rise, wages must also rise if workers are to survive. As wages rose, industrial profits were squeezed, and this fall in profits would eventually bring economic expansion to a halt. The obverse of the profit squeeze was the rise in the share of landlords' rents. Thus there was a clash of interests between the new class of industrialists and the landlords. As a temporary relief for this dilemma, Ricardo advocated reduction of import duties on imported food, which would keep wages down and postpone the profit squeeze.

Ricardo's argument is advanced in abstract arithmetic terms without reference to history or institutions.[18] Thus it is difficult to categorize his judgement of capitalist potential very clearly. However, it was certainly more optimistic than that of the young Malthus, and considerably less dynamic than that of Marx and Schumpeter, neither of whom had a two-sector model with scarcity of natural resources as a drag. Some of Ricardo's followers (e.g. J. S. Mill) assumed that his schema implied the advent of economic stagnation within the forseeable future, and that it would be a stagnation at income levels for workers, rather near to subsistence. This turned out to be a poor judgement on subsequent capitalist performance, though it can hardly be attributed to Ricardo himself. The other impact of Ricardo has been longer-term. He stimulated the use of two-sector models and theories that expect growth to come to a halt because of natural limits; e.g., Jevons's theory about coal shortage, the Club of Rome concern with natural limits and ecology, and contemporary pessimism about oil shortage. Ricardian thinking about the industrial sector as the more or less exclusive locus of rapid technical change has also had a tremendous influence on subsequent thought, e.g., the notion of an 'industrial' rather than a scientific-technical revolution, the intense concern of many economists with terms of trade between agriculture and industry, or with the dangers of de-industrialization.

There are many contradictions and paradoxes in the analysis of Marx and Schumpeter, and the following is restricted to what Schumpeter called their 'vision', unencumbered by detail.

Marx

Marx recognized, more clearly than most of his contemporaries, the enormous productive power of capitalism as compared with that of preceding epochs. He scorned Malthus, and rejected Ricardo's pessimism about the drag to progress associated with the pressure of population on resources. He stressed the enormous growth of productive power represented by the transition from manufacture to machinofacture, and the importance of accelerated accumulation of fixed capital as the mainspring of economic progress. He expected a continued expansion of trade and concentration of production into bigger units, both of which would provide continuing economies of scale. He clearly considered that European plunder and monopolistic trading exploitation of the rest of the world had been a necessary feature of merchant capitalism, but he did not make any substantial claim (as some subsequent Marxists have done) that it was a necessary feature of the capitalist epoch.

Marx speculated on the possibility that the momentum of capitalist productive performance might weaken because maintenance of productivity growth might be increasingly inhibited by the difficulty of sustaining technical progress. Sustained progress would require an increased ratio of fixed capital to output, and this might reduce the rate of profit in the long run. However, he put forward several reasons for thinking that this possibility might be offset by countervailing forces. Hence, though Marx expected capitalism's ultimate collapse in favour of socialism, his breakdown hypothesis is basically socio-political rather than economic. He expected increasing polarization of the interests of workers and capitalists, and the breakdown was expected as a result of the victory of the workers' interest, which would then abolish private property as a means of production. However, Marx did not present socialism as a stationary state, so under socialism, as with capitalism, Marx presumably would have expected the mainsprings of growth to be technical progress and capital accumulation. The main difference between capitalism and socialism would be a more equal income distribution, the elimination of unemployment, and a termination of business cycles.

Marx considered a 'reserve army' of unemployed to be a major prerequisite of capitalist economies. It was necessary to keep wages low relative to profits. Marx did not have a subsistence theory of wages, but a bargaining theory. When demand was high, as in business booms, the bargaining position of labour would improve and profits would be squeezed. In a depression the bargaining position of labour would weaken and the profit outlook would improve. He considered these oscillations in the labour market situation to be the major cause of cyclical fluctuations under capitalism, and he took a ten-year cycle to be typical.[19]

As Marx was not interested in the survival of the capitalist system, he was not really concerned with economic policy, except in so far as the labour movement was concerned. There, his argument was concentrated on measures to limit the length of the working day, and to strengthen trade union bargaining power. His analysis was also largely confined to the situation in the leading capitalist country of his day—the UK—and he did not consider the policy problems of other western countries in catching up with the lead country (as Friedrich List did). In so far as Marx was concerned with other countries, it was mainly with poor countries which were victims of western imperialism in the merchant capitalist era.

Schumpeter

Schumpeter gave greater stress to the role of technical progress and less to the role of capital accumulation than Marx did. He rejected completely the Malthus-Ricardo type constraints arising from pressure of population on fixed natural resources.[20] He also rejected the view that there was any necessary element of imperialist exploitation in capitalist development.[21]

Schumpeter made a sharp distinction between the way an economy would operate as a 'circular flow' if technology were static, and the way it operates in the real world of 'economic development' where 'technique and productive organization' are changing. In a capitalist economy, 'economic life changes its own data by fits and starts'; the system 'so displaces its equilibrium point that the new one cannot be reached from the old one by infinitesimal steps. Add successively as many mail coaches as you please, you will never get a railway thereby.'

Schumpeter stresses not the role of capital stock as the incarnation of technical progress, but rather the central role of the entrepreneur: 'Capital is nothing but the lever by which the entrepreneur subjects to his control the concrete goods which he needs, nothing but a means of diverting the factors of production to new uses, or of dictating a new direction to production.'[22] He distinguishes sharply between the entrepreneurial role of innovation and that of owning or managing assets. Only the entrepreneur creates profits as distinguished from 'interest', which is the return on ownership. Interest comes in a steady stream, but profits are 'transitory and ever-changing' because the entrepreneur can capture the benefits of innovation only temporarily. Once the viability of the innovation is demonstrated, it will be copied by imitators. It will cease to be an innovation and, having lost its freshness, will drop back into the domain of the circular flow.

Schumpeter regards innovation as 'difficult and only accessible to people with certain qualities'; 'only a few people have these qualities of leadership'. Hence innovation comes in jerks or 'swarms', discontinuously in time. The economy thus progresses through a series of cycles. One round of innovations gathers momentum as the innovator attracts imitators; then there is stagnation, which is eventually broken by some new entrepreneur. Thus the entrepreneur is the hero of economic development, and his heroism is all the more legitimate because in each wave new men emerge, as 'the function of the entrepreneur itself cannot be inherited' (p. 79).

Schumpeter described the nature of economic development as the 'carrying out of new combinations', which he defined rather widely as follows (in fact, only the first two of these represents what is conventionally included in the notion of technical progress):

1. introduction of new goods;
2. introduction of new methods of production;
3. opening a new market;
4. conquest of a new supply of raw materials;
5. new organization of an industry.

Schumpeter's provocative approach was a major break with the academic tradition in economics, which had ignored Marx and not taken much interest in growth problems for several decades. He put technical change at the centre stage of capitalist development, and in his discussion of the temporary character of innovation profit, brought out clearly the non-appropriability of knowledge which is the major reason it is so difficult to capture its role in a production function. One aspect of his argument that is difficult to accept is the notion that entrepreneurship is so scarce a factor of production.

His own later argument, that innovation can be institutionalized in large firms, itself contradicts the notion. If the entrepreneur is disenthroned in Schumpeter's schema, then we must fall back on capital as the vehicle for technical change.

Like Marx, Schumpeter was not interested in policy to promote growth in the way in which Adam Smith was, nor did he discuss problems of relative backwardness within the process of capitalist development. Because Smith was so heavily oriented to policy, his unit of analysis was the performance of particular nations. Marx and Schumpeter in their main theoretical work argue in more general terms, so their reference unit is not so clearly national, but in fact they were analysing the capitalist process in the lead country. One reason for the absence of policy discussion is that both Marx and Schumpeter expected the capitalist system to collapse for different reasons. However, it is a little odd that Schumpeter did not discuss patents, R and D, and invention, which must move one step ahead of the entrepreneurial act. Perhaps he thought that innovation normally occurs well within the frontier of potentially exploitable knowledge.

Other Insights into the Development Process

Apart from Marx and Schumpeter, the literature on economic growth for most of the nineteenth and early twentieth centuries is rather thin. One of the problems of earlier analysts of capitalist development is that they had to work without the benefit of the modern statistical revolution, which owes so much to the intellectual efforts of Simon Kuznets who developed the analytic framework of national accounts, and encouraged scholars in other countries to produce historical estimates of the major magnitudes. We are now, therefore, much better placed to see when the critical changes in the magnitude of economic growth took place than were earlier writers, using partial indicators such as industrial production or prices, or simply relying on imaginative hypothesis or metaphor. Thanks to pioneers like Colin Clark and Simon Kuznets, we now have an adequate conceptual basis for measuring aggregate economic activity in a national accounting framework. There are official GDP estimates for all our countries since 1950, and reasonably authoritative historical estimates back into the nineteenth century for many of them. The international comparability of these estimates has been enhanced not only by the adoption of common definitions but by extensive empirical work to facilitate comparison of levels of performance by adjustment for differences in the purchasing power of currencies. Here we owe a great deal to the work of Milton Gilbert and Irving Kravis.

There has been a resurgence of interest in economic growth and development in the postwar period, in relation to the problems both of advanced capitalist countries and of the poorer 'developing' countries.

The literature on the advanced countries has been largely technocratic, concerned with models and production functions, without the socio-historic sweep of the Smith-Marx-Schumpeter tradition. Within this literature there have been two important new ideas which have added to the possibility of analysing capitalist development. These are the notions of technical progress being 'embodied' in the capital stock, and of education as a form of 'human capital' embodied in the labour force.

The first of these ideas was presented in its most elaborate form by Salter.[24] He takes capital to be the major vehicle of economic growth because it embodies technical progress. This view led him to define the capital stock as an accumulation of successive 'vintages' of capital goods, which augment the productive power of investment year by year (whether it be for replacement, widening, or deepening) because of the progress of technique. He makes a distinction between 'best practice' productivity and average productivity, which is extremely helpful in identifying the nature of technological leadership, the reasons why other countries lag behind the productivity leader, and why follower countries can achieve faster growth than the leader. Salter made a sharp distinction between the contribution to growth of economies of scale and those of technical progress, the former being much less important than the latter. When Salter 'explains' economic growth performance, he does it in terms of labour productivity rather than of total factor productivity, as some later analysts in this tradition have done. My own approach to explaining growth has been strongly influenced by Salter, as is clear in Chapters 3 and 5 below.

Another significant development in this literature was the dramatization of the possible significance of education in economic growth by the introduction by Schultz of the concept of 'human capital'.[25] This idea had been adumbrated by Adam Smith, but neglected by Ricardo, Marx, and Schumpeter, who tended to treat all labour as homogeneous. However, the specific identification of the role of education in economic performance is very difficult; and some of the early enthusiasm of human capital pundits who explained wage differentials largely in terms of education, and sought to use the theory to give direct guidelines in educational policy, has met various kinds of scepticism and challenge from authors who think that differences in intelligence, social origin, luck, or credentials have a bigger influence on earnings than has the contribution of education to productivity. In this study we can do no more than acknowledge this factor as one that has obviously facilitated economic growth, but whose precise role cannot be identified, probably because a shortage of educated people has never been a serious drag on growth in advanced capitalist countries.[26]

Denison is the most ambitious and successful of the modern analysts who have used production functions to throw light on the relative importance of factors contributing to growth.[27] He does this by giving weights to the items that figure in our Table 1.1, which he derives from the share that each factor has in national product as measured in the national accounts. For each factor, e.g., land, labour, capital, he used indicators similar to those in our Appendices, except that he disaggregates more. He adjusts labour input for differences in age, sex, and education (*à la* Schultz), but he does not adjust capital stock (*à la* Salter). He makes allowance for gains owing to economies of scale, sectoral shifts in production structure, international specialization, and disembodied technical progress. He ends up with a measure of 'total factor productivity' and an unexplained residual.

All quantitative analysts of economic growth are greatly indebted to Denison, who has shown great ingenuity and sophistication in providing indications of the potential order of magnitude of particular influences on growth, and has demonstrated that respect for national accounting and its logic does not preclude intelligent guesswork. The rigour of his analysis, the meticulous detail of his research and his analytical mastery have done a great deal to spark off further useful work in this field.

Nevertheless, there are some major problems with Denison's method, which understates the weight of capital in the production process. He gives zero weight to government-owned capital, as no return is attributed to such capital in the national accounts. This means that capital invested in roads, schools, etc., is ignored because governments do not generally charge for use of such facilities. He also excludes depreciation from his capital weights. The third reason is more fundamental. As Schumpeter indicated so clearly, the rewards of technical progress can be appropriated only on a temporary basis in entrepreneur's profits, so that profits understate the role of capital in growth. The Denison approach also handles technical progress inadequately, because it is regarded as a separate contribution to growth, not embodied in capital. The Salter technique offers more promise in the long run if better measures of scrapping rates can be obtained which would throw more light on the actual rate of technical progress. Salter also makes the dichotomy between leader and follower countries clearer than Denison does.

I have tried to show how Denison understates the role of capital in growth, even within the limits of his own methodology, in a replication of his measures for nine countries for 1950-62. The average growth rate of GDP in these countries was 4.29 percentage points a year. Denison explained 0.87 points of this growth by capital inputs, 0.76 by augmented labour input, and the 2.66 points by total factor productivity. I found a growth rate of 4.39, with capital inputs 'explaining' 2.14 percentage points, augmented labour inputs 0.83 percentage points, and the rest 1.42 points.[28] I have not, therefore, used a total factor productivity approach in this study, though its devotees have some of the raw material to construct a rough version of such measures in the statistical appendices.[29]

Another major stream of postwar thought that is relevant to our interests is 'development economics', which deals with the growth problems of poor countries. This body of literature is both explanatory and prescriptive. It tries to explain why the poor countries are economically backward, and it sets out a number of alternative strategies for catching up with the developed world.

Four main types of explanation for backwardness are usually advanced: (1) the initial institutional setting of many of these countries was or is less favourable to capitalist development than those of western Europe and its offshoots; (2) various kinds of plunder and colonialism have retarded development; (3) in some developing countries (e.g. India and China) the pressure of population on natural resources was greater than in western Europe because the process of civilized human settlement was more ancient; (4) demographic growth in poor countries in the postwar period has been much greater than was ever the case in the advanced capitalist countries, and this has diverted savings into capital-widening rather than capital-deepening.

The prescriptive part of the 'development' literature is enormous, and is designed to cater to all political tastes and to apply to 160 countries with very different income levels and degrees of economic sophistication. As this study is concerned with advanced capitalist nations rather than with poor ones, the relevance of this literature is limited. The per capita income range of our sixteen advanced countries is now quite narrow, with the worst-off having an income level only 40 per cent below that of the lead country—the USA. Most 'developing' countries fall well outside this range, and the poorest of them had an income only a fortieth of that in the USA in 1978.[30] However, the income range within the advanced group has not always been so narrow, and even within the present dispersion there are important problems of relative backwardness. Hence, the following analysis also makes a sharp distinction between the growth policy problems of the lead country of the capitalist group and those of 'follower' countries.

The Role of Policy and Circumstance

Economic performance is often portrayed as an autonomous process, but in fact it is influenced by institutions and policy to a much greater degree than Marx and Schumpeter ever admitted. Marx obviously felt that some institutional changes in property relations were necessary to launch the capitalist process, but that thereafter government policy played no directly sustaining economic role in his schema. Schumpeter expected capitalism to collapse in part because of perverse policy (anti-trust, etc.), but generally considered government policy to be impotent. Adam Smith discussed policy and institutions in detail, but was mainly concerned with getting the institutions right and removing perverse policies, so that the economy could function according to market forces, which would promote a natural harmony of interests. Ricardo discussed monetary and foreign exchange policy, but his main prescriptive message was in favour of tariff reduction on food imports in order to cheapen the cost of labour and postpone the day when diminishing returns in agriculture would set in and grind the growth process to a halt by squeezing profits. He expected innovation to produce recurrent bouts of technological unemployment, but he rejected the notion that the level of aggregate demand might be inadequate to secure full use of resources.

It was not until after the 1929-33 depression that a problem of macroeconomic demand management was generally recognized to exist. The inevitability of recurrent unemployment during business cycles had previously been accepted even by analysts like William Beveridge, whose early book on unemployment made policy proposals to deal with frictional rather than cyclical problems. Even the catastrophic events of 1929-33 left Schumpeter unmoved. He regarded the depression as a process of creative destruction.

J. M. Keynes (1883-1946) was the economist who did most to dramatize the need for economic management—both domestically, in promoting full employment through fiscal activism, and internationally, by creating institutions to provide for crisis management and a workable international monetary system. Keynes's contribution was important both for his theoretical work, and because of his unique powers of persuasion. As a rich and successful speculator, bureaucrat, negotiator, statesman, patron of the arts, teacher, journalist, lobbyist, and newspaper proprietor, his ideas impregnated academic and government circles in the UK and USA and had a tremendous influence on postwar judgements on the role of policy.

In fact, the central concern of Keynes was not with economic growth or with factors determining potential output in the long term: he was concerned with removing the gap between performance and potential by eliminating involuntary unemployment. It was clear in the interwar period that these gaps can be very large indeed.

Subsequent experience in the period (1945-73) dominated by Keynesian-type policy suggests that successful demand management and international co-operation achieved a great deal more than was expected. Not only was unemployment reduced to residual levels in the European countries and Japan, but the experience of rapid growth and euphoric expectations of growth raised investment rates to unprecedented dimensions. Perhaps these unexpected results were due to the fact that these countries had an unusually large productivity backlog *vis-à-vis* the USA, but it is just possible that maintenance of high demand and high investment may help accelerate the pace of advance of the technical frontier in the capitalist process as a whole. This hypothesis cannot be fully tested until we have a country as technological leader that practices such a policy. In the postwar period, the US economy has not been run at high steam as have those of European countries. It has had levels of unemployment equal to the long-term norm (4.7 per cent for 1950-73, compared with 4.8 for 1920-9 and 4.7 for 1900-13); its investment rate has been lower than historical maxima; and its productivity growth has not accelerated.

In the 1970s there were some major changes in the problems facing economic policy. The international monetary system set up after the war collapsed rather messily between 1971 and 1973; the OPEC countries used their bargaining power to force up the price of energy to an extent that caused major problems of inflation, balance of payments, and structural adjustment; and a variety of other forces contributed to produce rates of inflation hitherto unknown in peacetime. This led governments to change their policy objectives. The full employment goal was dropped, and deflationary policies were pursued in an attempt to dampen inflation and bolster the balance of payments. The payments objective was in fact over-fulfilled. The balance of payments and international reserve position of some of the advanced capitalist countries was remarkably strong in view of the OPEC challenge. Several countries also brought the rate of price increase back to the 'tolerable' levels of the 1950-73 period. But in most cases, the deflationary policies were not carried far enough to break inflationary expectations, partly because of the strong commitment to provide income support to the unemployed and to dole out subsidies to firms that would otherwise go out of business. The alternative way of dealing with inflation through incomes policies was not successful because of disharmony of interest between the parties concerned. Thus the advanced capitalist countries have had to cohabit with a rate of inflation that brings considerable discomfort in spite of the big sacrifices of employment and output that have been made. The danger of running these economies below their potential is that it will weaken investment, slow down technical progress, and tempt some countries into the kind of beggar-your-neighbour remedies which cut down international trade in the 1930s. The trade-offs have hence been a good deal less comfortable than they were in the 1950s and 1960s, but the policy mix of the 1970s produced an uneasy stalemate with few rewards for the sacrifices made.

Finally, one must take adequate note of the role of non-economic events on the economic performance of capitalist countries. Economists generally devise more or less self-contained systems of explain economic development and do not like to give 'exogenous' events a major role. Some historians, by contrast, describe economic development as a chain of *ad hoc* events happening more or less by accident. Schumpeter probably came closest to building a schema in which unexplained events play a major role, but he postulated a rhythm in these events. The present approach is somewhat eclectic, in that it offers a schema (on the lines of Table 1.1) to explain why capitalist performance is superior to that of earlier economic epochs; but the major changes in the rhythm of development within the capitalist epoch are explained largely in terms of exogenous shocks and variations in the effectiveness of economic policy in coping with new circumstances, new social pressures, or new balances of international power. This is clear in Chapter 4 below, which rejects the idea of a general schema explaining variations in the pace of development within the capitalist epoch.

2

CHANGES IN ECONOMIC LEADERSHIP, 1700-1980

IN analysing capitalist development, it is important to distinguish between the growth potential of the 'lead' country, which operates nearest to the technical frontier, and that of 'follower' countries, which have a lower level of productivity. Since 1700 there have been only three lead countries. The Netherlands had top productivity performance until the 1780s, when the UK took over. The British lead lasted till around 1890, and the USA has been the lead country since then.[1] Leadership is defined here in terms of productivity (GDP per man-hour; see Graph 2.1 and Table 2.1).

It is useful to see why these countries attained their lead position, why the first two lost it, and whether the USA is now about to lose it. This should help to illuminate which factors are important in growth, and what the underlying growth potential is for the advanced capitalist group as a whole. However, the forces animating growth in the lead countries are more mysterious and autonomous than in follower countries, whose growth path can be more easily influenced by policies to mimic the achievements of the leader and exploit the opportunities of relative backwardness.

THE DUTCH CASE

The Dutch republic was the lead country for most of the eighteenth century. In 1700 its income per head was around 50 per cent higher than that in the nearest rival, the UK, and its economic structure was much more advanced. Only 40 per cent of the Dutch labour force was in agriculture as compared with 60 per cent in the UK (Table 2.2). The percentage of the population in urban areas was higher than in the UK. Its international trade was as big as that of the UK although its population was only a fifth as large.

Dutch agriculture was highly specialized, with exports of dairy products, large imports of live cattle from Denmark, and a quarter of its grain needs supplied by Poland. Non-food crops such as hemp, flax, bulbs, hops, madder, and tobacco were of considerable significance. The service sector had developed large-scale international

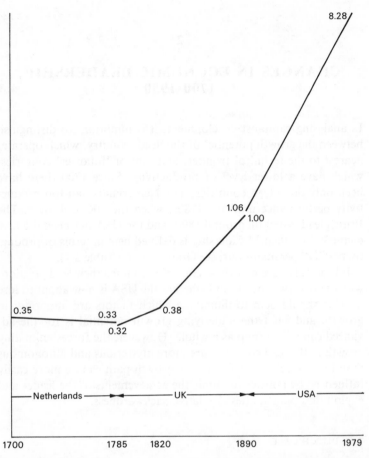

Graph 2.1. *Locus of Productivity Leadership, 1700-1979* (GDP per man-hour in 1970 US$)

transactions in banking, insurance, shipping, and warehousing. There was a diversified industry, with sophisticated processing (bleaching, printing, and dyeing), of English woollens and German linens, as well as a major domestic production of linen. Other significant industries were malting, brewing, distilling, ceramics, soap, bricks, tobacco cutting, tanning, sugar refining, shipbuilding and fisheries. The fuel of Dutch industry was peat, which was available at low cost compared with energy prices in other countries, because it could be transported by canal. Dutch industries therefore tended to be rather energy-intensive.[2]

TABLE 2.1

Approximate Growth Rates of Productivity and Capital Stock
per man-hour In Lead Countries, 1700-1979

Lead Country	Date	Annual average compound growth rate of:	
		GDP per man-hour	Gross fixed non-residential capital stock per man-hour
Netherlands	1700-1785	−0.07	(n.a.)
UK	1785-1820	0.5	0.0
UK	1820-1890	1.4	0.9
USA	1890-1979	2.3	2.4

Source: Appendix C, Tables C10, C11, and C12; Appendix D, Tables D12 and D13.

The investment rate was high by the standards of the epoch, with heavy investment in land reclamation, canals, urban infrastructure, windmills, shipping, and sawmills.[3] There was significant technological innovation in agriculture, shipping design, shipbuilding techniques and saw milling, hydraulic engineering, etc. Dutch universities had a high level of technical achievement, and the country had highly skilled artisans capable of making machinery, optical instruments, and clocks.

Sometimes the Dutch achievement is denigrated, as if the seven provinces were like a small city-state without any significant industry; e.g., E. J. Hobsbawm's remark that the Netherlands was in many respects 'a feudal business economy; a Florence, Antwerp or Augsburg on a semi-national scale. It survived and flourished by cornering the world's supply of certain scarce goods and much of the world's business as a commercial and financial intermediary. Dutch profits did not depend greatly on capitalist manufacture'.[4] There are three things wrong with this conclusion: (1) the Netherlands was not feudal; (2) it had 1.9 million people at a time when Florence had 80,000, Antwerp 60,000, and Augsburg 20,000; and (3) capitalist manufacture was as important a source of profits in 1700 as it is today.[5]

There were three main reasons for Dutch achievement in the merchant capitalist epoch. The first was the 'modernity' of Dutch institutions, which were highly favourable to capitalist enterprise, and the absence of a feudal past in most of the country.[6] Most land was owned by peasant proprietors or tenants with capitalist type leases and money rents. There was relatively little common land to constrain cropping practice or inhibit efficient livestock breeding. There was a rather small nobility of landowners, and virtually no church land after the departure of the Spanish. Political power resided largely in the urban bourgoisie. All land was clearly registered and mortgageable. This meant greater freedom than elsewhere to vary output patterns in agriculture. It also meant that urban activity was relatively free of guild restrictions.

Enterprise was further helped by religious tolerance and immigration of Protestant and Jewish refugees. The unusual character of Dutch society was not a product of the Protestant ethic, but was due to the unique origins of the country. It was a country of recent settlement—on land mostly retrieved from the sea and marshes. Hence Dutch views were deeply impregnated with the possibilities for rational manipulation of the human and material environment and a 'Faustian sense of mastery over man and nature', which characterizes capitalist attitudes to technological change.[7]

The second element that the Dutch turned to advantage was geography. The Netherlands dominated major rivers giving access to markets in the heart of Europe. There was scope for developing ocean ports, and possibilities for internal water transport were exploited to provide regular and frequent services for passengers and freight at lower cost than in any other country at that period.[8] They were short on timber, but turned peat into a major fuel, and used wind power imaginatively to operate drainage works and propel industrial machinery.

The third reason for success was the pursuit of mercantile policies. The seventeenth-century world was still a place with limited markets, in which the success of trading countries depended on beggar-your-neighbour practices. Thus the Netherlands blockaded Antwerp's access to the sea from 1585 to 1795, taking over its entrepôt trade and textile industry. Its successful struggle with Portugal was similarly responsible for Dutch monopolies in trade with large parts of Asia and Latin America. It should be noted that the bulk of Dutch trade (probably three-quarters) was of an entrepôt character, involving transhipment and warehousing in Amsterdam.

The main reason for loss of leadership was the destruction of monopolistic trading privileges in conflicts with France and the UK, who pushed the Dutch to the sidelines. Nevertheless, the economy did not collapse like an ancient imperialism. It simply entered on a long period of decadence throughout the eighteenth century.

Population growth slackened as the economy ceased to attract migrants. The importance of international trade declined. There was some de-urbanization with a growth in the proportion employed in agriculture. There was stagnation in population in the industrialized western Netherlands and substantial growth in the agricultural province of Overijssel. Agricultural output increased, with a fall in imports and a growth in agricultural exports. There was a major decline in production and exports of the leading industries of the seventeenth century. This included textiles (particularly the Leiden woollen industry), fisheries, and shipbuilding.[9] The volume of foreign trade dropped almost 20 per cent from 1700 to 1790 (before the French wars temporarily wrecked it almost completely). During this period UK exports rose almost four-fold in volume and French two and a quarter-fold.

Dutch service industries continued to play an important part in the economy, and there was a very large increase in overseas investment. In 1790 total Dutch foreign investment probably amounted to 800 million guilders at a time when national income was around 250 million. This suggests that foreign investment was over three times the size of domestic product. If the rate of return on foreign investment was around 4 per cent, then foreign income would have been around 30 million guilders, giving a national income about 12 per cent higher than domestic product.[10]

As a result of this extraordinarily high *rentier* income, the income distribution was disequalized, with pauperism and unemployment in the old industrial areas, and an increase in the share of the wealthy.

There seems little doubt that a contributory factor to Dutch decline in the eighteenth century was that the currency was overvalued in the new international trading situation. There were numerous complaints about the high level of Dutch wages in the eighteenth century and the huge efflux of capital speaks for itself. The exchange rate remained unchanged throughout 1700-75.[11]

Other explanations have been advanced for Dutch performance in the eighteenth century. It has been argued that the economy sank into complacent stagnation because of its 'high-level traditionalism'.[12] The argument is not very fully developed but it involves the idea that commerce was favoured at the expense of manufacture, and that the Dutch life-style was so satisfying and Dutch technology so close to the frontier of contemporary best-practice that there was little incentive to innovate. I think it is true that Dutch performance was closer to potential than has been the case for most capitalist economies since then, but I do not see that this should lead to loss of entrepreneurial dynamism. My own hunch is that the primary cause was British and French damage to Dutch foreign markets, together with an over-development of the banking interest which kept the currency overvalued and further weakened export potential.[13]

THE BRITISH CASE

At the end of the seventeenth and for a good part of the eighteenth century, British economic writers like Petty, Child, Temple, and Adam Smith advocated emulation of the Dutch model, in respect of institutions, technology, and the greater division of labour by international specialization.

In fact, most of British progress in the eighteenth century was a replication of the Dutch merchant capitalist model. British progress in this era depended heavily on Dutch technology. This was true in agriculture, canal building, shipping, banking, and international specialization. In agriculture and services, therefore, the UK was a follower not a leader.[14] By 1820, when the capitalist era began, UK income per head and productivity were only barely higher than the Netherlands had achieved in 1700, and its economic structure was similar (see Table 2.2). The crucial difference between the UK in 1820 and the Netherlands in 1700 was the emergence of rapid technical progress in cotton textiles, iron manufacture, and the use of coal which the UK pioneered but which were still a rather small part of the economy.[15]

The reasons for British technological advance in the eighteenth century were rather similar to those of the Dutch in the seventeenth. These were (1) the character of British institutions, which permitted economic change and enterprise in agriculture, industry, and commerce and favoured the development of scientific attitudes;[16] (2) some of the geographic advantages of the Netherlands with regard to sea transport and the same kind of challenge-response mechanism with regard to energy: shortage of timber drove the Dutch to peat and the British to coal; (3) the fact that the UK took over the Dutch leadership as a world trader. It was this latter characteristic of the merchant capitalist situation which probably

TABLE 2.2
Employment Structure in the Lead Countries, 1700-1979[a]
(percentages of total employment)

		Netherlands	UK	USA
		%	%	%
1700	Agriculture	40	60	(n.a.)
	Industry	33	15	(n.a.)
	Services	27	25	(n.a.)
1820	Agriculture	(n.a.)	40	(n.a.)
	Industry	(n.a.)	30	(n.a.)
	Services	(n.a.)	30	(n.a.)
1890	Agriculture	33	16	39
	Industry	31	44	27
	Services	36	40	34
1979	Agriculture	5.9	2.5	3.5
	Industry	31.3	38.5	30.7
	Services	62.9	59.0	65.8

[a] Agriculture includes forestry and fishing; industry includes mining, manufacturing, electricity, gas, water, and construction; services is a residual including all other activity, private and governmental (including military).

Sources: For the Netherlands, 1700 the figures are an average of the proportions given for the eighteenth century for Friesland and Overijssel by Jan de Vries, *The Dutch Rural Economy in the Golden Age, 1500-1700*, Yale, 1974, p. 230; and Slicher van Bath, *Een Samenleving Onder Spanning*, V. Gorcum, Assen, 1957, p. 126, respectively. Both these areas had remarkably high industrialization for such relatively rural provinces. We know that western Holland with its big towns had even bigger proportions in industry and services, see A. M. van der Woude, *Het Noorderwartier*, Wageningen, 1972, though the only occupational information given in the latter source is for 1811 (p. 270). For the UK 1700, I have used Gregory King's occupational listing for 1688 as a guide—see G. E. Barnett, *Two Tracts by Gregory King*, Baltimore, 1936, assuming that, at that period, the English distribution was a reasonable proxy for that of the UK. 1820 Great Britain estimates are available from P. Deane and W. A. Cole, *British Economic Growth 1688-1959*, Cambridge, 1964, p. 143, with Irish structure assumed to be as in 1700. UK 1890 derived from C. H. Feinstein, *National Income, Expenditure and Output of the United Kingdom 1855-1965*, Cambridge, 1972, p. T131. USA 1890 derived from J. W. Kendrick, *Understanding Productivity*, Johns Hopkins, Baltimore, 1977, p. 43. Netherlands 1890 derived from P. Bairoch, *The Working Population and its Structure*, Brussels, 1968, p. 110. 1979 figures from OECD, *Labour Force Statistics*, Paris.

did most to launch the UK into the new textile technology, for it greatly expanded the market in this field.

The rise of British trading monopolies and the dominance of world trade was also the decisive factor in Dutch decline. Thanks to mercantilist policy and a powerful navy, the British destroyed Dutch commercial supremacy in a series of wars at the end of the seventeenth century, and built up their own monopolies and privileges in North America, the West Indies, India, Brazil, and Spanish

America (the latter by virtue of the Methuen and Utrecht treaties). British merchants had long experience as textile traders, both in exporting domestic woollens and importing or reexporting Indian cottons. In 1760, when the wave of innovation in cotton textiles began, the UK was already the world's biggest trading country, and almost two-thirds of its exports were textiles. In textiles, the export market was as big as the internal market.

This emphasis on the mercantilist element in UK access to leadership perhaps understates Britain's technical virtuosity. However, the acceleration of technical progress before the nineteenth century was a gradual process, which covered a much wider area than textiles, which are usually given so much credit as a lead sector. It was the fruit of a cumulative process in western civilization, requiring slow institutional change and scientific advance in a number of countries. The wide diffusion of the process is clearest in agriculture, but even in cotton textiles, UK experience was not unique. Cotton textile output expanded rapidly in France as well as the UK, and the *ancien régime* in France did not prevent that country from experiencing significant economic development in the eighteenth century, albeit less than that in the UK.[17]

The textile innovations of the eighteenth century did not involve great scientific novelty or heavy investment, and many of them were made by artisans who did not have long experience of the industry. Their long-run significance for accelerated economic growth was less than new techniques in the use of coal and steam and those already mentioned in agriculture, and in some respects it is a puzzle why they were not developed earlier. Nevertheless, they were a spectacular demonstration of the potential profits from innovation. Hargreaves's Jenny (1764-7) permitted a sixteen-fold productivity increase in spinning soft weft, and was an immediate success in the home spinning industry. Arkwright's spinning frame (1768) could produce a strong warp and use water power. Crompton's 1779 'mule' could produce both weft and warp. Cartwright's 1787 power loom extended the productivity gains to weaving; and, finally, the American Eli Whitney invented the cotton gin in 1793 which substantially reduced the cost of raw cotton production.

The highly profitable experience with textiles spread new attitudes to innovation throughout the economy. Economies of scale and specialization within guaranteed mercantilist markets became transformed into capitalist growth through the profit incentive.

But the new wave of innovations in steam power, steel, and railways were of a different category from the textile inventions, depending more clearly on application of scientific principles and requiring much bigger investments for their application. They made a decisive change in the use of non-human power in the production process and in the capacity of transporting goods to much bigger markets. The process of innovation was rapidly diffused to these other countries, which were institutionally ripe for capitalist development.

Although British nineteenth-century productivity growth was faster than it had ever been in the Netherlands, we know in retrospect from US experience that the UK was not a particularly dynamic leader. Its productivity growth rate from 1820 to 1890 was fairly steady at 1.4 per cent a year, whereas American productivity averaged 2.3 per cent from 1890 to 1979.

The UK did little by way of government policy to foster either education or technical progress. An appreciable portion of its most ambitious people were siphoned into military bureaucratic posts overseas or were snobbish about entering domestic industry. Nor did it follow policies to stimulate high levels of domestic demand. Policy contributed to the high average level of productivity mainly by opening up the economy to international competition. This had obviously beneficial effects on productivity levels in a sector like agriculture, where British productivity was much higher than in other European countries, which had high protective barriers. It also meant that the UK economic structure was more efficient than in most countries because it concentrated on sectors in which it could perform well. Its service sector was highly developed, particularly the lucrative banking, shipping, and commercial services, which relied heavily on overseas markets and were helped both by the openness of the economy and the UK's position as an imperial power.

The domestic capital stock of the UK grew rather slowly during its period of productivity leadership. From 1785 to 1820 the capital stock per man-hour did not grow at all, and from 1820 to 1890 it grew by 0.9 per cent a year (see Table 2.1). Clearly, the UK was not pushing its investment effort as far as the USA was subsequently to do, and this is perhaps the major reasons why it did not open up the technological frontier as fast. The slow growth in domestic capital stock was not due to a shortage of savings. In the decade before 1914, UK foreign investment was as big as domestic investment, and in 1914 its foreign assets were 1.5 times as high as its GDP.[18] In 1913, income from foreign property meant that GNP was 9.4 per cent higher than GDP. In 1855 the difference was only 2.1 per cent.

At the time it was overtaken by the USA, there were strong signs that the UK was growing at less than its potential because its currency was overvalued. It became a massive exporter of capital, with foreign investment almost as big as that at home, and it experienced net emigration on a bigger scale than other European countries in spite of its higher income per capita. Its share of export markets declined. From 1820 to the mid-1850s, UK export prices had fallen more than import prices, from then onwards the external price movements were reversed. The check to profitability that overvaluation brings also inhibited domestic investment and labour productivity, which grew more slowly in 1890-1913 (about 1.1 per cent a year) than from 1820 to 1890.

The slackening of British productivity growth might have been alleviated either by devaluation or by tariff protection. The cost of the first move would have been considered too damaging to the UK's interests as the manager of the world currency system, and to its banking and commercial interests. It was therefore never openly discussed. The second option did become a political issue, but its pundits were not successful. Even if such action had been taken, the UK would still have lost its leadership to the USA.

The British 'climacteric' at the latter third of the nineteenth century has been extensively discussed. However, the extent of the problem is sometimes exaggerated. The UK lost its productivity lead to the USA in the 1890s, but it kept ahead of European countries until well after the Second World War.[19] It did not lose it for the same reasons as the Dutch did to the British. It was not thrust out of a monopoly position in a limited world market; nor did it suffer an absolute decline in GDP. The UK loss of leadership to the USA was in fact inevitable, given the greater dynamism of the US economy.

From the viewpoint of the rest of the world, the UK policy options were not unfavourable to growth. UK policy diffused the growth process to follower countries by removing restrictions on trade, by investing abroad, and by permitting export of skills and technology, which was not the case in the merchant capitalist era.

THE US CASE

The emergence of the USA as the technical leader was due to the fact that it had huge natural resources of land and minerals, which by 1890 had been opened up by improvements in transport and the creation of a vast internal market whose population was much bigger than that of any of the advanced European countries, and was growing much faster. It attracted immigrants on a very large scale, and enjoyed higher rates of investment. The rate of US domestic investment was in fact more than twice the UK level for the sixty-year period 1890-1950, and the difference in rates of growth of capital stock per worker was even bigger (see Tables 2.1 and 2.3).

At the time when leadership passed to the USA in 1890, American economic structure was less 'mature' than that of the UK. American productivity in 1890 was already appreciably higher than British in both agriculture and industry, and lower in services.[20] In agriculture and mining a good deal of the US advantage was due to its superior natural resource endowment.

The US economy was big enough to breed giant corporations with large research budgets, which helped to institutionalize the innovation process in a way in which the UK had never done. The USA strengthened its fundamental research by building up research departments of major universities, and making special provision in land grant colleges for agricultural research. It later attracted distinguished immigrants to its university faculties, particularly as a result of European wars.

During the period of American technical leadership, the nature of innovation changed because product innovation became more important. During UK leadership the big change was the switch in the production process from manufacture to machinofacture. Generally speaking, there was not much change in the nature of final consumer goods. In the US leadership period, the traditional pattern of consumption has been transformed, and the lead country has had to be active in product as well as process innovation. This has involved developments in the techniques of salesmanship, market research, advertising, consumer credit, etc., which had little counterpart in the UK period, and in which the USA has excelled.

US foreign investment was always rather small relative to domestic investment. In 1976 foreign assets were equal to less than a fifth

TABLE 2.3

*Ratio of Gross Fixed Non-residential Investment to GDP
at Current Market Prices, 1801-1979*

	UK	USA[a]	Japan		UK	USA[a]	Japan
1801-10	4.6			1891-1900	6.7	15.8	8.7
1811-20	5.3			1901-10	6.6	15.7	9.0
1821-30	5.5			1911-20	4.5	12.5	13.8
1831-40	6.4			1921-30	6.4	12.7	13.1
1841-50	8.3			1931-40	6.4	10.1	14.2
1851-60	7.4			1941-50	6.1	9.9	16.3
1861-70	7.5			1951-60	11.7	12.8	20.3
1871-80	8.0	11.5		1961-73	14.7	13.5	27.0
1881-90	6.2	12.2	6.3[b]	1974-9	15.3	13.1	24.1

[a] The first three entries refer to 1870-8, 1879-88, and 1889-1900, respectively; the last refers to 1974-8.

[b] Refers to 1885-90.

Sources: Estimates of non-residential investment for the UK up to 1860 from C. H. Feinstein, 'Capital Formation in Great Britain', in *Cambridge Economic History of Europe*, vol. VII, pt 1, 1978, p. 41 (with upward adjustments to include Ireland of 34.6 per cent for 1801-10, 30.2 per cent for 1811-20, 25.8 per cent for 1821-30, 18.5 per cent for 1831-40, 15.2 per cent for 1841-50 and 10.5 per cent for 1851-60. Ireland was presumed to have the same investment/GDP rates as Great Britain). Feinstein shows investment as a ratio to GDP at constant prices, p. 91. I use the same source (P. Deane) for GDP, but at current prices, including Ireland, and augmenting GDP to include the difference between Feinstein's investment figures and those of Phyllis Deane. In Table 21, p. 77, Feinstein compares these estimates with his earlier estimates in *National Income, Expenditure and Output of the United Kingdom 1855-1965*, Cambridge, 1972, pp. T4, 10, 11, 85, and 86. For 1856-60 his new estimates (with my adjustment) are higher at 6.5 per cent of GDP compared with 3.9 in the earlier study. I have assumed that his earlier estimates for 1901-49 are valid, but that his earlier figures need upward adjustment as follows: 2.06 per cent of GDP for 1861-70, 1.55 per cent for 1871-80, 1.03 per cent for 1881-90, and 0.52 per cent for 1891-1900. 1950 onwards from *National Accounts of OECD Countries* (1950-62 from the 1950-68 edn). USA to 1928 derived from J. W. Kendrick, *Productivity Trends in the United States*, Princeton, 1961, pp. 296-8; S. Kuznets, *Capital in the American Economy*, Princeton, 1961; R. Goldsmith, *A Study of Saving in the United States*, Princeton, 1955, pp. 619 and 623; and *Historical Statistics of the United States*, 1960 edn, pp. 379-80. 1929-70 from *The National Income and Product Accounts of the United States, 1929-1974, Statistical Tables*, US Dept of Commerce, pp. 2-3, 16-17, 124-5, 166-7, 326, 342, 345-6. 1970 onwards from *National Accounts of OECD Countries*. Japan: 1885-1904 GDP and non-residential fixed investment from K. Ohkawa, N. Takamatsu, Y. Yamamoto, *Estimates of Long-term Economic Statistics of Japan since 1868*, vol. I, *National Income*, Toyo Keizai Shinposha, 1974, pp. 186 and 200. 1905-61 K. Ohkawa and H. Rosovsky, *Japanese Economic Growth*, Oxford, 1973, pp. 278-9 and 290-1. 1962 onwards from *National Accounts of OECD Countries*.

of GDP. This is less than a fifteenth of the Dutch 1790 ratio or a seventh of that of the UK in 1914.[21]

The relative standing of the USA as a lead country was greatly strengthened during the First and Second World Wars. Both of these stimulated demand in the US economy and did almost no damage to American capital assets. Both events were major catastrophes for European countries, and in the Second World War Japan suffered as well. They involved not only physical damage to capital stock and manpower, but a narrowing of the scope for economies of scale through international trade. Thus the leader-follower gap among the advanced capitalist countries was swollen well beyond what it would have been in peacetime circumstances.

Normally the change of leadership from a slow UK to a more dynamic USA should have brought an appreciable acceleration of productivity growth within the advanced capitalist world. In fact, the average productivity growth rate did accelerate slightly in 1913-50 in spite of two wars. Without them, the acceleration would probably have been much greater.

Since the Second World War the European countries and Japan have greatly reduced the productivity gap between themselves and the USA. Since 1973, US productivity growth has decelerated rather sharply. There has been some slowdown in other countries, too, but less dramatically than in the USA. Chapter 5 below examines the possible causes of this slowdown in some detail, but we should note here that the gap in productivity between the USA and some of the European countries—Belgium, France, Germany, and the Netherlands—is now very small, and that if 1973-9 trends were to continue to 1985, all these countries would by then have over-taken the USA.

It is clear that the original reasons for US leadership have now largely disappeared outside agriculture. The USA is no longer so outstandingly advantaged in terms of natural resources, as its minerals no longer have their pristine richness, and innovations in bulk transportation technology have given European countries and Japan access to even richer resources than in the USA. The size of the US internal market is no longer such a unique asset, given the remarkable reduction of international trade barriers which has occurred in the postwar period. US population growth is no longer so much faster than in other countries.

Another possible reason for the waning of the US leadership position is the weakening research effort. Recorded research and development spending in the USA rose from 0.2 per cent of GDP in 1921 to a peak of 3 per cent in the mid-1960s. It declined to 2.3 per cent in 1975.[22] These figures probably exaggerate the rise and decline of the economically useful research effort because the 1921-69 rise includes a phase in which non-institutionalized effort was being institutionalized, and a build-up of government research on military and space technology with limited economic applicability, which was phased down in the 1970s.

The most fundamental reason for the erosion of US productivity leadership is that in the postwar period the European countries and Japan have run their economies at a much higher pressure of demand than ever before; unemployment has been at very low levels; and this induced very high rates of investment. The US economy has not been run at such high steam. Its business cycle experience and unemployment levels have been rather close to those in normal years in the past. The US level of investment has not been particularly high by its own historical standards.

Hence the most likely scenario for technical leadership is that it will pass from the US to a collective grouping including the most successful European countries as well as the USA. Japan may well join this collective leadership before the end of the century, and in certain sectors such as steel and automobile manufacture it has already done so.

In the long run, most interpreters of capitalist potential would expect the curve in Graph 2.1 to flatten out into an S-shape, because humanity will ultimately have pushed its economically useful knowledge close to the Promethean limits.[23] But with a collective technological leadership which includes countries which have shown such dynamism for thirty years, the technical frontier may for a time be pushed out faster than in the past; i.e., the next segment of the productivity frontier (Graph 2.1) may have a steeper slope than in the past if these countries maintain high investment rates, though one would not expect the new leaders to maintain anything like their productivity growth performance of 1950-73.

LONG-TERM CHARACTERISTICS
OF CAPITALIST DEVELOPMENT

THE year 1820 is chosen as the birthday of modern capitalism in this study because, since then, all these countries, with the exception of Japan and Italy, which were late-starters, have been involved in a process of substantial and sustained growth.[1] Before 1820 no country, not even the UK achieved growth rates equal to the minimum achieved since that date; and even the UK, the fastest growing country in the eighteenth century, was not breaking new ground in terms of level of income per head. It did not surpass Dutch seventeenth-century performance until the nineteenth century.

There are a number of gaps in the country coverage of the growth record between 1820 and 1870, which force us to concentrate on experience since the latter date, but the evidence available on output, foreign trade, and population growth indicates that average performance from 1820 to 1870 had much greater similarity to that from 1870 to 1913 than to experience before 1820.

Table 3.1 illustrates the very substantial increase in gross domestic product per capita since 1820. The average increase was thirteen-fold, or an annual rate of 1.6 per cent. Tables 3.1 and 3.2 show a breakdown of per capita and total output growth rates by sub-periods, and these make clear the essential fact of accelerated growth since 1820, in spite of the significant variations of growth momentum since then.

The per capita growth rates for 1820-1979 range from 1.4 per cent a year for the UK to 1.8 per cent for Germany, Japan, Norway, Sweden, and the USA. The UK, the pioneer in accelerated growth, has now been passed by all the other countries except Italy; whereas Japan, whose modern growth did not start until the Meiji reforms of 1867, has shown the fastest growth. However, the long-run experience of these countries falls into a rather narrow band, and their growth process has not differed as much in timing or amplitude as some analysts have suggested. Rostow suggested a spread in 'take-off' dates for these countries (excluding the UK) that ranged from 1830-60 for France to 1896-1914 for Canada. But his chronology was unsubstantiated and is now discredited.[2] Gerschenkron also

TABLE 3.1

Growth of Output (GDP at Constant Prices) per Head of Population, 1700-1979
(Annual average compound growth rates)

	1700-1820	1820-70	1870-1913	1913-50	1950-73	1973-79	1820-1979
Australia		(n.a.)	0.6	0.7	2.5	1.3	(n.a.)
Austria		0.7	1.5	0.2	5.0	3.1	1.5
Belgium		1.9	1.0	0.7	3.6	2.1	1.7
Canada		(n.a.)	2.0	1.3	3.0	2.1	(n.a.)
Denmark		0.9	1.6	1.5	3.3	1.8	1.6
Finland		(n.a.)	1.7	1.7	4.2	2.0	(n.a.)
France	0.3[a]	1.0	1.5	1.0	4.1	2.6	1.6
Germany		1.1	1.6	0.7	5.0	2.6	1.8
Italy		(n.a.)	0.8	0.7	4.8	2.0	(n.a.)
Japan		0.0	1.5	0.5	8.4	3.0	1.8
Netherlands	−0.1	1.5	0.9	1.1	3.5	1.7	1.5
Norway		1.0	1.3	2.1	3.1	3.9	1.8
Sweden		0.6	2.1	2.2	3.1	1.5	1.8
Switzerland		1.7	1.2	1.5	3.1	−0.2	1.6
UK	0.4	1.5	1.0	0.9	2.5	1.3	1.4
USA		1.4	2.0	1.6	2.2	1.9	1.8
Arithmetic average	0.2	1.1	1.4	1.2	3.8	2.0	1.6

[a] 1701/10-1820

Source: Appendices A and B.

TABLE 3.2

Growth of Output (GDP at Constant Prices), 1700-1979
(Annual average compound growth rates)

	1700-1820	1820-70	1870-1913	1913-50	1950-73	1973-9	1820-1979
Australia		(n.a.)	3.2	2.1	4.7	2.5	(n.a.)
Austria		(1.4)	2.4	0.2	5.4	3.1	2.0
Belgium		2.7	2.0	1.0	4.1	2.3	2.3
Canada		(n.a.)	3.8	2.9	5.2	3.2	(n.a.)
Denmark		1.9	2.7	2.5	4.0	2.1	2.6
Finland		(n.a.)	3.0	2.4	4.9	2.3	(n.a.)
France	0.6[a]	1.4	1.7	1.0	5.1	3.0	2.0
Germany		2.0	2.8	1.3	6.0	2.4	2.6
Italy		(n.a.)	1.5	1.4	5.5	2.6	(n.a.)
Japan	0.1	(0.4)	2.5	1.8	9.7	4.1	2.7
Netherlands		2.4	2.1	2.4	4.8	2.4	2.7
Norway		(2.2)	2.1	2.9	4.0	4.4	2.7
Sweden		(1.6)	2.8	2.8	3.8	1.8	2.5
Switzerland		(2.5)	2.1	2.0	4.5	-0.4	2.4
UK	1.1	2.4	1.9	1.3	3.0	1.3	2.0
USA		4.4	4.1	2.8	3.7	2.7	3.8
Arithmetic average	0.6	2.1	2.5	1.9	4.9	2.5	2.5

[a] 1701/10-1820

Source: Appendix A. The figures are adjusted to exclude the impact of boundary changes.

exaggerated the difference in growth experience of these countries in calling mid-nineteenth century France 'relatively backward', Germany a 'relatively late arrival', and Denmark 'very backward' at the middle of the nineteenth century.[3]

Measurement of output trends over such long periods means comparing the present situation with that of dead ancestors who had had no experience of air and motor transport, radio, television, cinema, or household electrical appliances. Such an assessment requires robust evidence and strong faith in the logic of index numbers and national accounts. My own conclusion is that such comparisons can be made with much greater confidence now than was the case a couple of decades ago, but that they should still be regarded as rough orders of magnitude. The detailed source notes provided in Appendix A show there is still scope for further research, and the estimates for countries such as Belgium, Finland, the Netherlands, and Switzerland may yet be subject to significant revision.[4] But the range of growth experience portrayed seems likely to remain valid, given the amount of statistical effort devoted to the two extreme countries, the UK and Japan.

In Chapter 1, the main forces accounting for or constraining capitalist growth were specified as follows:
1. natural resources;
2. labour supply;
3. the stock of capital and technical progress;
4. changes in the efficiency of resource allocation through economies of scale and specialization.

The importance of each of these is analysed below in quantitative terms as far as possible. In my view, the most important of these has been item 3.

NATURAL RESOURCES A CONSTRAINT?

We have seen that there is a wide range of views about the constraining role of fixed natural resource limits on economic growth. These vary from the extreme pessimism of Malthus to the insouciance of Schumpeter.

The long-run experience since 1820 suggests that Malthus was certainly wrong and Schumpeter was too cheerful, though he was nearer to the truth.

The stock of agricultural land in these countries grew in the nineteenth century because of expansion in the USA and Canada. But when this process ended forty years ago, agricultural productivity grew faster than ever before, and has indeed grown faster than that in industry in virtually all these countries since 1950 (see Tables 5.11 and 5.13 below). Advances in technology have overcome the problem that Ricardo feared, and the terms of trade of farmers have not improved but have worsened, so that in most advanced countries governments help prop up their incomes by various devices.[5]

Although Malthusian fears gradually faded with regard to agricultural land, there has been recurrent concern about other natural resources. In 1865, the English economist Jevons[6] predicted that a coal shortage would bring economic growth to a halt within a century because there would be no substitute. Jevons did not foresee how many coal reserves would be discovered or how good a substitute oil would be. But even after this was demonstrated conservationists continued to be gloomy about resource constraints and waste of non-renewable assets.

In the 1950s Colin Clark was worried about exhausting water resources, and the US government set up the Paley Commission because it was worried about mineral and metal resources. In the 1970s the fear that economic growth was running into constraints because of the exhaustion of fixed natural resources was reiterated in the Club of Rome study,[7] which was concerned with environmental limits owing to pollution as well as with physical constraints. The OPEC cartel has also used neo-Malthusian arguments as a kind of moral defence of its monopolistic pricing of oil.

In fact, however, prospectors usually discover new natural resources when prices rise, and technological progress has been rather successful in finding substitutes for scarce natural resources. In important cases, newly discovered resources have been richer than those discovered earlier. Rising prices check consumption and induce a switch to substitute products. Except in war situations, there are usually clear warnings of emerging scarcity as reflected in relative prices, and it is the rising relative price that induces technical change.

This past experience of successful adaptation to scarce natural resource positions makes one sceptical about the likelihood of resource constraints on growth in the long run. However, it is clear that the process of resource exhaustion and discovery affects the fate of particular countries. Geography and natural resources affected Dutch and British accession to economic leadership, and the USA had great natural advantages in wood, coal, and oil which enabled it to supply its energy needs from home sources. Since the 1960s, US external dependence for energy has greatly increased, which is a major reason for OPEC's success in imposing its monopoly power.

The sudden shocks caused by major increases in oil prices in 1973-4 and 1979 have been a very important check to growth, and the uncertainties in the OPEC bargaining position enhance the economic risks in searching for oil substitutes, or less energy-intensive modes of production and consumption. Nevertheless, as Table 3.3 shows, in energy, as with other resources, there has been a significant substitution between different sources, and also a sharp long-run decline in consumption per unit of real GDP, so the OPEC cartel is certainly not a permanent threat to the momentum of development.

TABLE 3.3

Primary Energy Consumption per $1,000 of Real GDP, 1850-1978
(GDP in 1970 US relative prices, energy in tons of oil equivalent)

| | Mineral fuels and hydro | | Fuel wood | | Total | |
	USA	UK	USA	UK	USA	UK
1850	0.43	1.71	4.20	(0.84)	4.63	2.55
1900	1.87	2.33	0.51	(0.10)	2.38	2.43
1950	1.76	1.55	0.05	(0.01)	1.81	1.56
1978	1.46	0.99	0.01	(0.00)	1.47	0.99

Source: 1978 from *Energy Policies and Programmes of I.E.A. Countries, 1978 Review*, Paris, 1979, p. 158. USA 1850-1950 from J. F. Dewhurst and associates, *America's Needs and Resources*, Twentieth Century Fund, New York, 1955, p. 1114. UK coal and oil consumption 1850-1950 derived from B. R. Mitchell, *European Historical Statistics 1750-1970*, Macmillan, London, 1975, pp. 361, 364, 408, 411. The figures for mineral fuels include coal, gas, and oil. The rough guess for fuel wood consumption in the UK is simply one-fifth of the US figure per unit of GDP. Some figures on US and UK lumber consumption for all purposes for 1799-1869 are provided by N. Rosenberg, *Perspectives on Technology*, Cambridge, 1976, p. 34, and on p. 252 he suggests a 5:1 per capita ratio.

LABOUR SUPPLY

Since 1820, population of these countries had increased four-fold— about 0.9 per cent a year, compared with 0.4 per cent in the mer-

TABLE 3.4

Rates of population growth, 1500-1979
(Annual average compound growth rates)

	1500-1700	1700-1820	1820-1979	1820-1913	1913-50	1950-73	1973-9
Australia	0.00	0.1	2.5	3.1	1.4	2.2	1.2
Austria	0.20	0.3	0.5	0.9	0.1	0.4	0.0
Belgium	0.14	0.5	0.6	0.8	0.3	0.5	0.2
Canada	0.01	0.8	1.7	1.7	1.6	2.1	1.1
Denmark	0.08	0.4	1.0	1.0	1.1	0.7	0.3
Finland	0.26	1.3	0.9	1.0	0.8	0.7	0.3
France	0.13	0.3	0.3	0.3	0.1	1.0	0.4
Germany	0.11	0.4	0.6	1.1	-0.8	0.9	-0.2
Italy	0.12	0.3	0.7	0.7	0.8	0.7	0.6
Japan	0.26	0.1	0.9	0.6	1.3	1.2	1.1
Netherlands	0.35	0.2	1.1	1.0	1.3	1.2	0.7
Norway	0.26	0.6	0.9	1.0	0.8	0.8	0.5
Sweden	0.42	0.6	0.7	0.8	0.6	0.6	0.3
Switzerland	0.20	0.4	0.8	0.8	0.5	1.4	-0.2
UK	0.37	0.7	0.6	0.9	0.3	0.5	0.0
USA	0.05	1.2	1.8	2.3	1.2	1.4	0.8
Arithmetic average	0.19	0.5	1.0	1.1	0.7	1.0	0.4
Total	0.18	0.4	0.9	1.0	0.6	1.1	0.6

Source: Appendix B. The estimates are not adjusted for changes in frontiers except for Austria. The figures for Australia, Canada, and the USA include an estimate of the indigenous populations.

chant capitalist epoch and 0.2 per cent in the period of expanding agrarianism in the sixteenth and seventeenth centuries. The marked acceleration in population growth in the capitalist epoch took place despite a major decline in birth rates. Fertility in the 1970s was only a third of that in 1820 and earlier, and the increase of population was due to a decline in premature death from disease and malnutrition. Average life expectation has risen from 37 to almost 73 years (see Appendix B). There is room for controversy about the relative role of better food, sanitation, medical knowledge, and facilities at different periods, but over the long haul all these have been the result of economic growth.

Graph 3.1 illustrates the experience of fertility and mortality over the past 240 years in Sweden (one of the best documented cases). It shows:

1. the gradual decline in 'normal' mortality from about 2.5 per 100 in the eighteenth century to around 1 per 100 of the population in the 1970s;
2. the disappearance of calamities caused by famine and disease which produced recurrent peaks in the mortality curve (and also reduced fertility by causing amenorrhea). The last of these was the peak in mortality during the influenza epidemic of 1919;
3. the very large decline in the birth rate.

Although Swedish mortality experience is reasonably typical of the long-term developments in these countries, there were significant national variations in fertility. Demographic developments were not independent of economic conditions. This is particularly obvious in the case of migratory movements, which were a major reason for the fast growth of population in Australia, Canada, and the USA, all of which initially had large natural resources relative to their populations and could offer immigrants better opportunities than they could find in most European countries. Thus there has been a very wide range of population growth experience, with Australian population up the most while French population has not even doubled since 1820.

We cannot easily compare the demographic 'norm' of the 1970s with that of the 1820s, as the birth rate is still subject to important fluctuation, the death rate could always be affected by a major war, and migration can also change the picture. However, certain things are clear.

1. The transition from high to low death rates before the fall in

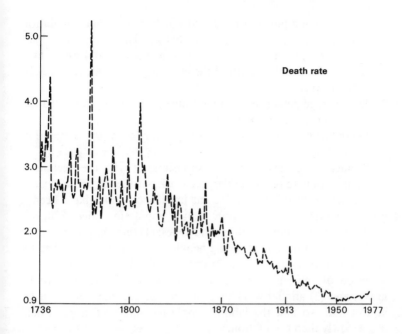

Graph 3.1. *Swedish Vital Statistics, 1736-1977* (*Sources*: H. Gille, 'The Demographic History of the North European Countries in the Eighteenth Century', *Population Studies*, June 1949; *Historical Statistics for Sweden*, vol. I, *Population 1720-1950*, CBS, Stockholm, 1955; and OECD, *Labour Force Statistics*, Paris, various issues)

birth rates temporarily produced much more rapid population growth than had ever been seen before. However, since 1973 population growth has fallen to an average of 0.4 per cent a year, which is only a sixth of the current growth rate in developing countries.

2. The average person lives much longer, which has expanded the span of potential working life.
3. There has been an increase in the proportion of the population of working age.
4. Women have fewer family responsibilities with the decline in fertility and are free to undertake work outside the home.

The net result of these different influences would have been a greater growth of labour supply than in population since 1820, but for three strong countervailing tendencies: (1) there has been a large decline in employment of young people, who are now absorbed by education rather than work; (2) virtually all old people now enjoy a period of retirement rather than working themselves into the grave; and (3) annual working hours per person have been cut by almost half, so that the labour supply has increased a good deal more slowly than population.

However, the first decades of capitalist development involved increased labour effort. We have already noted the more labour-intensive character of the new technology in agriculture, and working hours in industry were also very long. In fact, they appear to have been irrationally long from the point of view of efficiency. It was not until the 1860s that this was recognized and that hours began to fall. Before that, factory work often involved a more than ten-hour day and employers did not accept the argument that shorter hours would increase worker efficiency. Nassau Senior, the professor of economics at Oxford, defended their case by arguments which assumed that there is no efficiency gain from shorter hours.[8]

Most countries have accommodated themselves rather easily to the spontaneous elements in population change since 1820, and most of these were in a range that was not unfavourable to per capita income growth. In welfare terms, of course, the changes in demographic balance have been most welcome, with the reduction in early deaths which were a tragic occurrence in almost all families. The reduced burden of childbearing and the increased element of choice as to fertility have also transformed the lives of women for the better.

To an important extent, population growth has reflected deliberate policy, particularly in the traditional immigrant countries, Australia, Canada, and the USA, where large-scale immigration brightened investment prospects, attracted foreign capital, facilitated economies of scale, and added to the internal mobility needed to develop their natural resources. In emigrant countries, the loss of population was not a hindrance to economic development, and indeed helped to mitigate unemployment. In the years 1950 to 1973, several European countries also attracted immigrants on a large scale, and this contributed to their economic growth. Since 1973 migration policy has changed in many parts of Europe, just as it did in the USA in the 1920s.

CAPITAL

A necessary condition for exploiting the possibilities offered by technical progress is an increase in the stock of machinery and equipment in which this technology is embodied, and the buildings and infrastructure in which they operate. In the UK, where capital stock estimates are available for a longer period than elsewhere, the gross fixed capital stock (excluding housing and land) increased at an annual rate of 1.9 per cent from 1820 to 1978 and output (GDP) by 2.0 per cent; the stock of machinery and equipment grew by 2.6 per cent and that of non-residential construction more slowly— by 1.7 per cent. The evidence for other countries is less lengthy than that for the UK, but the same pattern is manifest, with total non-residential fixed capital and output growing more or less at the same pace over the long run but with machinery and equipment growing a good deal faster than the stock of buildings (see Appendix D for a more detailed analysis).

Before 1820, machinery and equipment was a fairly negligible item in the total capital stock. Thus, in 1760, machinery and transport equipment was only 8 per cent of the fixed non-residential capital stock in Great Britain and only 1.5 per cent of national wealth (including houses, land, and inventories). In 1830 these proportions had risen to 14 and 4 per cent respectively, and by 1975 to 45 and 29 per cent.

TABLE 3.5

Gross Non-residential Fixed Capital Stock
per Person Employed 1820-1978
(Dollars of 1970 US purchasing power)

	1820	1870	1890	1913	1950	1973	1978
Canada	(n.a.)	(n.a.)	(n.a.)	(n.a.)	16,279	29,760	33,553
France	(n.a.)	(n.a.)	(n.a.)	6,481	10,346	23,653	28,800
Germany	(n.a.)	3,597	5,311	7,888	9,386	26,733	34,877
Italy	(n.a.)	(n.a.)	2,059	3,150	6,151	16,813	20,178
Japar	(n.a.)	(n.a.)	713	1,178	2,873	14,172	20,103
UK	3,922	6,068	6,658	7,999	9,204	17,718	20,931
USA	(n.a.)	5,066	6,838	13,147	18,485	30,243	32,001

Source: Derived from Appendices C and D.

Table 3.5 shows the growth of capital stock per person employed. It illustrates the close relation between economic performance and capital. Thus one can see that the UK, which was the economic leader in 1820 and has since had the slowest productivity growth of the countries listed, had the biggest stock of capital per person employed and the slowest growth in this capital. Conversely, the table shows that Japanese capital stock per employee was initially the lowest and has grown the fastest, which is equally true of Japanese productivity experience. One also remarks that the US capital stock per employee outstripped that of the UK in 1890, when it overtook the UK in terms of productivity. US productivity leadership over nine decades is reflected in its superior level of capital; but by 1978, when this productivity lead was rapidly fading, it also lost its superiority in terms of capital per employee.

Graph 3.2 indicates the growth of per capita output, gross capital stock, and per capita labour input from 1880 to 1977 (as indices with 1880 = 100 in each case). It shows:

1. the broadly similar movement in capital and output over the long run, compared with the completely divergent movement in output and labour input. Labour input per capita has declined everywhere to a rather similar degree, but output and capital stock have increased at rates differing widely between countries but similar to each other in each country;

2. the much smoother movement of capital than of output. Output is affected strongly by the business cycle and by shocks such as

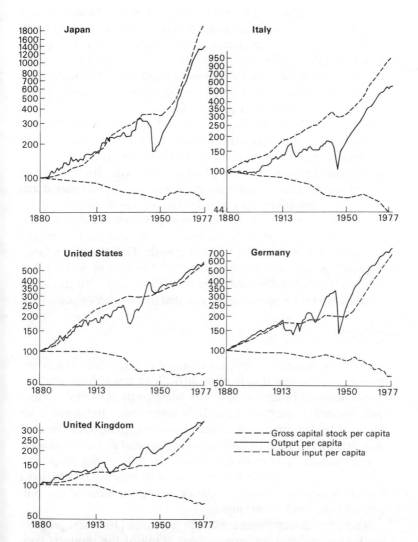

Graph 3.2. *Growth of GDP, Gross Fixed Non-residential Capital Stock and Labour Input per Head of Population, 1880-1977.* Indices: 1880 = 100 (pre-1950 capital stock figures for Germany refer to movement of net capital stock)

war. The capital stock moves more smoothly because it is a cumulation of assets assembled at different periods, so that even dramatic year-to-year changes in investment make little impact;[9]

3. a particularly interesting contrast in the movement of capital stock during wars, major depressions and their aftermath. Thus the US capital stock did not decline much in the early 1930s. Reactivation of unused capacity facilitated the rapid growth in US output during the Second World War. Similarly, in France, Germany, and Japan the rapidity of postwar recovery was possible because of the relatively intact capital stock;

4. the broad similarity in the phasing of growth rates for capital and output with a slackening in both in the 1913-50 period and an unprecedented acceleration in the post-war period.

5. Looking more closely at individual cases, we see that the UK was the country with the slowest growth in capital stock and output and Japan had the fastest growth. The USA had a faster growth in capital stock than the other countries up to 1913, but since then has performed more modestly. Since 1950 its capital stock has grown more slowly than that in the other countries.

TECHNICAL PROGRESS

Technical progress is the most essential characteristic of modern growth and the one that is most difficult to quantify or explain. It also interacts rather strongly with the growth of capital, so that their respective roles are difficult to disentangle. But there is no doubt of its importance in modern economic growth, or the contrast between its roles in capitalist and pre-capitalist development. A major driving force of modern economies is the strong propensity to risk capital on new techniques that hold promise of improved profits, in strong contrast to the defensive wariness of the pre-capitalist approach to technology.

Since the eighteenth century textile revolution, technical progress has been significant and continuous. Many of the products consumed today had no counterpart in the eighteenth century, and most production processes have been completely transformed. Furthermore, our economies are now geared to technical change in an organized and systematic fashion.

A good deal of research and development is now done in laboratories of large firms and by government departments. This trend started in 1876, when the Bell Telephone Company set up the first industrial research laboratory. Scientific and other research with ultimate economic applicability is carried out on a much larger scale now in universities than it was two centuries ago. The progress of technology is influenced to an important degree by the amount of investment that is carried out, because this involves improvement engineering and learning by doing, which are always necessary in the practical implementation of new techniques. As investment activity has increased enormously over the past two centuries, there is yet another reason to expect that technical progress is built into the economic system. The role of individual inventors who develop their bright ideas outside an institutional framework has not disappeared, though their share of the action has declined markedly.[10] In 1901 82 per cent of US patents were issued to individuals, but by 1970 the percentage had fallen to 21 per cent.[11] The institutionalization of innovation probably made the pace of advance of knowledge less erratic, and may have helped speed up the rate of growth of technical potential.

A rough proxy measure of the pace of technical progress is performance of the lead countries as described in Chapter 2 above. In 1820-90, when the UK was the leader, its productivity grew at 1.4 per cent a year, whereas US performance has been appreciably better—averaging 2.3 per cent a year from 1890 to 1979. Although in most decades the US pace of advance did not deviate too far from average, this has not been invariably the case. In 1929-38 and 1973-9, when demand was depressed, productivity growth fell well below the long-term trend, and in the war years, when demand was very high, it boomed at 4.1 per cent a year for twelve years (Table 3.6).

TABLE 3.6

Variations in Growth of GDP per Man-hour
in the USA, 1890-1979

Annual average compound growth rate			
1890-1900	2.0	1938-50	4.1
1900-13	2.0	1950-60	2.4
1913-29	2.4	1960-73	2.6
1929-38	0.7	1973-9	1.4

The slowdown in productivity growth since 1973 has led some observers to suggest that technical progress may be flagging. The evidence is analysed in some detail in Chapter 5 below, but it is not strong enough to warrant such a conclusion, particularly as the present slowdown is of rather short duration by historical standards and has also occurred before.

For individual industries there is a history of logistic development with initial slow development, rapid acceleration, and then retardation of growth. This process was analysed in some detail by Kuznets and Burns,[12] and interpreted in large part as being due to what might now be called the 'product cycle' of technical progress,[13] where the S-shaped trend reflects changing elasticity of demand, as well as fading possibilities for innovation.

The evidence of ultimately diminishing returns in these individual industry and product histories has given rise, from time to time, to pessimistic assessments about future trends for the economy as a whole. Thus Kuznets wrote in 1941:

In the industrialized countries of the world, the cumulative effect of technical progress in a number of important industries has brought about a situation where further progress of similar scope cannot be reasonably expected. The industries that have matured technologically account for a progressively increasing ratio of the total production of the economy. Their maturity does not imply a complete cessation of further technological improvements, but it does imply that economic effects of further improvements will necessarily be more limited than in the past.[14]

This conclusion of Kuznets turned out to be premature, because the USA found other industries to take over the previous dynamic role of waning sectors, and productivity growth in agriculture accelerated considerably.

It has certainly been true historically that technical progress has impacted unevenly in different parts of the economy (see Tables 5.11 and 5.13 below). There has been a longer-term tendency towards slower productivity growth in the service sector of the economy than in commodity production. This may well mean that technical advance faces greater problems in this sector than elsewhere, and if this continues it will certainly damp overall productivity growth in future because employment in services is now so high and demand for services is rising fast.

However, one should remain rather agnostic about current and future trends in technical progress. In the long run some slowdown seems likely, but there may well be shifts in demand towards more dynamic parts of the economy, and technical progress in services may well accelerate as it did in agriculture about forty years ago.

ECONOMIES OF SPECIALIZATION AND SCALE

In the merchant capitalist epoch, gains from trade, economies of scale, and specialization were regarded as providing the major opportunities for improvements in material prosperity. Adam Smith gave more space in his work to gains from these sources of growth than to capital accumulation and technical progress.

Until the nineteenth century, prosperity gained through trade usually involved a considerable beggar-your-neighbour element because of the limited size of the world market and its rather slow growth. There was a whole succession of, for the times, prosperous countries whose fortunes were gained at the expense of ousted rivals. Thus, Spain and Portugal displaced Venice and Genoa as major traders with the East by moving the trade routes to Asia away from the Mediterranean. Dutch prosperity was achieved by eating into the Portuguese and Spanish trading empires and by impoverishing the southern Netherlands (present-day Belgium). British and French trade expansion in the eighteenth century was to a significant extent at the expense of the Dutch. A much higher proportion of trade then than now was of an entrepôt character, involving re-exports of tropical products rather than exports of domestic manufactures. Trade of all the major countries involved monopolistic restrictions. Merchant capitalist attitudes were neatly summarized by a naval contractor overheard by Samuel Pepys in a London coffee house apropos of the Dutch: 'the trade of the world is too little for us two; therefore one must down'.[15]

However, there is no doubt that trade did expand appreciably under merchant capitalism (see Table 3.7), and this was the major source of productivity growth in that epoch—enlarging markets and degree of specialization in textiles, developing products of plantation agriculture such as sugar, tobacco, coffee and tea, and also diffusing technology. This experience gave both Smith and Ricardo their rosy liberal view of the potential of trade for economic development. Nevertheless, the UK's rise to world commercial supremacy in the eighteenth century was of a mixed character with both ecumenic growth-stimulating qualities and beggar-your-neighbour

TABLE 3.7

Volume of Exports 1720-1979

| | 1720-1820 | Annual average compound growth rates | | | | | |
		1820-70	1870-1913	1913-50	1950-73	1973-9	1820-1979
Australia		(n.a.)	4.3	1.3	5.8	3.9	(n.a.)
Austria		4.7	3.5	−3.0	10.8	7.9	4.0
Belgium		5.4[b]	4.2	0.3	9.4	3.5	4.3[c]
Canada		(n.a.)	4.1	3.1	7.0	3.2	(n.a.)
Denmark		1.9[c]	3.3	2.4	6.9	4.4	3.2[f]
Finland		(n.a.)	3.9	1.9	7.2	3.7	(n.a.)
France	1.0[a]	4.0	2.8	1.1	8.2	6.1	3.7
Germany		4.3[d]	4.1	−2.8	12.4	4.7	3.6[e]
Italy		3.4	2.2	0.6	11.7	7.1	3.7
Japan		(n.a.)	8.5	2.0	15.4	7.6	(n.a.)
Netherlands	−0.2	2.9	3.3	1.5	10.3	3.4	3.7
Norway		(n.a.)	3.2	2.7	7.3	6.9	(n.a.)
Sweden		(n.a.)	3.1	2.8	7.0	1.0	(n.a.)
Switzerland		4.1	3.9	0.3	8.1	4.3	3.7
UK	2.0	4.9	2.8	0.0	3.9	4.7	3.0
USA		4.7	4.9	2.2	6.3	4.9	4.4
Arithmetic average	0.9	4.0	3.9	1.0	8.6	4.8	3.7

[a] 1715-1820.
[b] 1831-70.
[c] 1844-70.
[d] 1836-70.
[e] 1831-1979.
[f] 1844-1979.
[g] 1836-1979

Source: Appendix F. Figures are not adjusted for changes in geographic boundaries.

elements. In this sense Friedrich List's positive evaluation of the contribution of the Navigation Act and other kinds of protection to British growth[16] is more persuasive than Adam Smith's arguments to the contrary.

Trade grew by 0.9 per cent a year from 1720 to 1820, and has since risen by 3.7 per cent a year. This compares with output growth in these periods of around 0.6 per cent and 2.5 per cent a year respectively. Over the long run, international trade has thus grown significantly faster than output, and this has improved resource allocation and productivity by better specialization and economies of scale. However, trade has been subject to major disturbances of a cyclical nature (see Table 3.8) and has not always moved faster than output (as can be seen by a comparison of Tables 3.7 and 3.2), so that its relative contribution to growth has been more important in some phases than others.

From 1820 to 1913, trade was an important stimulus to growth. The international economy was reopened after the blockades of the

TABLE 3.8

Amplitude of Recessions in Exports, 1820-1979

	Maximum Peak-Trough Fall or Smallest Annual Rise in Export Volume (Annual Data)				
	1820-70	1870-1913	1920-38	1950-73	1973-9
Australia		−32.2	−18.6	− 7.6	− 6.1
Austria		(n.a.)	−48.7	− 7.3	− 7.1
Belgium		−13.1	−31.8	− 9.6	− 5.7
Canada		−13.9	−40.6	− 6.1	−11.7
Denmark		−25.0	−20.3	− 6.7	− 3.9
Finland		−20.9	−15.7	−13.4	−17.4
France	−21.1	−12.9	−47.3	−12.0	− 4.0
Germany	− 22.9[a]	−14.2	−50.1	+ 2.3	−10.7
Italy		−30.6	−69.1	− 9.1	− 0.7
Japan		−23.7	−18.9	0.0	− 3.0
Netherlands		(n.a.)	−33.4	+ 2.6	− 3.4
Norway		− 7.7	−16.0	− 7.1	− 3.4
Sweden		−11.0	−37.0	−10.7	−10.7
Switzerland		(n.a.)	−50.2	− 4.2	− 7.9
UK	−14.1	−12.5	−37.7	− 8.0	− 0.7
USA	−28.7	−18.9	−47.8	−14.3	− 6.6
Arithmetic average	−21.7	−18.2	−36.5	− 7.0	− 6.4

[a] 1836-70.

Source: Appendix F.

Napoleonic wars; the UK moved to a policy of free trade; the German states created a customs union (*Zollverein*). A series of important treaties achieved substantial mutual reduction of tariff barriers. The mercantilist tradition of the eighteenth century was eliminated. The progress of technology favoured trade as freight costs fell (through development of railways, steamships, and exploitation of the Suez Canal). The growth of trade relative to output was somewhat less impressive from 1870 to 1913 than from 1820 to 1870, because continental trade policies became more protectionist, particularly for agricultural products; but trade restrictions in those days were rather mild compared with the experience that was to come.

The 1913-50 period saw a relapse into neomercantilism, with the blockades involved in two wars, the discriminatory policies, higher tariffs, quantitative restrictions, exchange controls, and other autarchic measures that were sparked off by the Great Depression of 1929-32 and the breakdown of international co-operation. As a result, trade grew at half the pace of output from 1913 to 1950. This impeded economic efficiency and acted as a drag on resource allocation.

After the Second World War, there was a succession of major moves to restore liberal trade regimes. Quantitative restrictions on non-agricultural products were dropped in the 1950s; successive multilateral negotiations in the GATT reduced tariffs very substantially; the European Community abolished tariffs between its members; and exchange controls virtually disappeared. These moves contributed to efficient resource allocation in a direct way. The establishment of institutional arrangements to guarantee continuation of a liberal international economic order bolstered confidence and was a major indirect stimulus to productivity because it helped create a climate conducive to high rates of investment.

Some of the growth-stimulating impact of trade faded in the 1970s as the once-for-all effect of trade liberalization was absorbed, but international trade has been better sustained than output since 1973, and pressures for a return to protectionism on a significant scale have been largely rejected.

The possible contribution to productivity of economies of scale within domestic markets was given considerable stress by Adam Smith, who cited their importance rather dramatically in the case of pin-making. It seems likely that this source of growth was relatively more important in the merchant capitalist epoch, when internal trade was being opened up on a national level, than it has been in the capitalist period proper. Nevertheless, there has been a growth in the market shares of large firms, and a growing standardization of products that have continued to make a modest contribution to productivity growth.

Structural changes figure quite frequently in growth analysis, but in the long run they do not have much of an independent causal role in influencing the pace of growth. They are usually manifestations of other more fundamental growth processes, being strongly influenced by the aggregate rate of growth of output and investment, the pattern of technical change, and the influence of demand patterns (including government demand) on technical change. They are also affected by changes in the openness of the economy to foreign trade. However, in the shorter run the role of sectoral shifts can be important in explaining productivity growth because some sectors, e.g. agriculture, may hoard labour in times of slack demand and disgorge it when the economy is buoyant. For this reason their influence in the period since 1950 is analysed in Chapter 5 below.[17]

4

PHASES OF DEVELOPMENT
WITHIN THE CAPITALIST EPOCH

IT is clear from the preceding analysis that the process of capitalist development has not been smooth. Within the capitalist period there have been distinct and important phases of development which are worthy of study, definition, and causal interpretation. I distinguish four phases, which I shall describe later, covering periods of unequal length; 1820-1913, 1913-50, 1950-73, and 1973 onwards. There have also been shorter-term fluctuations, usually called business cycles. My primary interest is not in these, but in major changes in trend which are distinguished from each other by changes in the institutional-policy mix and usually initiated by some sort of 'system shock' which upsets established patterns of international intercourse.

Before presenting my own diagnosis, it is useful to trace the history of cyclical or wave analysis, because my own quantitative empirical approach is not the only one available. In the past there have been a number of theories concerning the nature of long waves in economic activity. These were revived and augmented in the 1970s after a period when even the business cycle was considered obsolete and the long-wave hypothesis was regarded as quaint.[1]

The unfortunate thing about revivalist approaches to new problems is that the adherents are often single-minded enthusiasts, so that the analytical apparatus of the old theories is rehabilitated *in toto* in spite of remediable weaknesses.

CYCLE ANALYSIS

Cyclical analysis for the capitalist period started with Clement Juglar in 1856. He emphasized periodicity in economic activity whereas most earlier writers had tended to interpret interruptions to growth as random financial crises. Juglar also believed that cycles were roughly synchronous in France, the UK, and USA.[2] In his major work on cycles his attention was mainly concentrated on monetary phenomena—expansions or contractions in central bank activity, rates of interest, prices of key commodities, etc., plus narrative 'business annal' material. Although it is frequently asserted that Juglar found cycles of a characteristic length of nine years, this is not in fact true. His cycles for France average seven years with a range from three to eighteen years, and for the UK six years with a range from two to ten years.

For several decades the quantitative indicators available to cyclical analysts were similar to those used by Juglar, though they were later augmented to include price indices, and data on output and foreign trade. A more sophisticated causal analysis was also developed, such as one finds in the study by the Russian economist Tugan-Baranowsky on the nineteenth-century cycle in the UK.[3]

The ultimate refinement in statistical analysis of business cycles was the massive effort of the National Bureau of Economic Research (NBER) in the USA. The first phase was a comprehensive collection of narrative data stretching back to the beginning of the nineteenth century with a cyclical periodization for seventeen countries. The second phase was publication of a series of reference cycles for four countries (France, Germany, Great Britain, and the USA) based mainly on monthly quantitative data, which start in 1854 for the last two countries, in 1865 for France, and in 1879 for Germany.[4] The number of monthly series for the USA was nineteen for 1860 rising to 811 in 1942 (plus 161 annual indicators). The NBER derived its 'reference' cycles by plotting most of this information in de-seasonalized form, and by iterative procedures of inspection, deriving a cluster of roughly concurrent fluctuations. Thus its central concept of economic activity was a somewhat fuzzy cocktail rather than a clearly defined measure of aggregate economic activity. Its main use was as a sensitive warning indicator of turning points in business activity, with indicators classified as leading, coincident, or lagging. The reference cycle has become part of the official statistical armoury of the USA for forecasting purposes, though it is of course supplemented by the more articulate short-term models on which other countries place main reliance. For the period 1857 to 1978 the NBER established twenty-eight successive peak-to-trough movements for the United States, giving a recession on average every four years, with a variation from two-and-a-half to nine-and-a-half years. For other countries the average duration was found to be longer: fifty-three months for France, sixty-two for the UK and sixty-four for Germany for prewar years. The NBER cycles are not adjusted to eliminate trend, so they are not measures of oscillation in economic activity, and register recessions only when there is an absolute fall in the relevant indicators.[5] However, the NBER technique of using monthly and rather volatile series does pick up more cycles than would a GDP index based on annual data, and those reference cycles that do correspond with GDP movements do not always have exactly the same dates.[6] The NBER approach is a useful tool in interpreting quantitative economic history, but a major problem is that it yields no satisfactory measure of the amplitude of fluctuations because of the difficulty of producing a meaningful summary measure from such heterogeneous data. Thus one cannot use the reference cycle itself to distinguish major and minor cycles, in the same way that one can with simpler measures of industrial output or GDP fluctuations.

Hence my preference is for rather simple measures of annual movements in aggregate activity, which reveal clearly the big changes in the severity of recessions that have appeared systematically across our sixteen countries in the past century, as illustrated in Table 4.1. This table shows that peacetime business cycle history has been much milder since the Second World War than before, and that the 1920-38 period was much worse (except in Australia and Japan) than 1870-1913. Except in 1929-33, when the Depression hit every country, the weighted average of cyclical movements for the sixteen countries as a group is damped by the fact that individual country cycles are not synchronized. Before 1870 data on annual changes in GDP are not available for most countries, but it would seem that average cyclical experience was not too different from that of 1870-1913.[7] Table 4.2 shows supplementary cyclical indicators that I think are useful. They generally confirm the pattern shown by GDP movements, with notably smaller cycles since the Second World War. Also noteworthy is the significant change in price behaviour, where downward flexibility seems now to have disappeared. Graphs 4.1 and 4.2 are intended to show both cyclical volatility and differences in growth trends in different phases of capitalist development. The striking thing in Graph 4.1 is the great volatility of the 1913-50 period, and the markedly faster growth of GDP since 1950 in all countries except the USA. The price volatility of the 1913-50 period is also the most striking feature of Graph 4.2.

LONG-WAVE ANALYSIS

Although cyclical analysts had made distinctions between big and

TABLE 4.1

Amplitude of Recessions in Aggregate Output, 1870-1979

| | Maximum peak-trough fall in GDP or lowest rise (annual data) | | | |
	1870-1913	1920-38	1950-73	1973-9
Australia	− 19.4	− 8.2	+0.9	+2.1
Austria	− 2.3	−22.5	+0.1	−1.5
Belgium	− 0.2	− 7.9	−0.8	−1.8
Canada	−15.9	−30.1	−1.1	+1.1
Denmark	− 2.7	− 2.9	−0.7	−1.3
Finland	(n.a.)	− 6.5	−0.1	+0.3
France	− 6.2	−11.0	+2.5	+0.2
Germany	− 3.2	−16.1	−0.2	−1.9
Italy	− 5.1	− 6.1	+1.6	−3.6 ·
Japan	−7.3[a]	− 7.2	+5.1	−0.3
Netherlands	(n.a.)	− 9.1	−1.0	−1.0
Norway	− 3.0	− 8.3	+1.3	+3.2
Sweden	− 1.9	− 9.2	−0.2	−2.7
Switzerland	(n.a.)	− 8.0	−0.8	−8.6
UK	− 4.1	− 8.1	−0.2	−2.5
USA	− 8.2	−29.5	−2.2	−2.2
Arithmetic average	− 6.1	−11.9	+0.4	−1.3
Weighted average	−3.1	−17.3	+1.2	−0.6

[a] 1885-1913.

Source: Appendix A.

small recessions, and there had been some discussion of the Great Depression (in prices) in the last quarter of the nineteenth century, it is significant that the idea of recurrent long waves in capitalist development did not emerge until the First World War, i.e., about fifty years later than cycle analysis, and only after the rhythm of development had been very dramatically broken.

The main figures in long-wave analysis are N. D. Kondratieff, S. Kuznets, and J. A. Schumpeter. All of them drew heavily on cyclical-type indicators to test their ideas quantitatively.

Kondratieff

Kondratieff was a Russian economist, whose work on long waves was done in the 1920s as director of the Business Cycle Research Institute in Moscow. He distinguished three kinds of cycles: long ones of fifty years' duration, middle ones of seven to ten years',

TABLE 4.2

Amplitudes of Recessions in Other Economic Indicators, 1870-1978

	Maximum peak-trough fall or smallest annual rise (annual data)			
	1870-1913	1920-38	1950-73	1973-8
	Industrial production			
France	−10.6	−25.6	− 2.2	−6.5
Germany	− 5.7	−40.8	− 2.6	−8.3
UK	− 9.7	−32.4	− 2.6	−8.7
USA	−16.7	−44.7	−12.9	−9.3
Average	−10.7	−35.9	− 5.1	−8.2
	Consumer price index			
France	− 9.0	−10.4	− 1.1	9.1
Germany	− 5.1	−11.0	− 1.8	2.6
UK	− 6.2	−19.2	0.5	8.3
USA	− 9.4	−12.9	− 0.3	5.8
Average	− 7.4	−13.4	− 0.7	6.5

Sources: Industrial production, 1870-1913 from W. A. Lewis, Growth and Fluctuations 1870-1913, Allen & Unwin, London, 1978. 1913-59 from Industrial Statistics 1900-1959, OEEC, Paris, 1960; later years from OECD, Main Economic Indicators. The OEEC/OECD figures include manufacturing, mining, electricity, gas, and water, the Lewis figures include construction as well. Prices from Appendix E.

and short ones of three to four years'. He measured long waves by a double decomposition of time series—eliminating the trend and showing the deviations from it smoothed with a nine-year moving average. The nine-year average was enough to remove the influence of the two shorter types of cycle. His analysis covers the period 1770 to the 1920s and his long cycles fall into a range of forty to sixty years.[8]

Kondratieff's thesis was most clearly demonstrated by long-term movements in wholesale prices, where long waves were discernible without trend adjustment, though some of the long-term oscillation was obviously attributable to wars (e.g., the peaks in the Napoleonic wars and 1914-20). He analysed wholesale price developments for France, the UK, and the USA, and it is not surprising that in these relatively open economies he found that price trends were similar in the different countries, particularly as he adjusted the price indices to eliminate the effect of exchange rate changes which gives

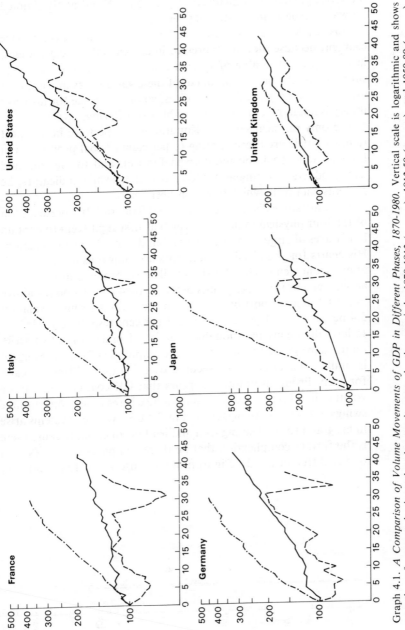

Graph 4.1. *A Comparison of Volume Movements of GDP in Different Phases, 1870-1980.* Vertical scale is logarithmic and shows growth performance; horizontal scale superimposes the three periods: 1870-1913 (———); 1913-50 (·········), and 1950-80 (— · —). Initial year of each period = 100. Decade intervals are marked on the horizontal scale.

the series greater resemblance.[9] On this basis Kondratieff claimed his waves to be an international phenomenon.

Most of Kondratieff's other indicators contain a strong price element, because they are expressed in current values: e.g., wages, interest rates, the value of foreign trade, and bank deposits. Not surprisingly, the price component of these value series moves in the same way as the general price indices, so this evidence for his wave theory is not in fact independent of his first offering.

The only physical series in Kondratieff's repertoire in his most famous article are those relating to per capita[10] coal production in England (and coal consumption in France), and to pig iron and lead production in England. Here, as with his value indicators, he presents data from which trend has been removed.

There are some distinct oddities about Kondratieff's presentation of the four physical indicators, which at first sight seem to contain long waves of large amplitude with a fair degree of synchronization. His charts for the physical indicators are shown as absolute deviations from trend. Thus he shows UK coal production 186 points above trend in 1869, 245 points below in 1894 and 164 points above in 1910. But in proportionate terms the deviations are much smaller: 5.4 per cent, −5.1 per cent, and 2.8 per cent respectively. He also follows the highly questionable practice of juxtaposing two series on the same graph to suggest that the amplitude of their movement is similar, this effect being secured by using quite different scales for each. From his graph it appears that UK coal output is more volatile than French coal consumption, whereas the proportionate swings in France were bigger than in the UK. Worse problems arise in his graph for British pig iron and lead production, because there is the further complication that he there compares two series with totally different trends. Pig iron output rose about four-fold over

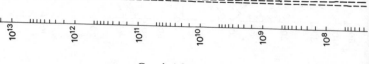

Graph 4.2 (contd)

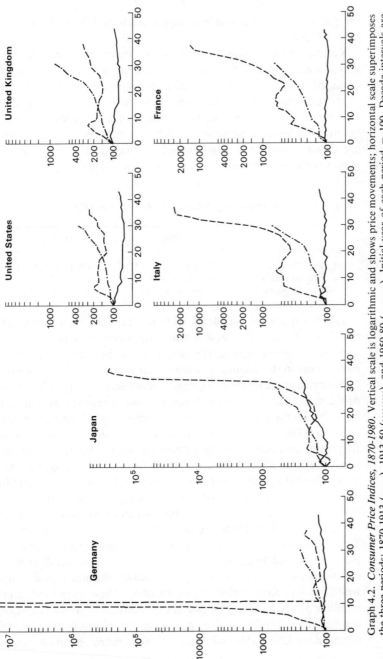

Graph 4.2. *Consumer Price Indices, 1870-1980.* Vertical scale is logarithmic and shows price movements; horizontal scale superimposes the three periods: 1870-1913 (———), 1913-50 (·········), and 1950-80 (– – – –). Initial year of each period = 100. Decade intervals are marked on the horizontal scale.

the period he covered, and lead output fell to less than a tenth of its original level.[11]

Kondratieff concluded tentatively that there had been three long waves in economic 'life' (a rather vague term, but one that is clearly intended to include output as well as price movements). His chronology refers not to particular years but to spans, and he distinguishes only two phases, the rise and fall, in each wave. He does not discuss the amplitudes of these waves, which vary between series, but they are clearly considered large enough to exclude the need for discussion of growth trends. His dating is as in Table 4.3.

TABLE 4.3

Kondratieff's Long-wave Chronology

	Rise	Decline
1. First long wave	1780s-90s to 1810-17	1810-17 to 1844-51
2. Second long wave	1844-51 to 1870-5	1870-5 to 1890-6
3. Third long wave	1890-6 to 1914-20	1914-20 to ?

There are several problems with Kondratieff's approach. The first is his failure to establish that long waves exist as more than a monetary phenomenon. He fails to show the existence of broad movements in the volume of output that even remotely correspond to our present measures of aggregate economic activity. The second problem is that the trend is taken out and discarded as if it were irrelevant to the discussion. Thus, in comparing UK and US growth between 1780 and 1980, one finds British GDP has risen about fifty-fold, and American by a thousand-fold. This fact is left out when the time series are decomposed for wave analysis, but such very different trends transform the nature and operational significance of any long waves that may be discerned. The third problem is that double decomposition of time series to eliminate trend and smooth out cycles blurs the impact of major historical events. Thus, Kondratieff's chronology pays no attention to the impact of the First World War, and later long-wave analysts tend to brush off the catastrophic 1929-33 recession and the Second World War as well. Finally, Kondratieff failed to offset these empirical shortcomings by giving plausible causal explanations as to why capitalist development should involve long waves as a systematic phenomenon. In the USSR this problem involved Kondratieff in ideological difficulties because his wave theory seemed to conflict with the more fundamental Marxist expectation of the ultimate breakdown of capitalism.[12]

There is no doubt that Kondratieff's contribution to long-wave analysis was fundamental in spite of its weaknesses,[13] because he fully adumbrates the three-cycle schema later developed by Schumpeter, and his statistical technique was the same that Kuznets later used to distinguish 'secondary secular movements'. Furthermore, he pointed to the likelihood of poor terms of trade for agriculture in periods of decelerated development—a point given major stress later by Arthur Lewis.

Kuznets and Abramovitz

Chronologically, the next development in long-wave analysis was Kuznets's work on 'secondary secular movements', published in 1930.[14] Kuznets's basic technique of identifying long waves was the same as Kondratieff's, i.e. to look at smoothed detrended series, though Kuznets made a special point of not eliminating population movements. His investigation was more detailed, involving careful analysis of fifty-nine series, most of which represented both physical output and the relevant price variance for particular commodities'[15] Kuznets did not claim that these indicators could be added to provide a meaningful picture of aggregate economic activity, and he did not use aggregative indicators for sectors such as agricultural or industrial production, which were available when he wrote.

His major conclusions are: (1) that 'secondary secular variations in production are in most cases similar to those in prices, the latter following a rather general course in agreement with the well-known historical periods of the rise and fall in the general price level' (p. 197); (2) he found a much shorter periodicity than Kondratieff, 'about 22 years as the duration of a complete swing for production and 23 years for prices' (p. 206); (3) most fundamentally, he did not think there was enough evidence to conclude that these secondary secular variations were major cycles. They were 'rather specific, historical occurrences' (p. 258). There is 'an absence of factors that would explain the periodicity' (p. 264).

Kuznets did not attempt to cluster his individual series to present a global chronology of long waves in economic life, nor did he analyse the synchronization of the series.[16] However, it is clear from other evidence that in the period Kuznets covered there were rather large depressions in the USA at intervals of fifteen to twenty years. This is directly observable in indices of industrial production (including construction), which Arthur Lewis has recently prepared (see Table 4.4). It is also clear that the recession/depression sequence

TABLE 4.4

Amplitude and Duration of Cycles in Industrial Production (including Construction), 1870-1913

	Peak year	Trough year	Percentage amplitude of peak trough movement	Duration of recession (years below peak)
France	1878	1879	− 0.7	1
	1882	1885	−10.6	6
	1892	1893	− 3.4	1
	1894	1895	− 4.4	1
	1899	1902	− 7.9	5
	1907	1908	− 1.4	1
	1909	1910	− 2.5	1
	1912	1913	− 2.1	1
	Average amplitude		− 4.1	
	Percentage of years below peak			39.5
	Trend growth rate		2.6	
Germany	1873	1874	− 0.5	1
	1876	1877	− 5.7	2
	Average amplitude		− 3.2	
	Percentage of years below peak			7.0
	Trend growth rate		4.3	
UK	1876	1879	− 4.1	3
	1883	1886	− 9.7	4
	1891	1893	− 6.3	3
	1902	1903	− 2.1	2
	1907	1908	− 8.0	4
	Average amplitude		− 6.0	
	Percentage of years below peak			37.2
	Trend growth rate		2.1	
USA	1872	1876	−14.8	6
	1883	1885	− 6.0	2
	1890	1891	− 1.5	1
	1892	1894	−15.9	2
	1895	1896	− 7.1	1
	1903	1904	− 6.3	1

Table 4.4 (contd)

	Peak year	Trough year	Percentage amplitude of peak trough movement	Duration of recession (years below peak)
	1906	1908	− 16.7	2
	1910	1911	− 4.2	1
	Average amplitude		− 9.1	
	Percentage of years below peak			37.2
	Trend growth rate		4.7	
Four countries combined = core	1873	1874	− 1.2	2
	1876	1877	− 0.4	1
	1883	1885	− 5.0	2
	1892	1893	− 5.2	2
	1899	1900	− 0.3	1
	1903	1904	− 2.1	1
	1907	1908	− 9.5	1
	Average amplitude		− 3.4	
	Percentage of years below peak			23.3
	Trend growth rate		3.6	

was different in France, Germany, and the UK, which is the major reason why the aggregate performance of these four countries (which Lewis calls 'the core', to distinguish them from 'the periphery'—the rest of the world) is more stable than they are individually. In comparing the cyclical performance of these countries, it is useful to keep in mind the differences in their long-run growth performance. A country like France or the UK, with slow growth, is likely to have more small recessions than Germany or the USA, which had much higher growth. A rough measure of how far recessions fell below the potential growth path is to combine the trend and the cyclical amplitude: e.g., the average French recession involved a fall of 6.7 per cent from trend (4.1 + 2.6 per cent), and the average German recession a fall of 7.5 per cent from trend (3.2 + 4.3 per cent).

After his early study of secondary secular movements, Kuznets moved on to fundamental definitional work on the rationale (scope, valuation, and net-ness) for GDP as an aggregate economic indicator within a system of national accounts, and produced historical estimates of US economic development which made it possible to analyse long-term movements in economic life on a much more satisfactory conceptual basis than the cocktail approach that virtually all economic analysts had previously been forced to use. Furthermore, Kuznets successfully stimulated and inspired replication of his work by scholars in many other countries. This accounting approach still has some drawbacks for cyclical analysis, because until recently data were available only on an annual basis, but it has revolutionized the study of growth and greatly facilitates testing of long-wave analysis.

From time to time since 1930 Kuznets has returned to long-swing analysis in a rather tentative way. Unlike his disciples, he himself never calls them 'cycles', as the word implies greater certainty about such phenomena and their periodicity than Kuznets concedes. In 1956 he did advance a tentative chronology of long swings in GDP, for eight countries,[17] but the periodization looks very odd, because the logic of the analysis calls for a declining phase in the decades following 1946, and Kuznets later dropped this one attempt to suggest a general chronology for long swings. He has not subsequently tried to incorporate international developments since the Second World War in his long-swing analysis.

Otherwise, Kuznets's work on long swings has been only a small part of his output and is concentrated on US experience. The most affirmative article is a 1958 study on population growth,[18] which finds the 'long-swing' hypothesis most plausible in relation to US population growth and to 'population-sensitive' components of capital formation such as housing and railway construction, and present in weaker and sometimes inverse form in other national accounting aggregates.

Kuznets has had several disciples in long-swing analysis whose work he has generally endorsed. Abramovitz is the most interesting of these,[19] because he has made the most ambitious attempt to discern long swings in aggregate US economic activity and has veered between more positive affirmation of long swings than Kuznets and a recantation, in the sense that he does not find valid evidence for the phenomenon in the postwar period. His work in this field has been almost entirely in relation to the US economy.[20]

Abramovitz distinguishes waves of acceleration and retardation in US growth with an average duration for the full swing of fourteen years and a variance from six to twenty-one years, using NBER business annal—reference cycle indicators back to the 1820s. He uses a cocktail of twenty-nine indicators including GNP. He smoothes his series by a rather complicated procedure, designed to eliminate NBER reference cycles, before removing the trend. He found that the turning points of his different series 'cluster in relatively narrow bands of years'. He therefore produced a general chronology with nine swings between 1814 and 1939.

Even at his most affirmative, Abramovitz was basically cautious about the nature of long swings. Thus in 1959 he wrote: 'It is not yet known whether they are the result of some stable mechanism inherent in the structure of the U.S. economy, or whether they are set in motion by the episodic occurrence of wars, financial panics, or other unsystematic disturbances.' By 1968 he concluded that Kuznets cycles were 'a form of growth which belonged to a particular period in history' (1840-1914), which had disappeared thereafter.

Schumpeter

The most complex cycle system was propounded by Schumpeter. He had a basic Kondratieff long wave of fifty years, on each of which he superimposed six eight- to nine-year 'Juglars', each in turn being crowned by three forty-month 'Kitchin' cycles.[21] Schumpeter insisted on the empirical regularity of his schema as if the basic facts about these three cycles had been well established, whereas there are great doubts about all three, as well as the legitimacy of his nomenclature. Kitchin's paltry contribution to the literature is lean meat indeed compared with that of the NBER, and Juglar never claimed to have demonstrated the existence of an eight- to nine-year rhythm. In fact, the NBER had already demonstrated rather wide variance in the length of cycles, so that there was little ground for distinguishing Juglars and Kitchins. Furthermore, Schumpeter distinguishes only the length of his three types of cycle and says nothing about their amplitude.

Schumpeter's treatment of statistical material is illustrative rather than analystic and is at times rather cavalier. He uses business annal material of the type favoured by his former colleague Spiethoff, or by Tugan-Baranowsky, both of whom had an obvious influence on his views. He also uses NBER type of statistical 'cocktail' material in pulse charts of industrial production, prices, interest rates, deposits, and currency circulation (p. 465). He makes passing reference to national income analysis (p. 561), but elsewhere refers to the concept of total output as a 'meaningless heap' (p. 484), national income as a 'highly inconvenient composite' (p. 561).[22]

Schumpeter's cycle analysis runs to 1,050 pages and is highly discursive. Judged on its statistical evidence alone, it would have been long discredited. Its power lies in the imaginative theory he supplies to explain the long waves and the highly illuminating commentary on many aspects of German, British, and American economic history. He argues that each wave represents a major upsurge in innovation and entrepreneurial dynamism. Although writing in the later 1930s, he was remarkably sanguine about the long-run productive potential of capitalism. For him, depressions were a necessary part of the capitalist process. They were a period of creative destruction, during which old products, firms, and entrepreneurs were eliminated and new products were conceived. In fact, Schumpeter dismissed the 1929-33 recession much too lightly. He says: 'the depression that ran its course from the last quarter of 1929 to the third quarter of 1932 does not prove that a secular break has occurred in the propelling mechanism of capitalist production because depressions of such severity have repeatedly occurred—roughly once in every fifty-five years.'[23] He then quotes the 1873-77 period as if it were a precedent for 1929-33. Such a comparison is totally misleading. In the earlier period the peak-trough fall in US industrial production was 14.8 per cent; in the later one, 44.7 per cent! There is no earlier parallel to the 1929-33 fall either in amplitude or in its international incidence.

Like most long-wave analysts, Schumpeter gives primary stress to autonomous features of the capitalist process and says very little on the role of government in economic life. Where he does mention government, it is usually to scorn its perversity, as in his attack on Roosevelt's New Deal—though he regards government as pretty impotent. For him the driving force in economic life is entrepreneur-

TABLE 4.5

Schumpeter's Long-wave Chronology

	Prosperity	Recession	Depression	Revival
1. Industrial Revolution Kondratieff (cotton textiles, iron, and steam power)				
	1787-1800	1801-13	1814-27	1828-42
2. Bourgeois Kondratieff (railroadization)				
	1843-57	1858-69	1870-85	1886-97
3. Neomercantilist Kondratieff (electricity, automobiles, chemicals)				
	1898-1911	1912-25	1925-39	?

ship, which he regarded as having been taken over more or less completely by large firms. The emphasis on entrepreneurship is present in Schumpeter's earliest work on capitalist development written in 1911, and is obviously influenced by the ideas of Max Weber and Werner Sombart, which were popular in that epoch.

Schumpeter's big-wave chronology was rather similar to that of Kondratieff, though he gave each of the big waves a name and divided each wave into four phases rather than two:[24]

The main weaknesses of Schumpeter's long-wave theory (ignoring his failure to demonstrate their existence in the real world) are three-fold: (1) he does not explain why innovation (and entrepreneurial drive) should come in regular waves rather than in a continuous but irregular stream, which seems a more plausible hypothesis for analysis concerned with the economy as a whole; (2) he makes no distinction between the lead country and the others, but argues as if they were all operating on a par as far as productivity level and technological opportunity is concerned. Thus his waves of innovation are expected to affect all countries simultaneously; (3) he greatly exaggerates the scarcity of entrepreneurial ability and its importance as a factor of production.

Schumpeter developed his ideas on capitalist development in another book published during the Second World War (*Capitalism, Socialism and Democracy*), which is not concerned with long waves but presents a breakdown theory for the capitalist system. This is rather paradoxical coming from an analyst who had such great faith in the robust character of capitalism, but his breakdown theory is sociopolitical rather than economic. He argues that there are four major forces destroying capitalism. In the first place, entrepreneurship is likely to be stifled by bureaucratization of management and decision-making in large firms. The second menace is the disincentive of progressive taxation and the increasing power of trade unions, which had already (he argues) retarded US recovery in the 1930s and was likely to become more stifling. The third threat came from the growing power of socialist ideas, and the fourth from the unpopularity of capitalism with intellectuals, who were continually engaged in denunciatory activities and harassments such as anti-trust suits.

Schumpeter's approach to long waves and the breakdown of capitalism has great fascination. It contains bold hypotheses and unsettling paradoxes, which gain in impact through his emotional detachment. His view of capitalist development is fatalistic, and he writes as if he were charting destiny. He dislikes most of what is happening in the real world, but does not advocate policies to remedy the predicted catastrophe. In fact, one is never sure with Schumpeter whether he is putting forward a specific hypothesis because he seriously believes it or because it is a stimulating illustration of his fundamentally dynamic and original conception of capitalist development.

Recent Long-wave Revivalists

The significant change in the momentum of economic growth since 1973 has revived the notion of long rhythms in economic life and a number of new long-wave pundits have emerged. Some of these have been vulgarizers of past long-wave theories, which they invoke uncritically in support of a fashionable gloom about the future;[25] others deserve critical inspection even though I have not found much in their work to shake my scepticism about long waves as a systematic phenomenon affecting output. The two revivalists examined here are W. W. Rostow and E. Mandel.[26]

Rostow is concerned with 'Kondratieff' movements, essentially in the sense of swings in the terms of trade of primary producers against those selling industrial goods. Thus he refers to the 1951-73 period as the 'downswing' of a fourth Kondratieff, and the OPEC-inspired price increases as the upswing of a fifth Kondratieff, which poses particular problems because of demographic pressures in the developing world. Although I myself feel uncomfortable about calling the 1951-73 period a 'downswing', the Rostow thesis in itself appears fairly reasonable, and Arthur Lewis has shown the interest in explaining this facet of Kondratieff's work. Furthermore, Rostow produces 800 pages of empirical material to back his argument, in welcome contrast to some of his earlier work. However, he complicates his argument by embedding it in a loosely integrated framework that features neo-Schumpeterian surges of innovation in leading sectors, demand changes as economies work themselves through a hierarchy of stages, and a reiteration of his earlier erroneous belief that there was a short, sharp take-off in Western countries which was staggered in time. Like Schumpeter, Rostow has little time for broad aggregates such as GDP, which to my mind are the central indicator to be used in measuring acceleration or deceleration of growth. GDP is not absent in Rostow, but its message is buried by disaggregation.

Mandel approaches long waves from a rather different ideological position from Rostow—being an erudite Belgian Marxist of Trotskyite persuasion. He asserts that there are long swings, roughly fifty years in length, caused by surges of new technology. In each swing there are two phases. In the first phase profit rates rise as the new technology is developed, and in the second phase profit rates fall as technical possibilities are exhausted. The timing, like the causality, is similar to Schumpeter's. The first (Industrial Revolution) wave is from the 1780s to 1847; the second, from 1847 to the 1890s, is attributable to a technological revolution dominated by 'machine production of steam motors'; the third, from the 1890s to 1939, is associated with the 'machine production of electric and combustion motors'; and the fourth, from 1940 to a future unspecified date, is associated with machine production of electronic motors and atomic energy. He suggests that the first phase of the fourth wave ended in 1967 and that we are now in the second phase. Unlike other writers in this vein, he does not refer to the waves as 'Kondratieffs', as he considers Kondratieff unoriginal as compared with van Gelderen (for whose work he has an exaggerated respect).

Mandel is mainly interested in theory and the empirical underpinning is very weak. He claims (p. 137) that 'economic historians are practically unanimous' in distinguishing expansions and recessions in the periods he uses in his periodization, but the only justification he gives for this is an article by Hans Rosenberg published in 1943, which itself contained no empirical material and was written before quantitative economic history began. He also presents estimates of industrial production for the UK, Germany, and the USA and estimates of world trade to buttress his argument. These are not deviations from detrended moving averages, but compound rates of growth between the years specified (which vary by type of indicator).

Table 4.6 shows Mandel's indicators for the second-wave downswing, which he calls a period of 'pronounced depression', and for the third-wave upswing, which he calls a period of 'tempestuous increase in economic activity'. The figures do not bear out such a dramatic conclusion, particularly if one uses the alternative measures in the bottom half of the table, which are drawn from more recent sources but cover exactly the same periods and refer to the same concepts as those of Mandel.

Mandel considers that there have been stages of development within the capitalist period; but, interestingly enough, although he

TABLE 4.6
Mandel's Evidence Scrutinized

| | | Annual average compound growth rates | |
		Second-wave downswing 'Permanent depression'	Third-wave upswing 'Tempestuous increase in economic activity'
Mandel's	UK	1.2 (1876-93)	2.2 (1894-1913)
indicators	Germany	2.5 (1875-92)	4.3 (1893-1913)
	USA	4.9 (1874-93)	5.9 (1894-1913)
	World	2.2 (1870-90)	3.7 (1891-1913)
	Average	2.7	4.0
Mandel	UK	1.4	2.4
replicated	Germany	4.0	4.2
	USA	4.9	5.0
	World	3.4	3.5
	Average	3.4	3.8

Source: First five rows from E. Mandel, *Late Capitalism*, New Left Books, London, 1975, pp. 141-2 (I have omitted his citation of Dupriez's 1947 estimates of world per capita output as these are much too shaky for serious use in this context). My indicators of industrial production including construction for the UK, Germany, and the USA are from W. A. Lewis, *Growth and Fluctuations 1870-1913*, Allen & Unwin, London, 1978, and for world trade volume from A. Maddison, 'Growth and Fluctuation in the World Economy 1870-1960', *Banca Nazionale del Lavoro Quarterly Review*, June 1962.

calls his book 'late capitalism', he claims that it is not a new stage but merely a development within the second stage of imperialist monopoly-capitalism, which Lenin distinguished from the first phase of 'free competition'.

At first sight this restraint is puzzling, for Mandel frequently refers to features of 'late capitalism' that seem rather different from those that Lenin distinguished, e.g., the enhanced role of the state in the economy, the formal ending of colonialism, the importance of military spending, and the changed international power locus. The reason for Mandel's position is explained towards the end of his book, where he makes it clear that he wants to avoid being classified with the type of 'revisionist' who claims that there is a new era of state capitalism with a mixed economy that can 'suspend the internal economic contradictions of capitalism'.[27]

Thus there is no real connection between Mandel's stages of growth and his long waves. The latter are the fruit of more or less exogenous technological development, and do not have the policy-institutional flavour that Schumpeter conferred on his by calling one 'bourgeois' and another 'neo-mercantilist'.

Although I disagree with Mandel's conclusion that he has found empirical evidence for long waves, his theoretical position has interesting elements of originality, and his discussion of the intellectual history of this field is also more stimulating than many other accounts.[28]

Conclusions on Long-wave Theories

My basic conclusion on long-wave analysis is that the case for believing that there are regular long-term rhythmic movements in economic activity has not been proven, although many fascinating hypotheses have been developed in looking for them. Nevertheless, it is clear that major changes in growth momentum have occurred since 1820, and some explanation is needed. In my view it can be sought not in systematic long waves, but in specific disturbances of an *ad hoc* character. Major system shocks change the momentum of capitalist development at certain points. Sometimes they are more or less accidental in origin; sometimes they occur because some inherently unstable situation can no longer be lived with but has finally broken down (e.g., the Bretton Woods payments system). I also feel that the institutional-policy mix plays a bigger role in capitalist development than do many of the long-wave theorists. A system shock will produce the need for new policy instruments, and these are not always selected on the most rational basis; or they may require a long period of experiment before they work properly. There may also be conflicts of interest within and between countries which prevent the emergence of efficient policies. Hence there may well be prolonged periods in which supply potential is not fully exploited. Some of these problems are faced in Schumpeter's analysis but usually as if their solution was a matter of destiny rather than choice.

It is also important to keep in mind that capitalist development since 1820, though it has a certain unity because the growth momentum has lain within distinctly higher limits than earlier epochs, has nevertheless seen rather big changes in the character of economic life which are bound to influence the type of fluctuations that are experienced. These changes have to be kept in mind in constructing any general theory of fluctuations or phases.

One of these is the change in the structure of production and employment that has resulted from increased levels of income and changed patterns of demand and productivity. In 1820, agriculture characteristically employed 55 per cent of the labour force in these countries, whereas the average is now down to around 7 per cent. Agriculture was and still is subject to erratic fluctuations in output owing to weather, and its products are generally sold in flexprice markets in which prices go down as well as up. This erratic element in economic life is now much smaller than it used to be. Industrial employment was probebly around a quarter of total employment around 1820 and rose towards a peak of somewhere round 50 per cent in most countries. Hence the process of capitalist development is often referred to as industrialization, with its first phase as the 'Industrial Revolution', and particular weight is often placed on industrial production as an index of growth. However, the industrial share in employment has been on the decline for the past twenty years, and has now regressed closer to the 1820 proportion than to its peak level. The big long-run gains have been in services, which had perhaps a fifth of total employment in 1820 against 60 per cent now. It was in the industrial sector that the business cycle was most marked in terms of stock-output supply adjustments and fluctuations in demand, but in the service sector both demand and supply are more stable, and this has dampened the amplitude of fluctuations in GDP.

A second major change in economic life has been the growing role of government. In 1820 government consumption was typically less than 10 per cent of GDP, but by 1980 it has risen to around 18 per cent. In addition, government intervenes on a similar scale to operate a vast network of social transfers, which change the distribution of income and the pattern of private spending. Finally, the government regulatory role in the economy has greatly increased. One result of the latter is that the stability of financial institutions has improved. Before the Second World War, depressions were often reinforced by major bank failures, but these are now much rarer and their impact is cushioned, though the potential for such disturbances still exists in the international field. As a result of these changes, government exercises both a propulsive and a compensatory role in economic life, which generally operated to stabilize the expenditure and income flow, and the aspirations of governments to act as managers of economic destiny have greatly increased. This has led some observers to speculate, perhaps prematurely, on a policy cycle as a successor to the business cycle.

There are also other changes to keep in mind when developing hypotheses intended to cover the whole capitalist period. One important one is the change in the average size of firms, and the growth of powerful trade unions to represent the interests of workers. Hence, the atomized market paradigm is no longer very relevant in wage and price fixing, which explains some of the change that has occurred in price behaviour. Another is the character of the international linkages between countries, which have varied a good deal over time and which have been the most exposed to what I call system shocks. One fundamental aspect of this is the nature of the international monetary system, which has a major impact on the type of policy weapons used domestically. Others are the level of trade, migration, and capital movements, and the scope for international transfers of technology.

PHASES OF GROWTH

Although I find no convincing evidence in the work of Kondratieff, Kuznets, and Schumpeter to support the notion of regular or systematic long waves in economic life, there have nevertheless been significant changes in the momentum of capitalist development. It is worthwhile to divide the 160 years since 1820 into separate phases which have meaningful internal coherence in spite of wide variations in individual country performance within each of them. In order to illustrate trends, cycles, and phases, I have made estimates for as many individual years as possible, including war years. I have also aggregated movements for the sixteen countries as a whole, showing both weighted and unweighted averages. For many purposes the unweighted average is the most relevant indicator of the characteristic experience of these countries, because countries are our basic unit of analysis. For some purposes a weighted average is a useful supplement, but it should not be forgotten that the USA has a very large weight in such averages, particularly for the twentieth century. For many indicators, information is poor before 1870. Hence the systematic presentation of data is restricted to the period following 1870. However, the evidence available suggests that in most respects the 1820-70 experience was similar to that in 1870-1913.

Table 4.7 gives a summary view of the amplitude of annual changes in GDP, which is our preferred measure of aggregate output, for the sixteen countries taken together. Table 4.8 gives

TABLE 4.7

*Year-to-Year Percentage Change in Aggregate
GDP of the Sixteen Countries, 1871-1981*

1871	3.1	1909	6.6	1946	−9.3
1872	4.2	1910	1.5	1947	2.9
1873	1.3	1911	3.8	1948	6.6
1874	4.0	1912	4.2	1949	3.9
1875	2.6	1913	3.5		
1876	0.6			1950	8.3
1877	2.2	1914	−6.2	1951	7.1
1878	2.3	1915	1.8	1952	4.0
1879	1.1	1916	7.2	1953	5.2
1880	4.3	1917	−1.2	1954	1.3
1881	2.8	1918	2.8	1955	6.8
1882	3.0	1919	−2.5	1956	3.7
1883	1.8	1920	−0.1	1957	3.2
1884	1.1	1921	−0.1	1958	1.2
1885	1.5	1922	6.5	1959	5.8
1886	3.0	1923	5.0	1960	4.9
1887	3.4	1924	5.2	1961	4.5
1888	1.8	1925	4.1	1962	5.2
1889	3.7	1926	3.4	1963	4.8
1890	4.2	1927	3.0	1964	6.2
1891	1.9	1928	3.1	1965	5.2
1892	3.4	1929	4.3	1966	5.5
1893	−1.0	1930	−5.4	1967	4.0
1894	2.4	1931	−5.7	1968	5.6
1895	5.1	1932	−7.1	1969	5.4
1896	1.3	1933	1.2	1970	3.6
1897	3.1	1934	6.2	1971	3.6
1898	5.1	1935	5.8	1972	5.5
1899	4.5	1936	7.7	1973	6.2
1900	2.6	1937	5.4		
1901	3.7	1938	2.1	1974	0.4
1902	1.2	1939	5.8	1975	−0.6
1903	3.5	1940	1.8	1976	5.4
1904	1.1	1941	7.6	1977	3.8
1905	3.8	1942	6.7	1978	4.0
1906	6.7	1943	7.0	1979	3.4
1907	2.8	1944	2.4	1980	1.3
1908	−3.7	1945	−9.5	1981	1.2

Source: Weighted estimates derived from Appendix A. 1871-1913 excludes Finland, Netherlands, and Switzerland. 1871-85 movement for Japan was estimated by extrapolation assuming steady growth. For the First World War there were some gaps in data for Austria, Belgium, and Switzerland for which rough estimates were made; this is also true for Belgium, 1939-47, Switzerland, 1944-6, and Japan, 1945-6.

a synoptic view of the incidence of recession by year, and by country. The biggest interruptions to growth occurred in the 1930-2 depression, and in the 1945-6 period of demobilization, dismemberment, defeat, and victory. All other disturbances had a much milder impact on output, including those of the First World War and its aftermath. The aggregate stability in the collective output of the group in peacetime has been quite impressive. In the forty-three years from 1870 to 1913, there were only two years of recession in aggregate output, and in the thirty-five years 1947-81 only one year. However, it is clear from Table 4.8 that individual countries have been much more unstable than the group as a whole (particularly before 1913). The cyclical experience of individual countries has not normally been synchronized, but rather compensatory. Cyclical experience in these countries has been synchronized only when they have been subjected to 'system-shocks' such as wars, or the collapse of longstanding international payments mechanisms.

My method of distinguishing phases of development is really quite simple. It involves collecting annual time series for major indicators of economic activity for the sixteen countries in as complete and comparable a form as possible, and by inspection of these and graphs derived from them, identifying fundamental turning points in growth momentum, and trying to establish growth and cyclical behaviour patterns that differ significantly between phases. The technique is not unlike that of the NBER in its attempt to identify reference cycles, and in particular does not involve elaborate decomposition of time series into different kinds of oscillatory movement. Simple techniques such as this are almost inevitable in handling information for sixteen countries, where each series, if it were available for the full 160 years, would involve more than 2,500 readings. Furthermore, it is necessary in this kind of comparative historical work to be very careful in making adjustments to enhance the comparability of the basic data. There is some danger in overprocessing results drawn too mechanically from such data.

In analysing the sequence of phases, the first problem is one of periodicity. Table 4.7 suggests that the period 1870-1913 has a certain unity in that growth was moderate and interrupted by recession, but not subject to the extreme shocks which struck three times between 1914 and the 1940s. There is also something special about the unprecedented secular boom which started in 1947 and

TABLE 4.8

Incidence of Recessions, 1870–1981
(Years and countries in which GDP fell)

Year	No. of falls	Countries affected	Year	No. of falls	Countries affected	Year	No. of falls	Countries affected
1871	3	AGI	1914	9	ACLFGIJNE	1950	0	
1872	2	CI	1915	6	ADLFGS	1951	1	D
1873	3	TDF	1916	1	F	1952	2	BK
1874	2	EG	1917	8	ADLFNWSE	1953	0	
1875	3	BCS	1918	7	DLFJNWS	1954	2	CE
1876	3	FGI	1919	4	AFGK	1955	1	D
1877	3	DGI	1920	5	CIJKE	1956	0	
1878	4	CFWS	1921	7	CDFIWKE	1957	0	
1879	4	TFGK	1922	2	JS	1958	5	BLNZE
1880	1	G	1923	2	TG	1959	0	
1881	1	I	1924	2	CW	1960	0	
1882	3	ACW	1925	1	D	1961	0	
1883	4	CFIW	1926	2	AK	1962	0	
1884	1	F	1927	2	FI	1963	0	
1885	2	TK	1928	1	A	1964	0	
1886	1	C	1929	4	ABLG	1965	0	
1887	1	S	1930	12	ATBCLFGIJZKE	1966	0	
1888	5	ATFIJ	1931	14	ATBCLFGINWSZKE	1967	1	G
1889	3	TCI	1932	10	TBCDFGNSZE	1968	0	
1890	1	A	1933	4	TCNE	1969	0	
1891	2	GJ	1934	1	B	1970	1	E
1892	4	ACIK	1935	2	FZ	1971	1	S
1893	4	ACFE	1936	0		1972	0	

n	Year	Codes	n	Year	Codes	n	Year	Codes
3	1894	CIE	0	1937		0	1973	
2	1895	AF	2	1938	BE	4	1974	DJKE
2	1896	JE	2	1939	LZ	9	1975	TBDGINZKE
4	1897	ACFI	7	1940	DLFJNWS	1	1976	Z
0	1898		5	1941	DFISZ	1	1977	S
2	1899	CJ	5	1942	FINWZ	0	1978	
1	1900	K	6	1943	FIJNWZ	0	1979	
5	1901	ALFGS	8	1944	ALFIJNWK	4	1980	CDKE
2	1902	LJ	9	1945	ACDLGIJKE	5	1981	BDGNK
2	1903	WK	6	1946	ACGJKE			
2	1904	WE	2	1947	KE			
2	1905	FJ	0	1948				
0	1906		1	1949	Z			
0	1907							
5	1908	ALIKE						
3	1909	TGJ						
1	1910	I						
0	1911							
0	1912							
0	1913							

Country code:

A	Australia	I	Italy
T	Austria	J	Japan
B	Belgium	N	Netherlands
C	Canada	W	Norway
D	Denmark	S	Sweden
L	Finland	Z	Switzerland
F	France	K	UK
G	Germany	E	USA

Source: Appendix A.

ended in 1973. Evidence of various kinds suggests that the nature of the growth process changed in the early 1970s, and particularly after 1973. I have therefore distinguished four phases: 1870-1913, 1913-50, 1950-73, and 1973 onwards. However, my hunch, based on partial indicators for a few of the countries, is that the first phase can be extended to include 1820-1913 as a whole.

Kuznets postulates five minimum requirements for acceptable stages of growth:[29] (1) they must be identified by characteristics that can be verified or quantified; (2) the magnitude of these characteristics must vary in some recognizable pattern from one phase to another ('stages are presumably something more than successive ordinates in the steadily climbing curve of growth. They are segments of that curve with properties so distinct that separate study of each segment seems warranted'); (3) there should be some indication of when stages terminate and begin and why; (4) it is necessary to identify the universe to which the stage classification applies; (5) finally, Kuznets requires that there be an analytic relation between successive stages, which, optimally, would enable us to predict how long each stage has to run. This seems to me too deterministic. It suggests that movements between successive stages are more or less ineluctable. As I cannot meet Kuznets's fifth requirement, my periods are 'phases' rather than 'stages'.

My growth phases fulfil the first four Kuznets's requirements as explained below.

1. The phases are identified by eight simple indicators showing both growth and cyclical characteristics: rate of growth of output, output per head, capital stock and export volume, cyclical variations in output and exports, levels of unemployment, and rate of price increase. These are the conventional macroeconomic indicators one might use for growth accounting or conjunctural monitoring. The results are shown in very aggregative form in Tables 4.9 and 4.10. Each phase also has five non-quantifiable 'system characteristics', by which I mean the basic policy approaches and institutional environment that condition growth performance. These include the government approach to demand management (i.e., the kind of trade-off that is made between unemployment and inflation), the bargaining power and expectations of labour, the degree of freedom for trade and international factor movements, and the character of the international payments mechanism. Changes in these between periods are summarised in Table 4.11.

TABLE 4.9

Growth Characteristics of Different Phases, 1820-1979
(Arithmetic average of figures for the individual countries)

| Phases | GDP | (Annual average compound growth rates) | | Volume of exports |
		GDP per head of population	Tangible reproducible non-residential fixed capital stock	
I ∫1820-70	2.2[a]	1.0[a]	(n.a.)	4.0[b]
∖1870-1913	2.5	1.4	2.9	3.9
II 1913-50	1.9	1.2	1.7	1.0
III 1950-73	4.9	3.8	5.5	8.6
IV 1973-9	2.5	2.0	4.4[c]	4.8

[a] Average for 13 countries.
[b] Average for 10 countries.
[c] 1973-8.

Source: Tables 1.3, 1.4, 5.4, 3.7.

TABLE 4.10

Cyclical Characteristics of Different Phases, 1820-1979
(Arithmetic average of figures for individual countries)

Phases	Maximum peak-to-trough fall in GDP (or smallest rise) annual data	Maximum peak-to-trough fall in export volume	Average unemployment rate (percentage of labour force)	Average annual rise in consumer prices
I ∫1820-70	− 6.7[a]	−21.7[b]	(n.a.)	0.2[b]
∖1870-1913	− 6.1	−18.2	4.5[c]	0.4
II 1920-38	−11.9	−36.5	7.3	−0.7[d]
III 1950-73	+ 0.4	− 7.0	3.0	4.1
IV 1973-9	− 1.3	− 6.4	4.1	9.5

[a] Denmark, France and UK only.
[b] France, Germany, Sweden, UK, and USA only.
[c] UK and USA 1900-13.
[d] 1924-38 for Austria and Germany, 1921-38 for Belgium.

Source: Tables 4.1, 3.8, C6 and 6.4.

2. Most of the characteristics are systematically different in the four phases identified. Generally, they are most favourable in phase III, second-best in phase IV, third-best in phase I and worst in phase II. This is true for six of the eight aggregative indicators

TABLE 4.11

System Characteristics of Different Phases

Governmental policy stance on unemployment/price price stability trade-off	Nature of international payments system	Labour market behaviour	Degree of freedom for international trade	Degree of freedom for international factor movements
I 1820-1913 'The Liberal Phase'				
No concern with unemployment	Gold (sterling) standard with rigid exchange rates exerts somewhat deflationary influence cushioned by wage flexibility	Weak unions; wages have some downward flexibility	Very free. No QRs but tariffs rise in second half of period	More or less complete freedom
II 1913-50 'The Beggar-Your-Neighbour' Phase				
Concern with price and exchange stability leads to conscious acceptance of large scale unemployment	Gold standard restored at nostalgic parities, and quarrels over government debt exert extreme deflationary influence and induce 1931 system collapse followed by move to moveable peg	Governments enforce downward wage flexibility involving a good deal of social conflict	QRs and tariffs raise very substantial barriers	Severe controls on both capital and labour
III 1950-73 'The Golden Age'				
Priority given to full employment	Fixed (but not rigid) exchange rate (dollar-based) system, international credit arrangements soften potential deflationary effects	Strong unions, no downward wage flexibility, social climate relaxed for most of period	Very strong move towards freer trade and customs unions	Gradual and substantial freeing of both labour and capital movement
IV 1973 onwards 'The Phase of Blurred Objectives'				
Lessened concern with full employment, more with price stability	System collapse followed by floating rates	Strong unions, strong upward bias in wage price expectations	Free trade maintained	Free capital movements remain, labour movement restricted

in Tables 4.9 and 4.10. The exceptions to the second-best rating of phase IV are the pace of price increase, where phase IV is worst, and export fluctuations, where phase IV shows best performance.

3. I have already indicated my choice of terminal points for phases. Here there is obviously room for argument as to which years to use for demarcation purposes, particularly as the use of annual data means that the periodicity has to be rather precise. I explained in Chapter 3 why I picked 1820 as the starting point for capitalist development; 1913 is clearly the last year of phase I, which ended with the outbreak of the First World War; and 1950 was chosen as a point where recovery from the Second World War was more or less completed in terms of recovery of the previous peak in output for the sixteen countries as a whole. However, four countries did not pass their wartime output peaks until 1954 (Japan), 1953 (Germany and the UK), and 1951 (USA), respectively, so one might well argue that 1953 rather than 1950 should mark the beginning of the postwar golden age. On the other hand, one might also argue for starting in 1948, which is when the ground rules for international co-operation within the capitalist group were set up by the Marshall Plan; so 1950 seems a reasonable compromise. It should be noted that use of 1948-73 or 1953-73 instead of 1950-73 would not affect the analysis seriously—the third phase would still appear as a period of secular boom on an unparalleled scale, and the second phase would still be the one with worst performance.

4. The dating of the fourth phase, from 1973 onwards, is perhaps the most controversial. There is always the danger of over-reacting to a recession and assuming that a new phase has begun when we are in fact faced with a temporary disturbance. However, the 1974-5 recession affected virtually all sixteen countries; the recovery has been slow, halting, and incomplete; and it was by far the biggest break in the postwar growth momentum. Although the recession in output was the most dramatic herald of change, there have been deeper causes, which probably mean that we live in a different phase from that of the 1950s and 1960s. The grounds for treating the post-1973 period as a new phase include observation of price as well as output behaviour, consideration of changes in the international monetary system, changes in government policy concerning the level of demand, changes in expectations in the labour market, and changes in the international economic power balance—some of which occurred just before 1973. The economic system behaves in

a different way, which creates major new tasks for economic policy, not all of which have been properly diagnosed. It is also more difficult now to reconcile different policy objectives.

Recognition of the phase phenomenon is important for growth analysis, because it forces consideration of factors operating for the group as a whole. Each phase is an orbit within which the countries are constrained to move. This does not prevent them from following different trajectories, but it means that their options are different from those they had in earlier orbits. Each phase has its own momentum which it is difficult to break, except by some collective happening. The breaks in trend between phases have in fact been caused mainly by system-shocks rather than by collective planning and foresight.

Growth analysis is an area of major controversy and can be carried out at several levels. One can subject the proximate causes to elaborate growth accounting as Denison has done. This approach is illuminating, but one cannot adequately interpret growth by concentrating entirely on supply factors, and Chapter 6 therefore looks at reasons for long-run variations in the buoyancy of demand or expectations, and at interactions between countries.

In my view, a good deal of the variation in growth performance between periods and countries can be proximately explained by differences in growth of capital stock and foreign trade; but growth in these areas depends on buoyancy of investment and export incentives, which depend on the level and stability of demand, which in turn are affected by the policy-institutional setting. The chain of causation is complex enough to make it difficult to separate symptoms from causes, but it is clear that there can be self-reinforcing interaction of different causes. Similarly, there are mutual interactions between countries which help create the phase patterns. There is obvious interaction between countries with regard to the aggregate momentum of foreign trade, and this is also true of capital formation.

The main conclusions I would draw about major fluctuations in the momentum of capitalist development are as follows.

1. There are distinct phases of economic performance, each with its own momentum.
2. Phases of growth are not ineluctable, and within each phase there is considerable scope for variation in country performance; but the policy-institutional framework is determined by

rather simple basic rules and expectations which have an inertia of their own.

3. The move from one phase to another is caused by system-shocks. These shocks may well be due to a predictable breakdown of some basic characteristic of a previous phase, but the timing of the change is usually governed by exogenous or accidental events which are not predictable.

4. A more specific conclusion is that developments since 1973 represent a new phase and not just a temporary interruption of phase III.

5. The present phase generally ranks as second-best. Performance is well below that in phase III in almost all important respects, but the economy has been a good deal more stable in real terms than before 1950, and the growth of output per capita is significantly better than in the first two phases. The two most discouraging features of the latest phase are the output record, which has been depressingly poor considering the relatively high growth of capital stock, and the price record, which is worse than in any of the other phases and has become a major pre-occupation of policy.

6. It is not easy to predict whether phase IV will continue to be second-best. Policy problems are particularly difficult in a new phase in which the ground rules are changed, and where there is uncertainty about the permanency of novel characteristics. The system changes from phase III to phase IV have been pretty fundamental: i.e., the move from a fixed to a floating exchange system, the change in expectations in labour markets, the auto-nomous shocks coming from OPEC, and the reduced importance given by governments to the goal of full employment. Freedom for trade and capital movements has been preserved but is under challenge, and freedom for migration has been seriously curtailed. The continuance of substantial slack in capital utilization will lower investment incentives, the future growth of capital stock, and the rate of technical progress. All this means that a return to phase III standards of performance is unlikely, and that a wide range of new policy issues will have to be solved if phase IV is to remain second-best.

5

PHASES OF PRODUCTIVITY GROWTH

ONE of the most intriguing questions about capitalist performance over the past 160 years is why average productivity performance accelerated so greatly in the third phase (the 'Golden Age'), from 1950 to 1973, and why the pace of advance slackened so markedly after 1973.

It is clear from Table 5.1 that from 1950 to 1973 output per man-hour rose at unprecedented rates—more than twice as fast as in the previous eighty years. The acceleration was sharpest in Austria, Germany, Italy, and Japan, where productivity was most adversely affected by the war and its aftermath, but the improvement in all European countries was very substantial. Indeed, the only exception to this generally euphoric situation, was in the lead country—

TABLE 5.1

Phases of Productivity Growth (GDP per Man-Hour), 1870-1979

| | Annual average compound growth rate | | | | |
	1870-1913	1913-50	1950-73	1973-9	1870-1979
Australia	0.6	1.6	2.6	2.6	1.5
Austria	1.7	0.9	5.9	3.8	2.4
Belgium	1.2	1.4	4.4	4.2	2.1
Canada	2.0	2.3	3.0	1.0	2.3
Denmark	1.9	1.6	4.3	1.6	2.3
Finland	2.1	2.0	5.2	1.7	2.7
France	1.8	2.0	5.1	3.5	2.6
Germany	1.9	1.1	6.0	4.2	2.6
Italy	1.2	1.8	5.8	2.5	2.4
Japan	1.8	1.3	8.0	3.9	3.0
Netherlands	1.2	1.7	4.4	3.3	2.1
Norway	1.7	2.5	4.2	3.9	2.6
Sweden	2.3	2.8	4.2	1.9	2.9
Switzerland	1.4	2.1	3.4	1.3	2.1
United Kingdom	1.2	1.6	3.1	2.1	1.8
United States	2.0	2.6	2.6	1.4	2.3
Arithmetic average	1.6	1.8	4.5	2.7	2.4

Source: Appendix C.

the United States—where postwar productivity growth to 1973 was no better than in 1913-50.

Since 1973, productivity performance has deteriorated in fifteen of the sixteen countries investigated. Average growth was 2.7 per cent a year from 1973 to 1979 as compared with 4.5 per cent in the Golden Age (1950-73). This is a very considerable slowdown even though generally better than historical experience before 1950. In all countries, faltering performance since 1973 is explicable in important degree by an adverse 'conjuncture' of more than usual cyclical dimensions which has impeded productivity growth by disturbing demand and resource allocation. And in Europe and Japan, longer-term considerations also help explain the productivity slowdown, because some of the specially favourable opportunies affecting supply potential in the 1950s and 1960s have been eroded. The productivity slowdown in the USA since 1973 has been relatively greater and more mysterious than in Europe because the longer-term productivity opportunities of the USA should have been improving, not deteriorating. The American productivity lead over some of the European countries (Belgium, France, Germany, and the Netherlands) has now been whittled down to the point where the US burden of technical pioneering and developing new consumer products can be shared with others (Table 5.2). In such a situation one might well have expected US productivity growth to accelerate rather than slow down. Instead, the retardation has been greater than in Europe. This raises an important question. Does it reflect a slackened pace of technical progress, which will ultimately constrain the growth possibilities for all countries as they catch up to the US level? I do not think this is likely. There are some special reasons for the American slowdown, and a similar retardation occurred in the 1929-38 period. I do conclude that the USA will lose its exclusivity as productivity leader and that there is a reasonable chance that the new collective leadership will prove more dynamic than the USA has been.

All the foregoing remarks relate to aggregate productivity. Movements by sector of the economy are considered towards the end of this chapter. However, it is worth noting that the slowdown of productivity, employment, and output since 1973 has been much more marked in industry than in services and agriculture.

Chapter 4 divided average experience since 1870 into four major phases during which the underlying pace of GDP growth differed

TABLE 5.2

Comparative Levels of Productivity, 1870-1979

(US GDP per man-hour = 100)

	1870	1890	1913	1938	1950	1973	1979
Australia	186	153	102	89	72	73	78
Austria	61	58	54	(47)	29	62	71
Belgium	106	96	75	70	50	75	88
Canada	87	81	87	67	78	87	85
Denmark	63	58	60	60	43	63	64
Finland	41	35	43	44	35	63	64
France	60	55	54	64	44	76	86
Germany	61	58	57	56	33	71	84
Italy	63	44	43	49	32	66	70
Japan	24	(23)	22	33	14	46	53
Netherlands	106	(92)	74	68	53	81	90
Norway	57	53	49	62	48	69	80
Sweden	44	42	50	59	55	79	81
Switzerland	79	70	60	70	52	62	62
United Kingdom	114	100	81	70	56	64	66
United States	100	100	100	100	100	100	100
Arithmetic average of 15 countries (excluding USA)	77	68	61	61	46	69	75

Source: Appendix C.

significantly. However, productivity growth has tended to be smoother than GDP. It has shown less cyclical sensitivity and has also varied less from one phase to another. Average productivity growth for the sixteen countries increased slightly in the 1913-50 period instead of slackening as output did.[1] Similarly, the slackening in the 1970s has been more marked for output than productivity (see Table 5.3).

TABLE 5.3

Summary Comparison of Growth Rates, 1870-1979

	Annual average compound growth rates—average for 16 countries			
	GDP	GDP per man-hour	Labour force	Total hours worked
1870-1913	2.5	1.6	1.2	0.9
1913-50	1.9	1.8	0.8	0.1
1950-73	4.9	4.5	1.0	0.3
1973-9	2.5	2.7	1.1	−0.1

FACTORS INFLUENCING PRODUCTIVITY GROWTH

Productivity growth is influenced by many factors, but I concentrate on six which have figured prominently in most discussions:

1. the degree of buoyancy and stability in *demand* and demand expectations;
2. the pace of *technical progress* as reflected by the movement of best-practice productivity in the lead country;
3. the growth of the *capital stock*, as the principal instrument for exploiting technical progress, and for reducing the technical lag between the leader and the followers;
4. *inter-country transmission* of pro-growth influences, in particular through trade;
5. *structural changes*;
6. other factors affecting the *efficiency* of resource allocation.

Each of these is discussed more fully in the following sections.

The Level and Stability of Demand

Demand conditions have their most direct impact on economic growth by affecting the degree of resource use. If the labour supply is not fully used, output will be below potential. This was most obvious in the early 1930s, when mass unemployment led to massive losses of output. In the 1950s and 1960s unprecedently high levels of demand reduced unemployment to extremely low levels. After 1973, slack demand reemerged as a serious problem.

The impact of demand conditions on employment was at the heart of prewar 'Keynesian' business cycle analysis. In the postwar period, it has become clear that the buoyancy and stability of demand can also be a major factor determining productivity growth. There was a backlog of opportunity on the 'supply' side which enabled productivity in these economies to respond very favourably once the right climate of demand and expectations of future demand had been created.

The impact of high and stable demand was cumulative. The short- or medium-term prospect of recession was reduced to negligible proportions. Price fluctuations were almost invariably upwards. Borrowing risks were reduced, the dangers of keeping liquid funds rather than assets increased. Real interest rates were very low. Experience of such a situation gradually changed entrepreneurial attitudes. Instead of worrying about investment risks, entrepreneurs became more aware of the consequences of not investing; i.e., a lack of capacity to meet expanding demand with consequent loss of market share to competitors, and rising labour costs owing to inadequate investment to raise productivity and offset rising wages.[2] After several years of very low unemployment, downwardly inflexible prices, and the virtual disappearance of the business cycle, entrepreneurial expectations became euphoric, and the aggregate rate of investment in these countries rose steadily. The 1950s were already a period of unprecedentedly high investment by historical standards, but the 1960s were even better.

The main instrument by which high demand created high productivity growth was by raising the rate of investment and the growth of the capital stock. Except in the United States, the growth of capital stock in 1950-73 proceeded at an unprecedented pace in all the countries shown in Table 5.4, and the average pace was more than three times that of 1913-50.

TABLE 5.4

Rate of Growth of Non-residential Fixed Capital Stock, 1870-1978

| | Annual average compound growth rate—average of net and gross stocks | | | |
	1870-1913	1913-50	1950-73	1973-8
Canada	(n.a.)	2.0[c]	5.5	5.0
France	(n.a.)	(1.0)	4.5	4.5
Germany	(3.1)	(1.0)	6.1	4.1
Italy	[2.5][a]	[2.2]	[5.1]	[4.2]
Japan	2.7[b]	[3.3]	9.2[d]	6.5[d]
UK	1.4	0.7	3.9	3.2
USA	4.7	2.0	4.0	3.0
Arithmetic average	2.9	1.7	5.5	4.4

[a] 1882-1913.
[b] 1880-1913.
[c] 1926-50.
[d] The net stock refers only to the private sector.

Note: All figures are adjusted to eliminate the impact of changes in geographic area. Figures in round brackets refer to net stock only; figures in square brackets to gross stock only

Source: See Appendix D.

There were other transmission mechanisms favouring growth in this virtuous circle situation, which were of lesser importance than accelerated investment but none the less significant in their contribution to growth. High demand flushed surplus labour out of low productivity occupations, both within countries and by promoting international migration; it improved efficiency, and induced economies of scale.

Since 1973 the virtuous circle has been put into reverse. There was a generalized recession in 1974-5 induced by the oil shock, and the subsequent economic recovery was incomplete when a second oil shock in 1979 induced a second period of recession. This prolonged *malaise* is not a business cycle in the classical sense, but the fruit of concerted governmental policies to restrict demand in the hope of mitigating price increases and payments disequilibria.

The causes of the new demand situation and the new policy responses of the 1970s are analysed in Chapter 6. Here I would simply note their adverse impact on productivity since 1973. In the first place, growth potential has been damaged because investment has been cut back. The growth of capital stock decelerated after 1973 (see Table 5.4), though it still exceeds peak prewar growth rates except in the USA.

In periods of slack demand, firms are generally slow to dismiss workers, and will hoard labour voluntarily to some degree and for some time. This has an adverse impact on productivity growth in most recessions. This tendency was reinforced in the 1970s by various kinds of employment subsidy or penalties for lay-offs. Several governments thus subsidized weak productivity firms which might otherwise have gone out of business. Employment in the government sector, which is now rather large and where productivity considerations are never strong, was expanded in the 1970s, in many cases with a view to providing some mitigation of the unemployment problem. All of the aforementioned practices tended to reduce the efficiency of resource allocation in ways that may or may not be recuperable when the macroeconomic climate improves.

Finally, any consideration of the conjunctural element in the productivity slowdown must include the price shocks administered by the OPEC cartel in 1973-4 and in 1979. The OPEC impact on productivity can be considered in two dimensions: direct and indirect. In the first place, there are the directly adverse effects on resource allocation in economies whose major source of energy increased in price by fourfold in 1973-4 and doubled again in 1979. This reduced the profitability and use of capital invested in energy-intensive buildings and machinery and caused a substitution of labour and materials for energy. There is considerable con-

troversy about the size of these directly adverse effects on productivity. Most of the estimates of the GDP loss relate to the USA
and cover a wide range. Using Denison's approach, the US productivity loss in this narrowly defined sense was only around 0.1
percentage points a year from 1973 to 1976. Other observers, such
as Rasche and Tatom, have advanced estimates more than ten times
higher than Denison's, which would attribute the whole of the US
productivity slowdown since 1973 to the direct impact of energy
problems.[3]

The direct impact of the energy price rise on productivity probably lies nearer to Denison's estimate than to that of Rasche and
Tatom, but a full accounting of the OPEC actions would be bigger
because these were a major cause of policies of cautious demand
management. The sudden rise in oil prices and the temporary oil
embargo contributed to inflation and inflationary expectations at
a critical point in 1973-4. It reopened inflationary fires in 1979. It
created large payments deficits and added greatly to uncertainties
about the financing mechanism to cover these deficits. These
factors were decisive in inducing cautious macroeconomic policies
in the major countries and are described in detail in Chapter 6
below.

The three 'conjunctural' elements in the productivity slowdown—i.e., the slowdown in investment, the general reduction in
efficiency associated with the sudden change of pace in demand,
and the special problems of energy—account for a sizeable part
of the productivity slowdown since 1973, but a full explanation
requires investigation of longer-term factors, whose influence is
more complex, and different in their incidence for the USA than
for the other countries.

Technical Progress

The most elusive problem in productivity analysis is the role of
technical progress. It is sometimes asserted that the postwar acceleration of productivity growth is due in large part to a faster pace
of technical advance. This argument often comes from those who
measure technical progress as a residual in production functions in
which the growth in capital stock is given only a third the weight of
labour input.

My approach is different. I assume that the pace of technical
progress is closely related to the rate of advance of best practice

productivity. This is not measurable directly, but as a rough proxy, I use the rate of growth of the average productivity level in the lead country—the USA. In fact, US productivity growth has been much steadier than that in the other countries. Most importantly, the USA has not had the postwar acceleration in productivity growth that has occurred in all the other countries. I conclude from this that the technical frontier has moved forward rather steadily. The productivity acceleration in most countries in the postwar period has, however, brought them much closer to the frontier.

Although I would not want to suggest that US productivity leadership on the macroeconomic level means that it has carried the whole burden of technical innovation for this group of countries, it is nevertheless clear from detailed cross-section studies that the aggregate US productivity advantage also applied until recently in most individual sections of the economy. Rostas found that, in 1935-9, United States output per man-hour was above that in the United Kingdom in all of the thirty-one industries in which he could make comparisons. He also found that the USA was ahead of Germany in all cases in a cruder comparison for 1936-7. I found the same all-round superiority of the USA in a comparison with Canada for twelve industries for 1935, and in 1963 West found only two out of twenty-nine industries in which Canadian net output per man-hour was unequivocally higher than in the USA.[4]

For 1950 we have a major study by Paige and Bombach of productivity levels in the UK and the USA. They compared performance in the major sectors of the economy and for forty-four individual industries. Although the US advantage varied a good deal from one area to another, it had an absolute lead in every case.[5] This in 1950—when the average UK productivity level was higher than that in all the other European countries, and four times as high as in Japan.

In a recent study for 1972 comparing physical output per employee year for sixty products in the USA and Japan, Yukizawa found sixteen cases where Japanese productivity exceeded that in the United States. The number is reduced to six when the comparison is restated in terms of man-hours, because Japanese worked 20 per cent more hours than Americans in 1972.[6] These results are somewhat surprising considering that aggregate Japanese productivity was only about half of that in the United States in 1972, but Japanese productivity levels by sector are more widely dispersed than in most other countries, and it would seem therefore that in a few areas Japan has claimed the mantle of technological leadership from the United States.

As European countries are now approaching the average US productivity level (and are closer to it than Japan), it is to be expected that they too will be increasingly taking over some areas of technical leadership.

Thus far, we have considered average productivity levels in different countries, either at the aggregate or industry level, and have used this as evidence of US technical leadership. But average productivity figures are only a proxy for the data we need. Technical leadership rests with the 'best-practice' plants or firms and not with the average. Within any country there is a wide spread of productivity performance among plants in a given industry as well as between industries. The US Bureau of Labor Statistics has developed figures on within-industry spreads of labour productivity from the 1967 US census of manufactures. These show the range between firms divided into quartiles. The ratio of top quartile to average value added per production worker hour is indicated in Table 5.5.[7] The mean ratio of best to average practice in the

TABLE 5.5
Productivity Spreads Within US Industries, 1967
(Quartiles)

	Ratio of productivity in 'most efficient' to average	Ratio of productivity in 'most efficient' to 'least efficient'
Hydraulic cement	1.71	2.97
Blast furnaces and steel mills	1.41	2.96
Steel pipe and tubes	1.58	2.89
Aircraft	1.28	4.54
Aircraft engines and engine parts	1.58	4.05
Other aircraft equipment	1.65	3.57
Cotton weaving	1.50	2.40
Women's hosiery, except socks	1.60	2.80
Knit fabric	2.20	4.90
Tufted carpets	1.90	5.20
Sawmills	1.70	4.10
Tyres	1.40	3.20
Aluminium rolling and drawing	1.50	4.00

Source: BLS, *Technological Change and Manpower Trends in Six Industries*, Bulletin 1817, Washington, 1974, and *Technological Change and Manpower Trends in Five Industries*, Bulletin 1856, Washington, 1975.

thirteen cases cited is 1.6; but this is the range only for quartiles. For individual plants the range would be wider than this.

These spreads within individual industries exist in all countries. Lundberg cites figures for Swedish pulp and paper which are ratios of performance in the top decile of plants to the industry average. For 1964 the ratio of best to average practice was 2.0 in pulp and 2.2 in paper. The spreads from best to worst deciles were 3.8 and 4.4 respectively.[8]

These interplant variations are due mainly (but not exclusively) to use in different plants of different vintages of capital, embodying technical knowledge of successive periods. Some of the differences will reflect variations in managerial or labour efficiency; but, generally speaking, the high-productivity plants have modern capital equipment and the low-productivity plants have old equipment. If technical progress were disembodied, and infusable into all existing capital stock as it occurs, then the systematic differences in productivity between old and new plants would be much smaller.[9] I am not suggesting that each successive vintage of capital is associated with a fixed productivity level throughout its life, and that optimum use prevails as from the date of installation. In fact, there may well be a considerable period in which performance is raised by what Arrow, echoing John Dewey, has called 'learning by doing'.

Technical progress in the USA has consisted in the process of investment in new plant which raises the level of best-practice technology. Every year some old plants are scrapped because new investment in superior equipment has over time gradually made them obsolete. They are scrapped when the saving in variable costs owing to installation of new capital becomes large enough to cover the extra fixed costs of buying the latter.

It is not possible to measure the pace of advance in best-practice productivity directly. In the short run it will move rather unevenly, and the lag between best and average practice will vary over time; but in the long run it probably moves more or less in line with average productivity. The movement in average productivity will be smoother than that of best-practice, because it reflects the cumulative impact of all vintages of technology currently in use, whereas best-practice productivity advances more or less in line with new investment. It is certainly true that the capital stock moves more smoothly than does new investment, as is clear from Graph 5.1.[10]

The most ambitious attempt to deal with inventive activity,

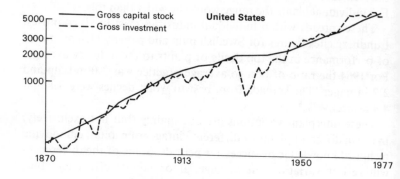

Graph 5.1 *Gross Non-residential Fixed Investment and Gross Non-residential Fixed Capital Stock in the USA, 1870-1977 (1870 = 100).* (*Source*: Table 2.3 and Appendix D)

innovation, and their relationship to economic growth is by Schmookler.[11] He argues that the development of new products and processes is induced by demand. The direction of change is determined by the desire to lower costs or conquer new markets. It is determined endogenously and not by the autonomous growth of scientific knowledge. Scientific discovery is 'far more a permissive than an active factor in the invention process'. If scientific capacity is limited in one field, a 'functionally equivalent invention' will be devised using knowledge from some other branch of science: 'mankind today possesses, and for some time has possessed, a multipurpose knowledge base. We are, and evidently for some time have been, able to extend the technological frontier perceptibly at virtually all points.' He argues even more strongly that 'the very high correlations obtained ... between capital goods invention and investment levels in different industries ... indicate that a million dollars spent on one kind of good is likely to induce about as much invention as the same sum spent on any other good.' He buttresses this argument with evidence drawn from US patent statistics (and chronologies of major inventions) covering a period of a century and a half, and he makes his demand-induced argument for capital goods, consumer goods, and new materials. In railways, he lists 232 'important' inventions between 1800 and 1957, and almost 99,000 US patents between 1837 and 1957. Hence the process of technical change for Schmookler is diffused, and certainly not concentrated in major waves. Schmookler says that 'long-term economic growth is primarily the result of the growth of technological knowledge', but the direction of its growth is induced by demand, and the pace of its growth seems to be determined by the rate of investment.

Schmookler is concerned almost entirely with the direction of innovation rather than with its pace of advance, but he seems to be saying that the latter is constrained only by the pace of demand and the degree to which it can be matched by investment. In effect, he says that there are constant returns to inventive effort. If you spend twice as much on technical progress you get twice as much progress—there are no diminishing returns. If this were so, then the pace of technical progress would presumably depend on the research effort and rate of investment that the lead country chooses to have. The Schmookler position would imply that, if the USA had pursued more aggressive policies to promote R and D and high investment, then technical progress would have been faster in the past. It also implies that, if the USA is superceded as leader by countries with more aggressive policies in this sense, then technical progress will be faster in future.

Rosenberg has challenged Schmookler's views on this issue.[12] His critique is concerned more with the applicability of Schmookler's highly ingenious arguments concerning the forces determining the direction of technical change, but it is even more valid as a critique with respect to the implications of Schmookler on the pace of technical advance in the lead country. Rosenberg's main point is that science and technology are not omnicompetent; that certain obvious long-standing human needs 'have long gone either unsatisfied or very badly catered for in spite of a well-established demand'; and that attempts to quicken the pace of technical progress run into decreasing returns because the necessary process of trial and error imposes constraints on the pace of development of knowledge. There are also limits on the size of the pool of technical skills available to develop and diffuse new techniques and get them operating successfully.

As far as the lead country is concerned, I agree with Rosenberg that these factors have been the ultimate constraint on the feasible pace of productivity growth. The follower countries are in a different situation. For them, the pace of productivity advance can be much faster and depends mainly on the rate at which they can increase their capital stock. This does not imply that US technical progress has proceeded historically at its 'warranted' or 'natural' rate. It is clear that the level of demand (as measured by the rate of unemployment) could have been substantially higher in a fair proportion of years in the past few decades. There were also quite a number of years in which investment rates were well below previous peaks.

For the follower countries, the problem of technical progress has been different from that of the USA. Over most of the range of production processes and product innovation, the other countries have not had to break new ground. They have had to imitate rather than innovate. One should not exaggerate the ease of this process. They have had to adapt known technology to their particular needs in terms of product mix, factor prices, resource endowments, labour relations, consumer tastes, export ambitions, size of plant, etc. All this requires 'improvement engineering', technical and managerial skills, and an ability to remain familiar with a range of technical practice that is constantly changing in the lead country. Nevertheless the followers have not faced the same risks and problems as the leader except in those small sectors of their economy—Japan with TV sets, the UK and France with Concorde—where they have surpassed or tried to surpass US performance.[13]

Follower countries catching up with US best-practice technology have been in the situation Schmookler described. They have been able to raise their rate of investment and pace of productivity growth without the ultimate constraints the USA faced. One might ask why the follower countries waited so long to reduce the gap between themselves and the leader. Presumably, the opportunities to overcome backwardness were open before the great productivity spurt that started after the Second World War. I think the answer is as follows. The USA developed its productivity lead initially in the period from the 1890s to 1913, at a time when its prospects were particularly bright because of its great natural resource advantages, huge internal market, and rapid population growth. This fostered higher rates of investment than in Europe and a faster growth of capital per employee. By 1913 the US productivity advantage over the UK—the old leader—was about a quarter. One cannot tell how wide this productivity gap would have become in 'normal' circumstances. Eventually, the forces making for US ascendancy would have faded, as indeed they now have. In the meantime, however, the productivity gap became very much bigger, mainly because of the two world wars—both of which stimulated the US economy and retarded the advance of the other countries. In 1950 there was an unnatural degree of dispersion between the USA and most of the other countries. This was why the latter did so well in growth terms simply by implementing sensible policies for full employment and freer trade. High demand propelled them into a situation of unprecedentedly high investment and eliminated a good deal of their technical backlog.

As other countries draw nearer to US productivity levels, their pace of development will be much more dependent on the pace of advance of the technical frontier, and to that extent can be expected to be slower.

Growth and Level of the Capital Stock

The productivity opportunities offered by technical progress cannot be exploited unless the capital stock per worker is renewed and expanded. Table 5.6 shows the growth rates of capital stock per man-hour in the seven biggest countries. The figures refer to the

TABLE 5.6
Rate of Growth of Non-residential Fixed Capital Stock per Man-Hour, 1870-1978

	Annual average compound growth rate—average of net and gross stock			
	1870-1913	*1913-50*	*1950-73*	*1973-78*
Canada	(n.a.)	1.8^c	3.4	3.0
France	(n.a.)	(1.7)	4.5	5.3
Germany	(2.1)	(0.9)	6.1	6.3
Italy	[2.3]^a	[2.6]	[5.4]	[6.3]
Japan	2.0^b	[2.9]	7.6^d	6.8^d
UK	0.6	0.8	4.0	4.3
USA	2.6	1.9	2.9	1.8
Arithmetic average	1.9	1.8	4.8	4.8

Note: All figures are adjusted to eliminate the impact of changes in geographic area. Figures in round brackets refer to net stock only; figures in square brackets to gross stock only.

^{a} 1882-1913.
^{b} 1880-1913.
^{c} 1926-50.
^{d} The net stock refers only to the private sector.

Source: See Appendix D.

fixed non-residential tangible capital stock (excluding land). They show quite clearly the sharp acceleration in the growth of capital stock per man-hour in Europe and Japan, and the much faster postwar growth of capital stock in these countries than in the USA. Since 1973 the capital stock has grown more slowly, as noted in Table 5.4 above, but except in the USA the growth of capital stock per man-hour has been remarkably well sustained. As a result of slack demand since 1973, there has also been slack use of capacity, which probably means that there is also some cyclical productivity slack which would be available when demand expands.

It is sometimes argued that the productivity performance of economies is highly dependent on the stock of 'educational capital' embodied in the labour force. The relationship of education to economic performance is obviously a rather subtle matter of both cause and effect, complicated by variations in the quality of education, by the existence of many opportunities for learning outside formal education, and by the fact that the roles of intelligence and education are difficult to disentangle. Estimates of the educational stock in 1976 in thirteen countries are presented in Table 5.7. The USA held the lead in education as it did in productivity, with a 10 per cent overall educational advantage over its nearest rival Canada, and an even more marked advantage in higher education. Italy was clearly the laggard, but Japan was near the top in terms of education, in spite of being at the bottom in terms of productivity.

TABLE 5.7

Average Years of Formal Educational Experience of the Population Aged 25-64 in 1976

	Total	Primary	Secondary	Higher
Belgium	10.30	6.00	3.68	0.62
Canada	10.54	5.83	4.15	0.56
Denmark	9.70	5.00	4.25	0.45
Finland	8.98	6.00	2.59	0.39
France	9.87	5.00	4.31	0.56
Germany	9.36	4.00	5.13	0.23
Italy	6.91	4.40	2.27	0.24
Japan	10.42	6.00	3.98	0.44
Netherlands	9.14	6.00	2.70	0.44
Norway	9.28	7.00	1.81	0.47
Sweden	9.33	6.00	2.68	0.65
UK	10.41	6.00	4.12	0.29
USA	11.60	5.80	4.75	1.05

Japan's 'surplus capacity' in this respect may well have been a necessary condition for its productivity leap in the postwar period, which required great capacity to adapt to changing techniques of production.

All countries have increased the educational qualifications of their populations significantly since 1950, but the economic significance of this is probably no greater than the changes that occurred from 1870 to 1950. In 1976 the average stock of formal education per person in these countries was 9.7 years; in 1950 it was 8.2 years. The evidence available for a few countries suggests that in 1870 the average stock of education per person in these countries was about 3 to 4 years, with substantial sections of the population illiterate and with very little higher education at all.

It does not seem, therefore, that the postwar acceleration of productivity growth was matched by an acceleration in the growth of educational capital. Similarly, it is clear that the slackening in productivity growth since 1973 is in no way due to a slowing down in the pace of growth of educational capital. Indeed, the evidence available shows more rapid growth in the educational stock in the 1970s than in the 1960s or 1950s (see Table 5.8).

International Diffusion Mechanisms

There are a number of dimensions in which growth influences can be diffused between countries. The discussion here is restricted to trade.

Trade is an important component of demand, and one that has been highly unstable at times in the past. Confident expectations about export markets are a key factor in general confidence, particularly as export markets are the ones generally pursued by the entrepreneurs most willing to take risks and invest. Conversely, uncertain or pessimistic export expectations will have an adverse general effect on demand. For any particular country, export demand will be determined by events in the world as a whole; but the degree to which the buoyancy of world demand is transmitted to it will depend upon its exchange rate. A country may create a depressed demand situation for its entrepreneurs if it retains a rate that overvalues its currency. Conversely, it may stimulate demand by undervaluing the exchange rate. In the postwar period the importance of trade as a factor in demand has been stressed by Beckerman and Lamfalussy,[14] who attributed the better performance

TABLE 5.8

Change in Average Per Capita Educational Experience of the Population Aged 25-64, 1950-80

| | Annual average compound growth rate | | |
	1950-60	1960-70	1970-80
Belgium	0.6	0.8	0.9
Canada	0.6	0.8	1.0
Denmark	0.3	0.5	0.6
Finland	n.a.	n.a.	n.a.
France	0.5	0.6	1.0
Germany	n.a.	0.5	0.2
Italy	1.1	1.4	1.6
Japan	1.1	1.1	0.8
Netherlands	0.4	0.7	1.0
Norway	0.3	0.6	1.2
Sweden	n.a.	0.8	1.2
UK	0.3	0.4	0.6
USA	0.8	0.9	0.9
Arithmetic average	0.6	0.8	0.9

Source: Derived from *Educational Statistics Yearbook*, vol. I, OECD, Paris, 1974, and *Education, Inequality and Life Chances*, OECD, Paris, 1975. The figures are derived from census material with adjustments to enhance the comparability of the classification by level of education.

of some countries to export-led growth and characterized under-valuation/overvaluation situations as creating virtuous/vicious circles which can last for a long time and produce a cumulative momentum towards euphoria/depression in entrepreneurs in a fixed rate system.

I think there is a good deal in this argument. It seems quite plausible that the UK suffered from an overvalued currency with brief intervals more or less continuously from the 1870s to 1967. The argument to this effect in the 1920s and 1960s is well known, but in the forty years preceding the First World War overvaluation[15] probably had a great deal to do with the very low rate of domestic investment, and the very large exports of capital and labour. The UK returned nostalgically to the prewar gold parity in the 1920s and was probably overvalued for a good deal of the 1950s and 1960s. This may well be an important reason for the UK's tortoise-like performance in the long run.

In the 1970s, there has been a drastic change in the payments system of these countries, with the move from pegged to floating exchange rates. The old system collapsed under the strain of widely different rates of inflation between countries, the openness of capital markets to large speculative movements, the desire of the reserve currency country to change its parity relative to other major traders, and the reluctance of the latter to revalue. The new system has worked reasonably well considering the nature of the disturbances involved; trade has continued to expand, and the vast size of the international capital market, which was a nuisance in a fixed rate world, has helped considerably in launching the new system— where flexibility, diversity, and anonymity were needed by the new OPEC creditors. In principle, the new system reduces efficiency slightly by raising transaction costs for traders, but it gives greater leeway for the pursuit of independent national policies for promoting full employment and economic growth. The latter possibilities have not yet been fully exploited, and the operation of the new system has been complicated to some degree by continued pursuit of policies more appropriate to a fixed rate system, and by efforts to modify and 'manage' the extent of the float.

There are several ways in which trade can help directly in improving resource allocation and productivity, but their relative importance is a matter of considerable disagreement. A lot depends upon the approach taken. One may take a 'counterfactual' viewpoint, and ask what would happen in the absence of international trade. The impact on productivity levels would be catastrophic in some of the smaller countries, whose trade ratios are very high, and whose productivity levels depend heavily on international specialization. Large countries would also suffer very badly, because several of them would be deprived of access to raw materials and energy, without which output and productivity would suffer a great deal. However, this approach is too apocalyptic, for the practical options are of a more incremental nature and involve taking a view of whether the postwar liberalization of trade, within the OEEC liberalization programme, the EEC customs union, the GATT rounds, the Canada-US automobile arrangements, etc., have made much of a contribution to growth.

The modalities by which such liberalization may affect productivity on the supply side include a greater degree of specialization of production in lines of comparative advantage, extra opportunities to exploit economies of scale, and stimulation of productivity through greater competition. All of these have obviously been facilitated by liberalization in the postwar period, which has raised the ratio of output that is traded. But, surprisingly enough, most of those who have analysed gains of this kind for the postwar period have attached rather low values to them.

Some authors have stressed the importance of trade as a vehicle for diffusing new technology. The literature on 'technology gaps' and 'product cycle' theories of international trade has stressed the acceleration of these processes in the postwar period. However, the acceleration of trade in new technologies is mainly a reflection of increased rates of investment rather than an independent causal factor in the diffusion process, which can also proceed through other channels, such as licensing agreements, payment for use of foreign patents, etc.

Denison estimated that reductions in trade barriers contributed 0.16 percentage points to growth in 1950-62 in Belgium, Italy, and the Netherlands, 0.15 in Norway, and less in other European countries. I have suggested elsewhere that his estimates are too low; because they are based on nominal rather than effective tariff incidence, they ignore the impact of removal of quantitative restrictions, economies of scale, and competition. In Table 5.9 I put forward alternative estimates[16] of the contribution of trade to growth for the 1950s (the decimal points are not intended to suggest a high level of accuracy!).

TABLE 5.9

Annual Average Percentage Point Contribution of Gains from Trade to GDP Growth Rate, 1950-62

Belgium	0.42	Netherlands	0.50
Denmark	0.26	Norway	0.48
France	0.17	United Kingdom	0.06
Germany	0.28	United States	0.01
Italy	0.39	Arithmetic average	0.29

These figures are intended to provide only a rough order of magnitude of the relative importance of gains from trade to productivity growth in the 1950s and the first part of the 1960s, when the EEC internal tariff barriers were still in course of removal. The gains were more important for the small than for the big countries.

In the 1970s, the scope for gains of this sort has been negligible, so that slower productivity growth in the 1970s is due partly to the waning importance of these gains from trade.

The relatively liberal trade policies of the postwar period and the reasonably co-operative attitudes of the countries in international payments matters (by interwar standards) have been a major influence in creating favourable growth expectations. They were the international component of the favourable demand climate in domestic markets, which nurtured high rates of investment and economic activity. This positive influence of trade on the demand and investment climate made a more fundamental contribution to faster postwar growth than the beneficial impact that removal of trade barriers made to the efficiency of resource allocation.

Impact of Structural Change

Changes in the pattern of demand, output, and employment have been very considerable in the past century, and should be taken into account in interpreting the nature of productivity growth.

The Sectoral Pattern of Employment and Output   Since 1870, there has been a massive reduction in the share of agricultural employment, a big increase in the share of services, and moderate growth in industry. The first two phenomena have operated more or less continuously in the same direction in all the countries. By contrast, the industrial share has risen and fallen, peaking somewhat below 50 per cent of the employed population.[17] In 1870 agriculture occupied half of the population of these countries; in 1979, only 7.5 per cent. Service employment now predominates, representing well over half of total employment.

TABLE 5.10
Structure of Employment, 1870-1979

	Average of 16 country shares		
	Agriculture[a]	Industry[b]	Services[c]
1870	48.8	27.5	23.7
1950	24.7	36.6	38.7
1979	7.5	34.5	58.0

[a] Includes forestry and fisheries.
[b] Includes construction.
[c] Includes military personnel.

Source: Table C5.

The timing of 'de-industrialization' has varied. In 1979 the industrial share was below its 1950 level in Australia, Belgium, Canada, Denmark, the Netherlands, Norway, Sweden, Switzerland, the UK, and the USA; it was about the same in France and Germany; it rose substantially only in Austria, Finland, Italy, and Japan. However, even in the latter group it is now past its peak. In several countries there has been an absolute drop in industrial employment over the past decade. In Austria, Belgium, Germany, the Netherlands, Sweden, Switzerland, and the UK, the peak absolute level was in the mid-1960s.

Table 5.11 shows rough estimates of growth of output per man (*not* man-hour) by sector for the postwar period. It also shows the pattern of employment and output change by sector. Productivity performance in the service sector has almost always been a good deal slower than in commodity production, and productivity in agriculture has grown faster than in industry in the majority of cases. At first sight it would appear that the structural shifts in employment have been unfavourable to productivity growth, as employment has fallen in agriculture and risen most in services; i.e., the employment movements are inversely related to the pace of productivity growth. However, the productivity effects of structural change do not derive simply from movements of employment between sectors with different growth rates: they also depend on the absolute level of productivity in different sectors. The productivity level in agriculture was much lower than that in the rest of the economy in 1950. Hence the outflow of labour from low-level productivity jobs in agriculture has generally been favourable to total productivity growth. Indeed, high productivity growth in agriculture in the postwar period was due in large degree to the 'pull' effect of high demand elsewhere in the economy, which provided an outlet for underemployed labour in agriculture— particularly in Austria, Finland, Italy, and Japan, where the proportion of labour in agriculture was very large in 1950. The disparity in sectoral productivity levels still exists, but is a good deal narrower now than in 1950 (see Table 5.11).

Structural changes reflect two basic forces that have operated on all the countries as they have reached successively higher levels of real income and productivity. The first of these is the elasticity of demand for particular products, which has been rather similar at given levels of real income (particularly as relative price structures have moved in similar directions). These demand forces have reduced the share of agricultural products in consumption and raised demand for the products of industry and services. The second basic factor has been the differential pace of technological advance between sectors. Productivity growth has been slower in services than in commodity production: partly because of the intrinsic character of many personal services; partly because of measurement conventions which exclude the possibility of pro-

TABLE 5.11

Growth of Productivity, Employment, and Output by Sector, 1950-78, and Levels of Productivity by Sector, 1950 and 1978

	Agriculture	Industry	Services	Agriculture	Industry	Services
	Growth of output per person employed by sector					
	1950-73			*1973-8*		
			Annual average compound growth rates			
France	5.6	5.2	3.0	5.4	3.5	1.8
Germany	6.3	5.6	3.0	5.0	3.3	2.8
Japan	7.3	9.5	3.6	1.2	4.4	2.1
Netherlands	5.5	5.8	2.4	4.9	3.5	2.0
UK	4.7	2.9	1.6	2.8	1.5	0.7
USA	5.5	2.4	1.8	1.2	0.6	0.2
Average	5.8	5.2	2.6	3.4	2.8	1.6
	Growth of employment by sector					
			Annual average compound growth rates			
France	− 3.5	0.9	1.8	− 4.2	− 1.2	1.9
Germany	− 3.7	1.4	2.3	− 3.8	− 2.2	0.3
Japan	− 3.8	3.9	4.1	− 2.1	0.4	2.1
Netherlands	− 2.3	0.4	2.0	− 1.7	− 2.2	1.3
UK	− 2.0	0.0	1.0	− 1.9	− 1.5	1.1
USA	− 3.5	1.4	2.2	− 0.3	1.0	2.9
Average	− 3.1	1.3	2.2	− 2.3	− 1.0	1.6
	Growth of output by sector					
			Annual average compound growth rates			
France	2.0	6.1	4.9	0.1	2.2	3.8
Germany	2.3	7.1	5.3	1.0	1.0	3.1
Japan	3.2	13.8	7.8	− 1.0	3.7	4.2
Netherlands	3.1	6.2	4.4	3.2	1.3	3.4
UK	2.6	2.9	2.6	0.9	0.0	1.8
USA	1.9	3.8	4.1	0.9	1.6	3.1
Average	2.5	6.7	4.9	0.9	1.6	3.2

Table 5.11 (contd)

	Agriculture	Level of output per person employed by sector 1950		Agriculture	1978	Services
		Industry	Services		Industry	
		Percent of average for whole economy				
France	41	88	156	58	104	104
Germany	34	97	145	51	115	93
Japan	40	80	214	37	137	90
Netherlands	58	72	137	92	112	94
UK	47	78	126	88	92	106
USA	31	109	111	63	109	98
Average	42	87	148	65	112	98

Source: GDP by sector from *National Accounts of OECD Countries*, various editions. In some cases adjustments were necessary to achieve consistency of treatment in the linked series. Official figures of Japanese output by sector in constant prices are not published and our estimate is derived from physical output indicators for agriculture and industry, with service output treated as a residual. The distribution of employment between sectors in 1950 was derived from OECD publications for Netherlands, and the USA; from P. Bairoch, *The Working Population and Its Structure*, Brussels, 1968, for Germany; and otherwise from sources used in Appendix A for aggregate output. The German figures are adjusted to include West Berlin throughout.

ductivity growth in some services; partly because the government share of service employment is significant, and governments generally give little heed to the productivity of their employees.

The pattern of employment is also affected by international trade. Trade proportions vary because of the size, climate, natural endowment, and competitiveness of the different economies, and this is a major reason for variations in employment structure between countries at the same level of income, though there are some constraints on the range of variation because a good part of consumer demand is for items that are difficult to trade internationally. Institutional arrangements, past economic history, and policy can also affect structures differentially. Hence, countries that entered the postwar period with a large amount of underemployed labour in agriculture—particularly Austria, Finland, Italy, and Japan—were able to enjoy structural changes particularly favourable to growth, because for a given growth in total labour supply they were able to switch more labour into the high-productivity sectors.

Table 5.12 provides a rough idea of the extent to which structural changes have affected productivity growth since 1950. It shows what the growth rate of output per man would have been if the

TABLE 5.12

Impact of Structural Shift in Employment on Growth of GDP per Person Employed, 1950-78

	Actual rate of growth of GDP per person employed		*Rate of growth of GDP per person employed assuming employment structure unchanged and with actual in-sector productivity growth*		*Impact of proportionate sectoral shift in employment on growth of GDP per person employed*	
	1950-73	*1973-8*	*1950-73*	*1973-8*	*1950-73*	*1973-8*
France	4.6	2.9	4.1	2.7	0.5	0.2
Germany	4.9	3.1	4.5	3.1	0.4	0.0
Japan	7.3	3.1	6.0	3.2	1.3	−0.1
Netherlands	3.9	2.6	3.9	2.8	0.0	−0.2
UK	2.2	1.2	2.2	1.1	0.0	0.1
USA	2.4	0.4	2.2	0.4	0.2	0.0
Arithmetic average	4.2	2.2	3.8	2.2	0.4	0.0

Source: As for Table 5.11.

structure of employment had not changed, and if productivity growth in each sector remained as actually experienced. From 1950 to 1973, structural change generally favoured productivity growth, but its impact was uneven as between countries. Structural change was very favourable to Japanese productivity growth and quite favourable in France and Germany, but in the Netherlands and the UK structural change had no productivity impact. Structural change had less impact from 1973 to 1978, though the situation varied from country to country.

In the period 1870-1950, evidence on productivity growth by sector is rather scanty. Table 5.13 presents evidence for six countries. The pattern of structural change in employment was in the same direction as in the postwar period, but the switch out of agriculture was much slower. The general pace of productivity growth in each sector was slower, and agriculture was not the prime productivity performer it has been in the postwar period. It seems likely, therefore, that structural change was generally less important in its contribution to productivity growth in this period than it was after 1950.

TABLE 5.13

Growth of Output per Person and Employment by Sector 1870-1950

| | Annual average compound growth rates | | | | | |
| | Output per person employed, 1870-1950 | | | Rate of growth of employment, 1870-1950 | | |
	Agriculture	Industry	Services	Agriculture	Industry	Services
France[a]	1.4	1.4	0.7	−0.8	0.2	0.7
Germany[b]	0.2	1.3	0.7	−0.1	1.4	1.5
Italy	0.5	1.4	0.6	0.1	0.7	1.2
Japan[c]	0.7	1.7	0.5	0.1	1.7	1.9
UK	1.4	1.2	0.2	−1.1	0.9	1.3
USA[d]	1.3	1.6	1.1	−0.3	2.3	2.6
Arithmetic average	0.9	1.4	0.6	−0.4	1.2	1.5

[a] 1896-1949.
[b] 1871-1950.
[c] 1906-1950.
[d] 1889-1948.

Source: Estimates generally derived from same sources as those indicated in Appendix A for GDP. US from J. W. Kendrick, *Understanding Productivity*, Johns Hopkins, Baltimore, 1977, pp. 39 and 43. Japanese employment estimates kindly supplied by M. Umemura.

The significance of structural shifts requires careful interpretation. The in-sector productivity movements are not independent of the sectoral shifts (as we have already noted for agriculture), and the division of the economy into three sectors is somewhat arbitrary. The apparent impact of structural shifts can be changed by disaggregating the economy in a different way, or by using GDP deflators with a different weighting base. The service sector poses particular difficulties.[18]

The acceleration of productivity growth within sectors and the switch of employment between sectors are interrelated phenomena, which reflect the operation of deeper causal factors that have accelerated productivity growth: i.e., higher and more stable demand, an increase in the pace of capital formation, and the impact of accelerated world trade. The main respect in which structural change of the type discussed above has had an independent causal role in growth is the degree to which countries were able to exploit a reserve of labour under-utilized in agriculture.

Age and Sex Structure of Employment In this study, all employed persons have been treated as equal. Other productivity analysts have made adjustments for differences in the quality of labour because of changes in employment by age and sex, and have generally used relative wages as an adjustment factor.[19] This seems reasonable, though wage differentials are influenced by legislative and institutional factors as well as productivity differences, and there may be quite large variations in fringe benefits which are often significant. In the present study, which covers such a wide span of countries and time, such refined adjustments were not feasible on a systematic basis.

However, it does not appear that the slackening in productivity growth in the 1970s is due to a shift in the composition of labour input less favourable to productivity than occurred in 1950-73. In most countries in the 1950s and particularly in the 1960s, there was an unusually large increase in the teenage and youth population, and a general rise in activity rates for women. In the USA the youth share rose particularly sharply, because US youth tend to combine work with education, whereas in Europe and Japan the impact of the surge in the youth population on the labour market was cushioned by increased educational enrolment. In the 1970s a greater proportion of the increment in labour supply has consisted of prime-age males in most countries, and the proportion can be expected to increase further in future.

I tried elsewhere[20] to form an idea of the difference that changes in the age-sex composition of the labour force have had on the growth of productivity, and concluded that this phenomenon is of minor importance. Most of its impact is already covered in other dimensions of productivity analysis. The lower productivity of women, youth, and older workers is due partly to the fact that they work shorter hours than do prime-age males. This is already reflected in hours-worked figures, so there is some degree of double counting when age-sex composition is given as a separate component of productivity. The increase in female participation in the labour force also affects sectoral productivity growth differentially because female employment is heavily concentrated in the service sector. Here again, some of the impact of the change in sex structure is covered under the rubric of sectoral change.

Regulatory Constraints Another 'structural' reason for the slowdown in US productivity growth in the 1970s has been an increase in expenditures designed to improve the quality of life (or to prevent its worsening), rather than to increase output as conventionally measured. There has been a proliferation in government regulations regarding the environment, work safety, and health. All these require diversion of workers and capital to activities not reflected in the measure of output. The general increase in crime and in air piracy have also led to both mandatory and voluntary expenditures to protect public safety and mitigate property damage. Denison has estimated that these types of problem reduced US output per unit of input by 0.3 per cent a year in the 1970s, but had a negligible effect in the 1960s.[21] There are differing interpretations of this situation. Some would argue that economic development has reached a stage where environmental constraints and social disintegration have become powerful impediments to further growth. Others might argue that regulation has been pushed to unreasonable lengths by over-zealous lobbyists, or that the regulatory intent could be achieved at a lesser cost to productivity by greater use of the price mechanism. Similar problems have curtailed productivity growth in other countries, to an extent that has not been quantified, and it is possible that this new productivity depressant will remain as a permanent feature of advanced capitalist development.

Changes in Efficiency

There are a number of influences on productivity that arise from changes in the efficiency of resource allocation. As technology is constantly changing, it is natural to assume, as Arrow and Lundberg have done, that the process of 'learning by doing' is continuous. Methods of using equipment may well continue to be improved until the machines are scrapped, and then the process starts all over again with new machinery. The optimum use of resources assumed by neoclassical growth theorists may never be achieved in practice. It is not the case that the 'entrepreneur instantly perceives and adopts the best line of action in any given situation. Instead he is seen as perpetually groping in a mist of uncertainty, gradually and imperfectly learning his way on the basis of experience accruing to him.'[22] Given the accelerated pace of investment in the postwar period, it seems likely that the amount of learning by doing has increased.

The learning process is difficult to dissociate from economies of scale, which have been given particular emphasis by Kaldor as a source of growth in manufacturing.[23] I feel that Kaldor exaggerates the importance of this source of growth, which may have been more important in the time of Adam Smith than in the postwar period. Some authors stress the importance of changes in managerial and labour efficiency in the growth process. Personally, I doubt whether these have been a major influence in growth in the long term, but they vary cyclically, as do the other aspects of efficiency mentioned above. Hence, an important part of the slackening in productivity growth since 1973 is the result of inefficiency in resource allocation induced by the recession and subsequent inadequate recovery and by the OPEC shock, as we have already stressed.

SUMMARY AND CONCLUSIONS

Productivity growth accelerated greatly in the postwar period, increasing more than 2.5 times as fast on average as in the eight decades 1870-1850. This acceleration affected all countries except the USA. The US productivity lead, which has existed since the 1890s, has been greatly reduced. The US level is still a third higher than the average for the other countries, but four European countries

(Belgium, France, Germany, and the Netherlands) seem likely to overtake the USA in the 1980s.

The major forces for the postwar acceleration were high and steady levels of demand, both nationally and internationally, and the acceleration in the growth of capital stock—which high demand induced. Improvements in resource allocation because of the elimination of underemployed labour in agriculture and elimination of international trade barriers gave an extra once-for-all boost to productivity growth in Europe and Japan.

There is no evidence that the postwar acceleration was due to a faster pace of technical innovation. The frontier of technology lay predominantly in the US economy, whose pace of productivity growth did not increase. The acceleration of growth outside the USA is basically explicable in terms of a reduction in the technical lag. This raises interesting questions for the future, when other countries catch up to US productivity levels. Will their investment pace slacken as the burden of pioneering new techniques and products falls more heavily on them? This seems likely, as the risks will be higher and profit expectations lower; but the technical frontier may expand faster than in the past, because the USA will no longer be there alone. The momentum of the other economies and their rate of capital formation when they hit the frontier may well be higher than has historically been the case in the USA.

Since 1973 productivity growth slackened sharply for the following reasons:

1. Slack demand conditions and restrictive government policies constrained productivity growth in two main ways: they reduced the growth of the capital stock (particularly in the USA), and they reduced the efficiency of resource allocation.
2. The OPEC shocks, which raised energy prices ten-fold, also had a directly adverse effect on productivity.
3. Regulatory controls for environmental and safety reasons had an adverse impact on measured productivity.
4. The importance of structural shifts out of agriculture and gains from international specialization did not contribute to productivity growth as they had in the golden age of 1950-73.
5. The European countries and Japan were operating closer to best-practice technology, which made productivity gains more difficult to obtain.

The productivity outlook is a good deal less favourable than the performance achieved from 1950 to 1973. The basic 'supply' factors still seem to warrant future rates of productivity growth higher than prewar experience; but if the climate of demand and expectations are weakened enough to lower investment incentives at a stage when the challenge of technical pioneering and risk-taking has to be faced on a much wider front, then the productivity momentum of the European economies and Japan could be considerably weakened. Past experience demonstrates clearly enough that the possibilities of growth offered by technical backlogs can be squandered by inadequate demand policy. The postwar situation, which favoured high and relatively steady expansion of demand, has been interrupted by new challenges to which policy has not yet adequately responded.

6

THE ROLE OF POLICY IN ECONOMIC PERFORMANCE: AN ASSESSMENT IN THE LIGHT OF EXPERIENCE SINCE 1950

In the 'Golden Age' of the 1950s and 1960s economic growth in the advanced capitalist countries surpassed virtually all historical records. After 1973 performance deteriorated significantly. The pace of inflation more than doubled, as Table 6.1 makes clear, and the growth rate for GDP fell by half from 4.9 to 2.5 per cent a year.

TABLE 6.1

Indicators of Macroeconomic Performance, 1870-1979

	1870-1950	1950-73	1973-9
Annual average growth of GDP	2.3	4.9	2.5
Average annual rise in consumer prices	0.1*	4.1	9.5

* Average for peacetime years.

Source: Appendices A and E.

The slowdown in growth rates and the acceleration of price increases raise three major types of question which this chapter tries to answer:

1. It leads first to a re-examination of the 1950s and 1960s. To what extent was favourable performance then due to luck or policy? In so far as it was due to policy, how did policies differ from those practised earlier?
2. What caused the deterioration in the 1970s? To what degree was it due to a cluster of accidents and policy mistakes, or to the inevitable termination of previously favourable circumstances?
3. Given the new circumstances of the 1970s, what was the degree of success or failure of economic policy? What was the scope for doing better?

CHARACTERISTICS OF THE GOLDEN AGE (1950-73)

Several special characteristics enhanced economic performance in the 1950s and 1960s. Some of these required enlightened policy, some are attributable to temporarily favourable circumstance. They were:

1. successful re-application of liberal policies in international transactions;
2. governmental promotion of buoyant domestic demand;
3. policies and circumstances that kept inflation relatively modest in conditions of very high demand;
4. a backlog of growth possibilities, which made the supply response of the European and particularly the Japanese economy very sensitive to high levels of demand.

The first three characteristics are analysed in this section; the last one was examined in Chapter 5.

Managed Liberalism in International Transactions

Perhaps the least controversial assertion one can make about the Golden Age is that it involved a remarkable revival of liberalism in international transactions. Trade and payments barriers erected in the 1930s and during the war were removed, and the new style liberalism was buttressed by an ambitious set of arrangements for articulate and regular consultation between Western countries, and for mutual financial assistance. Prior to 1914, the governmental role in the economy was minimal. Fiscal policy was concerned with balancing the budget and the major economic policy weapon was Bank rate. International co-operation was limited to *ad hoc* bilateral measures.

Between the wars there was more conflict than co-operation. There were quarrels over war debts and reparations, no regular institutional arrangements for mutual credit or consultation except in the BIS, a shortage of liquidity, fundamental disequilibrium in exchange rates, and pursuit of beggar-your-neighbour commercial policies after the 1929-31 crisis.

The postwar international payments system provided a workable mechanism for the promotion of freer trade. The adherence to virtually fixed exchange rates was a handicap in some respects but there was an adequate supply of liquidity to ease countries over payments difficulties. Reconstruction was greatly eased by Marshall Aid, which prevented quarrels over war debts and reparations and established the habit of organized mutual consultation and mutual financial support. Trade was freed by abolition of quantitative restrictions in OEEC, reduction of tariffs on a regional basis in EEC, and, more globally, in GATT. International migration also revived, and after 1958 the increasing degree of convertibility of currencies led to a revival of the international capital market which had collapsed in 1930.

The results were impressive. In the years 1950-73, the exports of these countries rose 6.7-fold. They were a major force sustaining demand and productivity growth and keeping prices in check. In 1938, by contrast, exports of these countries had been lower than in 1913.

The creation of the EEC attracted a greater amount of direct American private capital to Europe in the 1960s than the US government has provided earlier in Marshall Aid. In 1950 the US private direct capital in Europe was valued at $1.7 billion, and by 1973 it had risen to $40 billion. This investment helped to strengthen European productivity and competitiveness. It was a major vehicle for technological transfer from the productivity leader, the USA.

Between 1950 and 1973 there was net immigration of 9.4 million people into Western Europe, compared with an outflow of 4 million from 1914 to 1949. This eased supply constraints. It facilitated output growth, and moderated inflation.

Managed liberalism added greatly to the buoyancy and resilience of the Western economies. These policies of enlightened self-interest and mutual support were due not only to intelligent digestion of the lessons of the 1930s, but to the urgency of Cold War pressures and to the overwhelming power of the USA to enforce its views in the immediate postwar years.

Governmental Promotion of Domestic Demand Buoyancy

A fundamental innovation in postwar policy aspirations was the commitment to full use of resources. In the USA the idea was enshrined in the Full Employment Act of 1946, though it was not fully implemented until the 1960s. In the UK and Scandinavia, the Keynesian gospel of fiscal activism and the primordial commitment to full employment gained wide acceptance in academic, political, and bureaucratic milieux. In France, the objective of full resource use was expressed in more *dirigiste* idiom, with less explicit emphasis on full employment, but with an earlier and stronger commitment to growth as expressed in its planning process. Italy and Japan had not participated in the Keynesian tradition, but they also aimed at rapid and ambitious rebuilding of their economies through government action and intervention whenever necessary. Germany gave greater emphasis to price stability than to buoyant domestic demand, but proclaimed the full employment goal in its Stabilization Law of 1967. In any case, it achieved fuller employment than most countries by export-induced growth.

There was a general move away from the prewar idea that the budget should be balanced irrespective of the state of the economy. In all these countries the national accounting framework was developed as an instrument for assessing the macroeconomic impact of government policy, and at the beginning of the 1960s the OECD countries set themselves an ambitious collective growth target.

Before the war, great importance was attached to price stability in many, but not all, countries. In the Golden Age it was often cited as a rhetorical target, but in fact the aim was generally to keep the pace of price increase within limits that did not put too great a strain on international competitiveness. When the outcome of demand management policy was unclear, the tendency was to take the upside risk. Lipsey stated a common view about the dangers of what might now be called 'overshooting' in demand management policy:

I should regard anyone who opposed this policy because of fear of inflation as having either an insufficiently thought-out position or a set of value judgements that were definitely perverse judged by any common standard. The *possibility* of incurring a once-for-all rise in the price level of one or two percentage points cannot be regarded as a high price to pay in order to discover by how much unemployment can be reduced by using the relatively simple tools of fiscal policy.[1]

There was a major increase in the proportionate size of government expenditure, which gave government a propulsive role in the growth of demand, and when combined with the commitment to use the budget for macroeconomic policy objectives transformed the nature of the business cycle, which was often dominated by swings in government policy rather than movements in the private sector. The growth of government revenue and expenditure increased the leverage of government discretionary policy, added to the automatic stabilizing effect of government, and strengthened the buying power of low-income consumers who were covered by income transfers.

Government policy played a significant role in stabilizing output,[2] but there were enough errors, lags, and uncertainties to prevent fine tuning. The main achievement was not the finesse of stabilization, but success in nurturing a buoyancy of demand which had been created during the war and Marshall Plan period and which kept the economies within a zone of high employment. The clear bias in favour of growth and employment, the lowered attention to risks of price increase or payments difficulties, and the absence of crassly perverse deflationary policies were the most important features differentiating postwar demand management from prewar policy. The pay-off was much bigger than could reasonably have been anticipated. The absence of downside risks in terms of output, and the buoyancy that continuous price increases gave to profits, nurtured a secular investment boom; and, given the favourable supply factors in Europe and Japan, growth performance reached unparallelled proportions.

There have been some dissenting views about the impact of policy on postwar performance. Robin Matthews was sceptical about its role in the UK[3] and suggested that faster growth was due mainly to a spontaneous investment boom, sparked off perhaps by government wartime spending but sustained in peacetime by the backlog of wasted investment opportunities and by an assumed quickening in technical progress. He rejected the idea that postwar government policy had been stimulative because the budget was in surplus for most of the period he considered, and he rejects the increased size of government spending as a contributory influence, because increased government spending was offset by higher taxes. Although he admits that Keynesian attitudes may have prevented governments from making deflationary policy mistakes in the postwar period, he does not give this much weight because he attributes interwar UK problems to structural changes in the pattern of world trade, rather than to British and foreign governments' policy mistakes.

In fact, the role of budgetary policy was generally supportive of growth in the Golden Age, and the UK situation which Matthews analysed was exceptional, as Table 6.2 makes clear. In the second place, I feel that Matthews dismisses too lightly the influence of the greatly increased size of government spending on goods, services, and transfers in the postwar period (see Table 6.3), which has strengthened expectations of high and expanding demand in many

TABLE 6.2

Impact of Budgetary Changes on GDP at Constant Prices, 1955-73

| | Average of annual impacts | |
	1955-65	1965-73
Canada	(n.a.)	0.49
France	0.25[a]	0.12
Germany	0.24	0.32
Italy	0.40	0.95
Japan	(n.a.)	0.24
Netherlands	(n.a.)	0.34
Sweden	0.42	0.55
UK	0.00	0.52
USA	0.07	0.28

[a] 1958-65.

Source: B. Hansen and W. W. Snyder, *Fiscal Policy in Seven Countries 1955-65*, OECD, Paris, 1969, and OECD, *Occasional Studies* (supplement to *Economic Outlook*), July 1978, p. 31. Positive figures indicate a supportive effect. The estimates include only the first-round multiplier.

TABLE 6.3

General Government Current Expenditures on Goods, Services, and Transfers as Percentage of GDP, 1950-77

	1950	1977
Austria	21.2	39.8
Belgium	19.6	43.5
Canada	19.2	37.0
Denmark	18.0	42.8[c]
Finland	19.7	35.6
France	26.7	40.9
Germany	28.3	41.3
Italy	20.7[a]	42.5
Japan	14.6[b]	22.3
Netherlands	23.9	52.3
Norway	21.9[a]	46.2
Sweden	23.6	55.6
Switzerland	19.4	30.4
UK	30.1	40.8
USA	20.0	32.6
Arithmetic average	21.8	40.2

[a] 1951.
[b] 1952.
[c] 1976.

Source: *National Accounts of OECD Countries*, 1960-77, 1950-68, and 1950-61 eds, OECD, Paris; and *Statistics of Sources and Uses of Finance 1948-58*, OEEC, Paris, 1960. Figures are at current market prices.

ways. Third, his structuralist interpretation of the problems in the interwar period understates the role of errors in domestic and international economic policy in that period.

Harry Johnson went much further than Matthews in rejecting any role for activist fiscal (or other) policy in postwar Western performance as a whole. It needs no explanation because it is alleged to be typical capitalist performance. He said:

> there are good reasons, rooted both in the 'real' analysis of the economic historians and in monetary theory, as to why capitalist economies should be expected in normal circumstances both to maintain a high level of employment and to enjoy some non-negligible rate of economic growth.[4]

He quotes Matthews as representative of the economic historians, even though Matthews never suggested that historically the UK had maintained high levels of employment. Quite the contrary: he pointed out that UK unemployment averaged 10.5 per cent in the interwar period, and 4.5 per cent before 1914. On monetary theory, Johnson states simply that 'monetary analysis assumes as a matter of empirical fact that the economic system tends towards a rational full-employment allocation of resources so long as the management of money is well behaved and can only be thrown off course by severe monetary mismanagement.' However, this hypothesis does not correspond with the facts. In the world of well-behaved money from 1870 to 1914, economic growth rates were half of these for 1950-73, and unemployment rates were appreciably higher.

Not all monetarists would go as far as Harry Johnson did, but they often seem to assume that, because Friedman showed perverse monetary policy to have made the US slump worse in the early 1930s,[5] this single one-country error of monetary policy was the only cause of the world slump of that epoch. There is well documented evidence of more complicated causality, including the deflationary fiscal policy errors of the Laval, Brüning, and McDonald governments in France, Germany, and the UK and of counter-productive animosities in international economic relations.[6]

It was this kind of instinctively deflationary official policy that was successfully discredited by Keynesian-type ideas. But there is now a clear tactic by monetarists and some Keynesian revisionists to suggest that such deflationary views were not influential in the prewar period,[7] and that Keynes was attacking a straw man!

The Role of Policy and Circumstance in Moderating Price Increases

Those who had contemplated the possibility of achieving full employment in the postwar period had predicted serious inflationary problems,[8] and the outcome was indeed quite different from the previous peacetime price record. The average rate of price increase from 1950 to 1973 was 4.1 per cent a year, compared with 0.4 per cent for 1870-1913, and a fall of 0.7 a year in the interwar period (see Table 6.4). But in most countries, inflation fell within bounds felt to be tolerable, and there was no very firm attempt to achieve stable price levels. The gentle upward crawl in prices was considered a reasonable trade-off for low levels of unemployment.

In retrospect, one can identify several reasons why price increases in the Golden Age were so modest in conditions of such high demand. Some of these are related to the exceptional supply factors operative in that period, some to policy-institutional features that will not be easily repeatable. They are as follows.

1. The fixed exchange rate system operated to impose a certain

TABLE 6.4

Average Rates of Change in Consumer Price Level, 1870-1979

		Annual average compound growth rates				
	1870-1913	1913-20	1920-38	1938-50	1950-73	1973-9
Australia	0.3	8.0	−0.7	4.7	4.6	12.0
Austria	0.1[a]	92.7[c]	2.1[c]	18.1	4.6	6.4
Belgium	0.0	20.0[d]	4.4[f]	11.5	2.9	8.4
Canada	0.4	10.6	−2.4	4.0	2.8	9.1
Denmark	−0.2	15.3	−2.0	5.1	4.8	10.9
Finland	0.6	37.2	0.5	22.3	5.6	12.8
France	0.1	20.5	3.6	28.1	5.0	10.7
Germany	0.6	39.3	−0.1[g]	3.8	2.7	4.7
Italy	0.6	24.4	0.3	38.4	3.9	16.3
Japan	2.8[h]	10.5	−0.3	82.4	5.2	10.0
Netherlands	n.a.	9.9	−2.9	7.4	4.1	7.2
Norway	0.6	17.4	−3.1	4.3	4.8	8.8
Sweden	0.5	15.5	−2.7	4.1	4.7	9.8
Switzerland	n.a.	12.5	−2.8	4.0	3.0	4.0
UK	−0.2	13.9	−2.6	5.3	4.6	15.4
USA	−0.6	10.1	−2.0	4.5	2.7	8.2
Average	0.4	22.4	−0.7	15.5	4.1	9.5

[a] 1874-1913. [b] 1879-1913. [c] 1914-1920. [d] 1914-1921. [e] 1923-1938. [f] 1921-1938. [g] 1924-38.

Source: Appendix E.

price discipline in countries where export prices tended to rise most. It was not as strict as that of the gold standard system operating before 1914, because devaluation was not entirely ruled out, and fairly large credits were available to countries in payments difficulty; but balance of payments crises and speculative capital outflows led governments to restrictive action and were also felt as constraints by business and trade unions in fixing prices and wages. This discipline was least operative in Finland and France, which did not stick to the fixed exchange rate protocol, and devalued several times. The system's constraints worked in the opposite direction in Germany, which imported inflation by not revaluing often enough to offset its low domestic propensity to price increases. However, there were enough important traders in the low-export price league (e.g., Italy, Japan, Belgium, Netherlands, and Switzerland) to ensure that the world market trend was modest. A number of smaller countries, and particularly Scandinavia, tended to drift with world price trends.[9]

2. From 1952 to around 1966, the economy of the biggest country, the USA, whose currency was the lynchpin of the international payments system, had comparatively high rates of unemployment and low rates of resource utilization, which led to low rates of price increase. This happened because of the hypercautious demand management policies of the Eisenhower administration. The slack was reduced in the Kennedy administration, but it was not until the Johnson administration, with its social programmes and the war in Vietnam, that the economy came under strain, in 1967. The Eisenhower caution was inspired by domestic aspirations to price stability, but its balance of payments consequences prolonged the viability of a fixed dollar exchange standard in a period when other countries became increasingly more competitive with the USA.

3. The removal of trade barriers and reopening of these economies to international trade after the autarky of war and prewar years was a significant factor in promoting postwar productivity growth in the manufacturing sector of these countries. The fastest expansion of exports was achieved by countries whose export prices were rising modestly or actually falling. The average rise in export prices for 1950-73 was only 2.1 per cent a year—half the rise in domestic prices.

4. Some key commodity prices were remarkably stable from

1950 to 1970. US agricultural policy kept international food prices low or falling because of a domestic support system that created huge domestic stocks. World petroleum prices were also stable, in spite of the massive expansion in consumption. This was due to the large reserves of cheap oil in Arab countries and US regulations to protect its domestic oil production, which delayed the upsurge of imports into the USA. By the end of the 1960s, it was clear that the countries that had formed OPEC in the 1960s had acquired considerable bargaining power, which was likely to be used once the Arab countries had shed their semi-colonial status. The price of non-ferrous metals was not as stable as those for wheat and oil, but sales from the US strategic stockpile put a damper on price movements. Finally, the gold price was stable for most of the period. There was a flurry in 1960 when the London gold market reopened, but the major countries fed the free market with gold up to 1968, which kept the price near the official $35 an ounce and helped keep down pressure in speculative markets generally. For this reason, the 1952-70 period was remarkably free of external price shocks.

5. An important factor in price stability was the easy expandability of the labour supply, both by using immigrants and by running down the excess stock of labour in agriculture. Countries in this situation were able to ease bottlenecks in particular sectors that might otherwise have given trade unions much greater power. The countries that made most explicit use of migrant labour as a cyclical stabilization device were Switzerland and Germany. In Switzerland unemployment was zero and in Germany less than 1 per cent of the labour force in the 1960s, and yet wage pressures were modest. In several other countries, immigrant labour was a lesser but significant factor in easing inflationary pressures. Italy and Japan were the two countries in which the large domestic supply of surplus rural labour performed the same function as immigration in Germany and Switzerland.

6. The climate of wage bargaining in the 1950s and most of the 1960s was rather mild. By prewar standards, there was a very low level of social tension. Several reasons contributed to this: the unprecedented increases in real income; the effect of East-West tensions in consolidating Western societies internally; the solidaristic feelings promoted by wide social security provisions and income transfers. The climate can be best recalled by citing some of the social critics of that epoch whose judgements now seem so

inappropriate. In books published between 1956 and 1960, Crosland, Galbraith, Bell, and Myrdal all proclaimed the unimportance of distributive issues, the increasing internal harmony of Western societies, the rise of legitimate meritocratic elites, etc.[10] The welfare state was in its heyday; there was no New Left, no neo-Marxist renaissance; Hayek was quiescent on current issues; Harold Macmillan said we'd never had it so good, and was believed.

7. A final factor damping price increases was the fact that institutions and expectations had not properly adjusted to the fact of continuous inflation. People were suffering from 'money illusion' which in the long run would be eroded. Friedman suggested in 1968 that such a phenomenon could well last for a couple of decades, after which expectations would become more rational and decidedly more explosive unless unemployment increased.[11] Indeed, it is rather surprising that money illusion was not broken by wartime experience and by the Korean War boom of 1950-1.

THE BREAKDOWN OF THE GOLDEN AGE SYSTEM

The Golden Age system broke down for a complexity of interacting reasons which are not easy to disentangle. Four major elements are distinguished here which go a good way towards explaining the acceleration of inflation and the reasons why growth potential came to be underutilized in the 1970s:

1. the rather messy collapse of the Bretton Woods fixed exchange rate system and its replacement by *ad hoc* floating currency arrangements and by the EMS;
2. the erosion of price constraints, and the emergence of strong inflationary expectations as a prime element in wage and price determination;
3. the various kinds of shock deriving from the more than ten-fold rise of oil prices in the 1970s, which was heavily concentrated on 1973-4 and 1979. This had adverse effects on the price level, the trade balance, the terms of trade, problems of structural adjustment, and consumer and investor confidence;
4. a weakening in governmental commitment to Keynesian-type demand management when faced with a spontaneous weakening in demand outside the range of previous postwar experience and in conditions of great price pressure. This was further sapped by the increased influence of monetarist economic theories, which,

like prewar economics, have little concern for growth and full employment.

It should also be added that some of the exceptional factors on the supply side, which permitted such high growth in Europe and Japan in the 1950s and 1960s, waned in the 1970s.

In my view, the first three of these changes that came in the 1970s were not a cluster of accidents or policy mistakes that are reversible.[12] Rather, it seems probable that the factors influencing growth and inflation in the advanced capitalist countries have undergone permanent modification for the worse.

The Breakdown of the Bretton Woods
International Monetary System

In the Bretton Woods international monetary system, the dollar was the unit in which other countries kept their reserves, and to which they pegged their exchange rates. The USA started the post-war period with a gold reserve very much bigger than all the other countries combined, and this, together with its strong balance of payments, was the basis of their confidence in the dollar, because ultimately the USA was willing to give gold in exchange for dollars to foreign central banks. Between 1949, when most countries devalued against the dollar, and August 1971, when President Nixon ended its convertibility into gold, there were very few changes in exchange rates, so that investment and marketing decisions concerning international trade faced little uncertainty on this score.

In the course of time, the increasing competitiveness in trade of the European countries and Japan led to a weakening of the US payments situation, particularly as the USA also had major payments abroad for military purposes, aid, and foreign investment. As a result, the international reserve position changed totally. In 1950 Germany, Italy, and Japan together had reserves of only $1.4 billion; by 1970 they had $23.8 billion. In the same period, US reserves fell from $24.3 billion to $14.5 billion.

This change in the reserve asset position meant that the rest of the world had more than adequate liquidity, but the long-run vulnerability of the reserve currency country with fast growing obligations and steadily declining gold reserves became increasingly clear. Its capacity to supply gold for dollars was obviously not going to last, unless there was a significant change in exchange rates. However, if the USA had taken the initiative by devaluing the dollar, it would have reduced the gold value of other countries reserves, which both the USA and the other countries would have considered a breakdown of the system, creating too much tension to make the outcome predictable, because the other countries might well have followed an American devaluation to preserve the value of their reserve assets.

A better solution would have been a revaluation of all the surplus countries against the dollar, combined with a much bigger upvaluation of gold, which would have increased US reserves. In fact, Germany revalued twice by a total of 15 per cent, but the willingness to go further was inhibited by the refusal of other strong currency countries and, particularly Japan, to revalue. The possibility of an official revaluation of gold was not seriously considered in the USA.

In the absence of any convincing evidence of reform in the system, there was a whole series of speculative crises against existing exchange parities. These were all the easier to mount because of the dismantling of exchange controls in Europe and the huge growth in the Eurocurrency market. From negligible levels in the 1950s, the net short-term foreign lending of banks in Europe rose to \$57 billion by end 1970.[13] It was easy to borrow in this market for speculative purposes, and speculation was not risky in a fixed-rate world because the penalty for mistakes, i.e. misjudgement of the date of devaluation, was very small, and the potential gain very large.

Until its 1967 devaluation, speculation was concentrated mainly on sterling, which deflected attention from the dollar. After that it became increasingly clear that a realignment of the dollar would be necessary, particularly as the US economy was no longer operating below potential. The reluctance of the strong currencies to revalue significantly made it clear that the change was unlikely to be achieved by international agreement.

The Bretton Woods system eventually collapsed by unilateral action on the part of the USA, which refused to defend its weak payments situation in 1970-1 in the standard deflationary way. It allowed a huge accumulation of dollars by other countries, and as a proxy devaluation imposed a 10 per cent import surcharge in 1971.[14] The rest of the world was thereby compelled to accept the US devaluation against gold in August 1971. The Smithsonian agreement of December 1971 patched up the fixed exchange system with agreed currency realignments, but this broke down again finally in 1973, because the repeated and perceived inadequacy of fixed-rate realignments in a world where international speculation was so easy made it impossible to defend a fixed rate without having a crisis every few weeks.

Given the present freedom for international payments transactions and the differences in national growth and price performance, it is clear in retrospect that the Bretton Woods system of pegged rates could not survive. One could imagine a prolongation of the system, given more good will.[15] There might have been less strain if France had tried a persuasive rather than a patronizing tone about revaluing gold early in the 1960s, and if the strong currencies had been more willing to revalue.

The Erosion of Price Constraints

The tactics that the USA used to enforce the devaluation of the dollar had inflationary consequences for other countries, particularly those such as Germany and Japan; these countries had the option of revaluation at an earlier stage, which would have reduced their export surplus, reduced their import prices, and curbed the influx of foreign capital. The German situation is described by Otmar Emminger, President of the Bundesbank, in an excellent analysis of the breakdown of Bretton Woods:

As one who participated in (and was partly responsible for) the decision of West Germany to go over to floating in March 1973, I can testify that the main reason for this decision was the effort to shield the German monetary system against further inflationary foreign exchange inflows, after the central bank had to absorb a dollar inflow worth more than DM 20 billions within five weeks, equivalent to more than double the amount of new central bank money required for a whole year.[16]

But, as Emminger points out, the system in its breakdown phase was also inflationary in the deficit countries. This was true of the United States itself, and in the UK there was an almost berserk feeling of liberation from the old constraints of stop-go which led to the adoption of a wildly expansionist policy:

for two years beginning in September 1971 control over the stock of money in the United Kingdom was non-existent. Bank credit to the private sector rose by 50 per cent, most of it financing either consumer outlays or real estate transactions. Simultaneously, on the fiscal side, total borrowing by the public sector moved from a small negative figure to an annual rate of 6 per cent of GDP.[17]

The collapse of the Bretton Woods fixed exchange rate discipline and the subsequent easing of demand management constraints had a sizeable role in the unusually large and synchronized boom in world output in 1972-3. This was the fastest two-year period of expansion since 1950-1 in the aggregate GDP of the advanced capitalist countries;[18] and, thanks in part to the easy availability of credit to finance imports, the boom was even bigger in the communist countries and parts of the Third World. In 1973 Soviet GDP rose by 7.6 per cent, Chinese by 10 per cent and Brazilian by 13.9 per cent.

The boom in output put the normal type of cyclical pressure on the price of manufactured goods, which were in such high demand. But a deeper change had occurred. The exceptional forces that in the 1950s and 1960s had kept the rise in export prices well below domestic price rises were no longer operative. The once-for-all efficiency gains of trade liberalization were now much smaller, and the pressures that the fixed exchange rate regime imposed to shave profit margins had greatly eased with its demise. This is clear from Table 6.5, which shows an average increase in export prices of 2.1 per cent in 1950-73, which is about half the 4.1 per cent a year increase in domestic prices. In 1973-79, the average increase in export prices (10.2 per cent) was, by contrast, higher than the domestic price increase (9.5 per cent).

The price pressures in primary commodity markets were even bigger than for manufactures, again for both cyclical and longer-term reasons. The gold price was now free, and its spectacular rise contributed to speculative fever. The world food price situation also changed drastically after twenty years of stability. During the late 1960s US policy had changed and its stocks dropped.[19] Because of *détente*, the USSR was able to buy large amounts of cereals from the USA, and did so in 1972 when it had a poor harvest. As a result, the price of cereals doubled in 1973. After twenty years close to or under $2 a bushel, wheat rose to $3.80 in 1973 and $4.90 in 1974. All agricultural prices rose in sympathy, and the impact on cost of living indices around the world was more or less immediate.

Given the way in which the Bretton Woods system collapsed, the ending of the special Golden Age price constraints, the impact

TABLE 6.5

Movement in Export Prices (in National Currencies), 1950-79

		Annual average compound rate of change	
		1950-73	1973-79
Australia		0.5	(10.8)
Austria		1.8	4.4
Belgium		1.2	7.7
Canada		2.2	13.2
Denmark		2.3	8.6
Finland		5.6	15.4
France		3.8	10.7
Germany		1.8	5.3
Italy		0.9	20.0
Japan		0.9	4.2
Netherlands		1.2	7.8
Norway		2.0	11.4
Sweden		3.0	13.0
Switzerland		0.5	2.5
UK		3.5	17.9
USA		2.7	10.9
Average		2.1	10.2

Sources: *Yearbook of International Trade Statistics 1979*, UN, New York; UN *Monthly Bulletin of Statistics*.

TABLE 6.6

Key Commodity Prices, 1950-80
(Yearly average)

	Gold (London) $ per fine ounce	Petroleum (Saudi Arabia) $ per barrel	Wheat (USA) $ per bushel
1950	35.00	1.75	2.23
1960	35.00	1.87	1.99
1970	35.98	1.95	1.48
1971	40.97	2.34	1.58
1972	59.14	2.46	1.90
1973	100.00	3.29	3.81
1974	102.02	9.76	4.90
1975	160.96	10.72	4.06
1976	124.82	11.51	3.62
1977	147.72	12.40	2.81
1978	193.24	12.70	3.48
1979	306.67	16.97	4.36
1980	612.59	28.67	4.70

Source: IMF, *International Financial Statistics*.

of the 1972-3 boom, and then of the oil shock, it is not surprising that wage-price expectations changed in the 1970s. The processes of wage bargaining and price fixing were no longer dampened by money illusion, but were geared much more explicitly to take account and correct for recent inflationary experience. Thus, when demand weakened in 1974-5, very strong pressure for price increases continued, dominated by inflationary expectations which now acted as a fan instead of a dampener. This was quite different from the situation after the Korean War boom of 1950-1, when expectations quickly relapsed to 'normal'.

Monetarists explain this change in expectations rather simply and technocratically as a predictable adaptation to a continuous process of exposure to inflation. More complex explanations seem necessary to explain the big inter-country differences in the pace of wage and price advance that emerged in the 1970s. These differences had been greatly narrowed in the days of fixed exchange rates.

There are in fact quite a number of ingenious theories to explain this change in socio-economic climate.[20] It is clear that any explanation that is to deal satisfactorily with the differences between countries is bound to be complex and eclectic.

The Oil Shock

Most of these causes were more or less endogenous to the Western economies, though not all of them were purely economic. Then at the end of 1973 came the exogenous shock of the OPEC oil price increases. In 1974 the price of crude oil was four times as high as the average for 1972. This was a commodity on which the Western countries had become increasingly dependent in a quarter-century of rapid growth during which the price of oil had been remarkably stable. In 1973, oil imports of the Western countries were more than seventeen times their 1950 level. Oil in 1973 represented half of energy consumption, compared with a quarter in 1950. Part of the price stability was due to the low cost of extracting oil in the Middle East, and the fact that Saudi Arabia and the Persian Gulf countries producing oil were in a semi-colonial status with pricing policy fixed to a large extent by Western oil companies. It is likely that this situation would have changed in the long run in any case, but the big increases were sparked off by Arab irritation at US policies in support of Israel. For this reason, the oil price rise was backed by a partial embargo on oil supplies, which greatly increased its economic repercussions—particularly in Japan, which was most dependent on imported oil.

The oil price increase had a significant direct impact on the general price level, and contributed considerably to inflationary expectations, coming as it did at the high point of what was already an inflationary boom.

The oil shock had several other important repercussions. Its adverse effects on trade balances were a major reason for the stringency of restrictive policies in 1974 in most Western countries. Even though it was evident that the OPEC countries would accumulate reserves on a large scale and not use a good part of their extra income on imports, it was not clear at first how efficiently these OPEC surpluses would be recycled by the international capital and money markets. In 1974 and 1975 there was a considerable shift in the terms of trade, which further lowered real incomes in Western countries at a time when domestic output fell for the first time in the postwar period. This exacerbated tension in wage bargaining, particularly in Italy and the UK, where wage indexing (under the *scala mobile* and phase III respectively) arrangements made no exceptions for changed terms of trade.

The oil shock was a major reason for the depth of the 1974-5 recession. Its immediate impact was to draw off purchasing power into OPEC reserve accumulations, and the big structural change in prices also had a deflationary impact on demand. Demand for motor cars was badly hit, and the investment outlook became very uncertain, particularly where the price rises were accompanied by embargoes on oil shipment. The oil situation induced both an important spontaneous recessionary element and a deeper restrictiveness in official fiscal and monetary policy by governments worried about inflation, the oil-induced deficit in their current balance of payments, and the unpredictability of OPEC policies for locating their huge new foreign exchange reserves. The consequence was much deeper spontaneous forces for recession than had been previously experienced in the postwar period, and a simultaneity of recessionary trends which was more pronounced than the synchronization of the 1972-3 boom.

Given the rather special situation, it is not surprising that 1974 and 1975 were years of both recession and very high price increase. Over the two years, the combined real output of these countries fell by 0.2 per cent and the terms of trade loss reduced real income by another 1.3 per cent. Thus, the total real income loss was 1.5 per cent over the two years. The average price increase for the sixteen countries was 13.2 per cent in 1974 and 12.1 per cent in 1975.

Changed Policy Aspirations

Because of the change in expectations and the major payments problems created by the oil price rise, virtually all governments have changed their policy aspirations and tactics. Virtually all of them have had much more cautious policies than they would otherwise have had in face of such a slackening in the use of resources. Most of them did in fact pursue contracyclical budget policies to counteract the impact of the 1974-5 recessions, though not enough to offset the large spontaneous recessionary forces at work. In the 'recovery' period 1976-9, the average fiscal posture was one of restraint in spite of the obvious weakness of demand. Monetary policy was also tighter than in the early 1970s, with a rather self-conscious adoption of targets for monetary aggregates. The overall economic effect of budgetary measures is shown in Table 6.7, which aggregates both discretionary and automatic budgetary impacts. In fact, budget outcomes were often more expansionary than governments would have wished because of the wide coverage and high benefit levels of unemployment pay and other types of income support, the indexing of civil service pay, and social benefits.

Although the adjustment to payments difficulties was eased by floating rates, and easy possibilities of borrowing in international

TABLE 6.7
Impact of Budgetary Changes on GDP at Constant Prices, 1973-80

	1973	1974	1975	1976	1977	1978	1979	1980
Canada	−0.3	−0.1	2.6	−0.9	−0.5	0.7	0.5	0.1
France	−0.0	0.6	2.2	−1.0	−0.3	0.7	−0.8	−0.5
Germany	−0.7	2.0	2.6	−1.0	−0.8	0.3	0.1	0.3
Italy	1.3	0.0	3.4	−0.6	0.5	1.1	0.1	−0.9
Japan	−0.5	0.9	2.2	1.0	0.3	1.6	−0.5	−0.4
Netherlands	−0.4	0.4	0.9	1.1	−0.0	n.a.	n.a.	n.a.
Sweden	0.5	1.5	−0.1	−2.7	0.2	n.a.	n.a.	n.a.
UK	1.3	0.6	0.1	0.5	−0.6	0.5	−0.6	−0.6
USA	−0.3	0.3	3.4	−2.0	−1.1	−0.9	0.0	1.5

Source: OECD *Economic Outlook*, various issues. Positive figures indicate a supportive effect, negative ones a restrictive impact. See notes to Table 6.2.

markets, the developed countries generally made much less use of these borrowing possibilities than developing countries did;[21] and in some cases deficit countries have followed more deflationary policies than their internal situation would suggest in order to keep their exchange rate from deteriorating too far—most notably the UK in 1976, when it borrowed from the IMF and engaged in an austerity programme, in spite of the Social Contract agreements to mitigate wage increases and the early prospect of oil self-sufficiency.

This cautious policy stance was adopted in the hope that slack in domestic labour and goods markets would help break the expectational momentum that was pushing up wages and prices, and would permit exports to rise to meet payments deficits. There was also a hope that collective restraint would ease pressure on primary commodity markets, which it did.

During the 1960s, various experiments had been made to supplement the macropolicy armoury with direct appeals to mitigate wage/price pressure by price/incomes policies. There was a great variety of experiments with such policies in the 1960s, both mandatory and voluntary, and on the whole their success had not been too great. In the early 1970s they had been discredited in the UK and USA by the mandatory controls imposed by the Heath and Nixon administrations. Rather little use was made of this policy instrument in meeting the oil shock, except in Canada and the UK. In the UK, the voluntary Social Contract arrangement between the government and the unions lasted three years, from August 1975 to August 1978, and deserves a good deal of the credit for reducing UK inflation rates from Latin American levels to 8 per cent in 1978.

As the British government did not use this opportunity to follow more expansionary policies, the trade unions dropped their co-operation in 1978.

At the same time as they followed cautious macro-policies to break inflationary pressures, many governments also stepped up labour market and industrial intervention to mitigate the unemployment and bankruptcy that macro-policy necessarily involved if it was to achieve its purpose. Thus, the UK government subsidized British Leyland and Chrysler and provided various kinds of wage subsidy; the Japanese government helped firms in difficulty; Germany and Switzerland encouraged immigrants to leave; Sweden and France encouraged workers to withdraw from the labour force. Most of these interventionist measures were in flagrant contradiction to the avowed aims of macro-policy, and it would have been more sensible to have dispensed with them and to have been more expansionary on the macro-level.

A major problem was the greater uncertainty about the impact of particular measures, and about the objectives of policy itself. The explosiveness of wage-price expectations and the uncertainty about the exchange rate are important examples. But there was also greater uncertainty about the degree of labour slack now that cosmetic devices were concealing unemployment and uncertainty as to how much the rise in energy prices had reduced the effective capital stock, or was likely to affect consumer demand for cars. The meaning of international reserves was blurred in a floating system where the private short-term foreign assets were so large in relation to official holdings. Governments were giving top priority to reducing inflation and the payments deficit, but it was not clear what inflation target was reasonable, or what payments deficit was acceptable.

All of these uncertainties enhanced the legitimate margin of caution, but with almost all countries being cautious at the same time it is not surprising that the recovery from the 1974-5 recession was a faltering one.

To some extent, the caution at policy-making level has been enhanced by the theoretical challenge to traditional Keynesian demand management from monetarists, Keynesian revisionists, the new micro-economics, and the Hayek resurrection. The monetarist challenge has been the most far-reaching. Having successfully criticized early postwar neglect of monetary policy, and predicted an acceleration of inflation and the viability of floating exchange rates, Friedman and his disciples have a much better hearing than was the case in the Golden Age, and have had some impact on both the rhetoric and reality of policy, particularly in the UK, which has been the most ardent and least successful practitioner of fiscal activism and the country where official rejection of the importance of monetary policy was most total in the 1950s. Extreme monetarist views about the efficacy of simple monetary guidelines and the impotence of fiscal policy have not prevailed in official circles in most Western countries, but the relative indifference to real output, the suggestion that small errors in an expansionary direction are likely to lead to hyperinflation, and that a good deal of unemployment is voluntary, have had a significant unfortunate impact.[22]

The main new policy problems of the 1970s were:
1. living with the new international payments arrangements;
2. living with OPEC;
3. trying to break inflationary expectations.

Here we attempt to assess the degree of success in meeting these problems and the costs in terms of unemployment and output forgone.

Viability of the New Payments Arrangements

The major change in payments arrangements since 1973 is that, with the exception of rates between the members of the EMS, countries do not commit themselves to defend a particular exchange rate, but rather use floating rates as an instrument of balance of payments adjustment. As there have been major balance of payments disequilibria and great scope for international capital movements, this system has been less harmful to real output than any attempt to stick to pegged rates would have been. Furthermore, the private international capital market has greatly expanded. Short-term foreign lending in the Eurocurrency market totalled $475 billion by the end of 1979, and the total of Eurobond issues was also very large. Finance from this market was another new source of payments adjustment that reduced the need for official payments financing. In any case, official reserves rose very rapidly in the 1970s' The gold, foreign exchange, and IMF resources of these countries rose from $68 billion at end 1970 to $576 billion at end 1979 (see Table 6.8).

The essential elements of postwar trade liberalism have been kept intact, with none of the developed countries using beggar-your-neighbour commercial policies, and with world trade recovering fairly well after the 1974 setback. There have been some blemishes in the shape of steel quotas, subsidies to exporters, etc., but there is no comparison with the catastrophic collapse of world trade in 1929-33. The spirit of mutual co-operation and the degree of mutual consultation have also remained unshaken, again in sharp contrast with 1929-33.

Nevertheless, there remain major problems with the working of these arrangements. They have had to operate in such inflationary conditions, and with such a large deficit *vis-à-vis* the OPEC

TABLE 6.8

Total International Reserves, 1950-79
($ billion, end-year position)

	1950	1970	1973	1979
Australia	1.5	1.7	6.2	5.3
Austria	0.1	1.8	4.3	14.9
Belgium	0.8	2.8	8.1	22.9
Canada	1.8	4.7	7.3	14.2
Denmark	0.1	0.5	1.5	4.1
Finland	0.1	0.5	0.7	2.0
France	0.8	5.0	15.6	59.5
Germany	0.2	13.6	41.5	99.7
Italy	0.6	5.4	12.2	47.9
Japan	0.6	4.8	13.7	31.9
Netherlands	0.5	3.2	10.4	30.1
Norway	0.1	0.8	1.6	4.8
Sweden	0.3	0.8	2.9	6.4
Switzerland	1.6	5.1	14.3	59.1
UK	3.4	2.8	7.9	29.2
USA	24.3	14.5	33.7	143.2
Total	36.9	67.9	182.0	575.5

Source: IMF, *International Financial Statistics*. The figures include SDRs and IMF positions as well as gold and foreign exchange. The IMF shows reserves in terms of SDRs with gold at 35 SDRs an ounce. In revaluing in dollar terms, the London end-year price for gold was used here, i.e. $112.25 in 1973 and $512 an ounce in 1979. In 1950 and 1970 gold is valued at $35 an ounce.

countries, that the exchange rate changes necessary to achieve significant adjustment had to be very big. A change in the rate has a substantial feedback on the internal processes of wage and price formation, and floating rates have therefore tended to exacerbate the dichotomy between countries with slow and fast inflation rates. At the same time, the degree of payments disequilibrium between the developed countries themselves has been very large, larger than in the 1960s. There are risks of financial collapse in the rapid and uncontrolled growth of private international capital markets, where some of the borrowers are not too creditworthy. There are, of course, possibilities of co-operation in the IMF and IBRD, which did not exist in prewar years, and which can help prevent or mitigate governmental default such as occurred in 1929-33; but greater joint regulation of international capital markets is desirable, and it would seem sensible to use gold more actively as an official reserve asset to dampen fluctuations in the gold price.

Finally, there are clearly mixed feelings about the desirability of the floating rate system. The European Community countries, with the exception of the UK, have established a system of pegged rates within the European Monetary System (EMS). The commitment to fixed rates in a world with open capital markets and large changes in interest rates has had deflationary consequences for the domestic economies of EMS members, which could have been avoided only by greater co-ordination of economic policy, particularly the policy on interest rates.

Living with OPEC

Until 1973, virtually all the major economic problems of these countries were responsive to their domestic policy or amenable to their international co-operation. But the OPEC problem is one over which they have little control, given the heavy dependence on imported oil and the difficulty of finding a substitute for it. Political tension in the Middle East and Iran make it difficult to negotiate arrangements for oil supplies and pricing that might have been more in the economic interest of all parties than what happened after 1973.

The OPEC cartel's pricing policy damaged Western economies in three ways. The first was the direct loss in real income because of higher oil prices. Over 1973-80, real output per head grew at 2 per cent a year in our countries, but real income growth averaged only 1.5 per cent. The difference was a transfer of resources to OPEC countries. The second loss arose from structural changes in demand and output because relative prices moved so greatly and so suddenly in 1973-4 and in 1979. This produced adjustments in consumer demand and investment intentions and rendered part of the capital stock obsolete. Hence powerful temporary forces for recession were transmitted to the private sector in both 1974 and 1979. The third effect of OPEC pricing policy was to augment inflationary pressures and create very big problems of balance of payments adjustment. This induced goverments to follow very cautious macro-policies, which did more to inhibit income growth than did the direct impact of OPEC measures.

All of these problems involved larger short-term adjustments than are normal in peacetime. The direct transfer to OPEC through terms of trade loss was equivalent to multiplying foreign aid several times over. The structural adjustment problem was very severe, and most governments tried to mitigate it by reducing the proportionate importance of taxes on oil products. The USA and Canada went further and used import controls to keep domestic energy prices below world prices. These North American efforts to mitigate structural adjustment proved to be mistaken, because they inhibited both economies in oil consumption and the development of North American energy production.

As far as the third problem is concerned, Western governments were probably too deflationary in reacting to the OPEC challenge. Given the size of the OPEC current surplus over the six years 1974-9 ($224 billion), the Western countries as a whole were obliged to have a payments deficit. In fact, the cumulative collective net deficit of the sixteen Western countries over these six years was relatively modest, at around $48 billion, and their international reserves actually grew by almost $400 billion (if gold reserves are valued realistically at market prices). On balance of payments and international reserve criteria, the policy stance appears to have been over-cautious, particularly in the four countries that had a bigger surplus after the first OPEC shock than they had had in the Golden Age (Germany, $28 billion; Japan, $18 billion; Switzerland, $17 billion; and Netherlands, $5 billion—see Table 6.9 for proportionate balances).

TABLE 6.9

Current Balance of Payments as percentage of GDP
in Current Prices, 1961-78
(Average for years cited)

	1961-73	1974-8		1961-73	1974-8
Australia	−2.2	−2.3	Italy	1.6	−0.7
Austria	−0.4	−3.0	Japan	0.4	0.6
Belgium-			Netherlands	0.5	1.5
Luxembourg	1.6	−0.1	Norway	−1.9	−8.9
Canada	−0.8	−2.0	Sweden	0.1	−2.3
Denmark	−1.9	−3.0	Switzerland	−0.1	4.4
Finland	−1.5	−3.3	UK	0.1	−1.7
France	−0.2	−0.8	USA	0.4	−0.1
Germany	0.6	1.3	Arithmetic average	−0.2	−1.6

Source: Economic Outlook, no. 26, December 1979, and National Accounts of O.E.C.D. Countries 1952-1977, OECD, Paris, 1979.

It can be seen from Table 6.10 that the long-term trend towards energy economy was given a further push by the rise in relative prices from 1973 to 1974. This push was sharpened by the second round of oil price increases in 1979, particularly in the USA, where domstic oil prices have finally been decontrolled. The only country with a perverse oil price policy is now Canada: she still has a large programme to subsidize domestic energy consumption, which is higher than in any other Western country.[23]

Realistic energy pricing has also increased production of substitute products for OPEC oil: e.g., North Sea, Alaskan, and Mexican oil; US coal; and atomic energy generally. However, various kinds of ecological restrictions still hinder many of these developments, and the costs and benefits of these obviously need to be re-assessed.

Although one may argue that the OPEC challenge might have been handled in a way that was somewhat less damaging for

TABLE 6.10

Energy Consumption per $1,000 of Real GDP, 1929-79[a]
(GDP in 1970 US relative prices, energy in tons of oil equivalent)

	1929	1950	1973	1979
Austria	0.95	0.97	0.91	0.85
Belgium	1.83	1.31	1.09	1.00
Canada	2.26	1.87	1.85	1.71
Denmark	0.81	0.78	0.96	0.93
France	1.15	0.91	0.82	0.75
Germany	2.09	1.37	1.01	0.93
Italy	0.47	0.44	0.76	0.71
Japan	0.81	0.99	0.85	0.74
Netherlands	0.84	0.79	1.16	1.12
Norway	2.24	1.65	1.30	1.23
Sweden	0.90	1.04	1.31	1.28
Switzerland	0.67	0.67	0.82	0.86
UK	1.83	1.55	1.08	0.99
USA	1.98	1.76	1.59	1.43
Arithmetic average	1.35	1.15	1.11	1.04

[a] All figures exclude fuel wood.

Source: 1929-50 from W. S. and E. S. Woytinsky, *World Population and Production*, Twentieth Century Fund, New York, 1953, p. 941; 1973 from International Energy Agency, *Energy Conservation*, OECD, Paris, 1981, and *Economic Outlook*, OECD, July 1979; 1979 from *Energy Balances of O.E.C.D. Countries*, IEA, Paris, 1981. GDP from Appendix A.

Western economies, it is clear that there is a substantial element of political conflict of a beggar-your-neighbour kind in the international oil situation which is likely to continue to impose serious and erratic constraints on growth in Western countries of a type familiar from 1913 to 1945 but absent in the period of *pax americana* that ended in 1973.

Deceleration of Inflation

Table 6.11 shows that there was appreciable success in moderating the pace of inflation after the 1974-5 peaks, but the pattern of deceleration divided rather sharply between two groups of countries. In the first six, price increases decelerated to rates within the norms of the 1960s. This A group includes Germany and Japan and four smaller countries: Austria, Switzerland, Belgium, and the Netherlands. The average price increase for these six countries was 3.9 per cent in 1978-9—less than a third of the peak rates.

TABLE 6.11
Deceleration of Inflation and Output Growth

	1978-9 average annual rate of price increase	1974-5 peak annual price increase	1973-9 annual average GDP growth	1950-73 annual average GDP growth
A: *Countries back to 'acceptable' inflation rates*				
Switzerland	2.3	9.8	−0.4	4.5
Germany	3.6	7.0	2.4	6.0
Austria	4.0	9.5	3.1	5.4
Netherlands	4.2	10.2	2.4	4.8
Japan	4.3	24.5	4.1	9.7
Belgium	4.7	12.7	2.3	4.1
Average A	3.9	12.3	2.3	5.8
B: *Countries not back to 'acceptable' inflation rates*				
Norway	6.6	12.0	4.4	4.0
Finland	7.7	17.6	2.3	4.9
Australia	8.2	15.1	2.5	4.7
USA	8.3	11.0	2.5	3.7
Sweden	8.6	11.0	1.8	3.8
Canada	8.8	10.9	3.2	5.2
Denmark	9.9	15.0	2.1	4.0
France	10.0	13.7	3.0	5.1
UK	10.3	24.2	1.3	3.0
Italy	13.5	19.1	2.6	5.5
Average B	9.2	15.0	2.6	4.4

Source: OECD *Economic Outlook, Main Economic Indicators*, and *National Accounts of O.E.C.D. Countries*.

The other ten countries clearly fell into a different camp, with some deceleration below peak rates, but with a rate of inflation in 1978-9 well above 'acceptable' norms of the 1960s.

After six years of cautious policy, their average inflation rate was 9.2 per cent—more than twice as fast as the norms of the 1960s. This group includes all the Scandinavian countries, whose inflation performance in the 1970s has been true to form, drifting somewhere near the mode for the group as a whole. It includes Australia, Canada, and the USA, with three big European countries—France, the UK, and Italy—in the extreme position, not able to decelerate below double-digit inflation.

What is the reason for the difference in price performance between these countries?

In the first place, it is clear from Table 6.11 that the members of group A decelerated their economic growth more than group B. Their GDP growth rates in 1973-9 averaged 2.3 per cent a year, down from 5.8 per cent a year in 1950-73. Group B also experienced a major deceleration, but it was smaller.

To some extent, this difference in inflationary momentum may be attributable to more cautious demand management in Group A than Group B. But a more fundamental reason why group A was able to break the wage-price spiral is that these countries have a different socioeconomic climate and different attitudes, which come from a complex variety of historical factors. In Germany and Austria memories of hyperinflation had a therapeutic effect on wage and price discipline; the Netherlands has a long postwar record of moderation in wage claims and a Social Compact atmosphere; Switzerland has a long history of price stability, and was willing to make greater sacrifices of output to achieve this goal than any other country; Japan has always had greater wage and price flexibility than the other countries.

In the other group, the four Scandinavian countries have never set great store by price stability, and their wage-price decision process tends to make them drift with the central tendency in their trading partners. In the USA, the price peaks of 1974-5 were dampened by internal controls on oil prices, and the subsequent process of decontrol hindered price deceleration. The three worst performers are beset by a decidedly non-consensual atmosphere in wage negotiations. France and Italy being the only Western countries with important communist parties and the UK having labour relations problems of a unique kind.

Thus we have two groups of countries, in most of which governments have followed policies of cautious expansion. In one group this has been crowned with success; in the other the results have been mediocre.

The most extreme cases of divergence from the cautious demand management strategy were Switzerland and Norway. The former country had to follow a sharply deflationary policy to achieve its top position in the low-inflation league, whereas Norway was the only country retaining a full-employment strategy. As a result, Norwegian economic growth scarcely faltered after 1973, yet its rate of inflation was the smallest of group B countries.

The Norwegian achievement was due partly to a solidaristic social atmosphere which kept wage claims relatively moderate and mitigated domestic inflationary pressures in spite of full employment. However, Norway was much less concerned than other countries about its external payments deficit, both because it expected large future earnings from oil and because it had traditionally been a foreign borrower.

Table 6.9 shows the extreme positions of these two countries in respect of the foreign balance, with Switzerland having an average surplus equal to 4.4 per cent of GDP in 1974-8 and Norway running a deficit equal to 8.9 per cent of GDP.

In fact, the majority of Western countries faced inflationary forces that they could not break by deflationary policy. In the first place, having tolerated creeping inflation for a quarter-century before 1973, no one expected a return to long-term equilibrium of zero inflation. Second, there were inflationary consequences of the OPEC problem which had to be absorbed, and these were usually bigger than could be assessed by any mechanical calculation of what oil prices added directly to price increases. The third reason is that virtually all Western countries now operate a highly developed welfare state, which provides substantial income cushions to the unemployed and to others suffering income losses owing to recession. In most countries there has been a substantial rise in social transfer expenditures since 1973 even where governments have been most committed to budget-balancing rhetoric. Apart from automatic stabilizers, many governments have intervened with subsidies to firms that might otherwise have gone bankrupt, and a good deal of this discretionary action has taken place in countries like Sweden and the UK under conservative governments, contrary to their own professed ideology. Hence there are strong contradictions between the professed objectives of macro-policy and the social or industrial policy of governments. There are similar perverse effects from some of the policy weapons used; e.g., very high interest rates restrict activity, but they also have a direct price raising effect, increase the budget deficit, and increase the flow of interest payments to OPEC creditors.

There is no doubt that deflationary policy had some impact in mitigating the pace of price increase, but given the above-mentioned constraints, the degree of success was meagre; and the cost, in terms of output and employment forgone, was large.

The Sacrifice of Employment and Output

Since 1973, unemployment has risen substantially in these countries, though the rise has been smaller than in the 1929-32 depression: from 1929 to 1932 unemployment in these countries rose from an average of 4.0 to 12.3 per cent of the labour force; from 1973 to 1980 it rose from 2.5 to 5.5 per cent. The difference is due partly to the fact that recession in output was much milder in the 1970s than in the 1930s, but it is also true that unemployment is no longer a very good indicator of the degree of slack in labour markets. Contemporary governments do more to dampen the downswing in income and output in recession than used to be the case, and they also do more to muffle the labour market repercussions of the demand swings that do occur. This accounts for the mildness of unemployment in the recession and also for its persistence in recovery. The labour slack diverted into other channels has to be re-absorbed in the recovery period and hinders the reduction of unemployment. The other reason for the persistence of unemployment is that the recovery in demand was weak and was interrupted by the second OPEC oil shock in 1979-80: it was clearly less vigorous than the recovery of 1934-7, as Table 6.12 shows.

Three significant cushions mitigated unemployment: curbs on immigration; reduction of labour force participation; and cuts in working time. These are not all of the same importance in different countries. In Switzerland and Germany a reversal of migration flows kept unemployment low; the Netherlands reduced activity rates by classifying people as handicapped; Sweden reduced

TABLE 6.12

Unemployment and Growth Rates: Prewar and in the 1970s

	Average of individual country unemployment rates	Average of individual country GDP growth rates		Average of individual country unemployment rates	Average of individual country GDP growth rates
1926	5.1	3.0	1968	2.5	5.2
1927	4.8	4.1	1969	2.1	6.3
1928	4.3	4.0	1970	2.2	5.2
1929	4.0	3.5	1971	2.5	3.8
1930	6.1	−1.3	1972	2.7	4.9
1931	9.2	−4.6	1973	2.5	5.7
1932	12.3	−2.9	1974	2.8	2.2
1933	12.1	1.9	1975	3.9	−0.4
1934	10.2	4.7	1976	4.2	4.5
1935	8.9	4.1	1977	4.5	2.3
1936	8.6	4.2	1978	4.8	2.8
1937	7.2	5.1	1979	4.6	3.6
1938	7.0	3.7	1980	(5.5)	(1.8)

Source: Appendices A and C. In all cases except prewar unemployment rates the figures are unweighted averages of the rates for the sixteen countries. For prewar unemployment, France and Japan are not included, Italy is not included for 1926-8 and 1935-6, and Switzerland is excluded for 1926-8.

unemployment by keeping significant numbers in training schemes.

It is difficult to make detailed estimates of the slack in labour markets, because present methods of monitoring the situation are inadequate. Perhaps the simplest measure of the overall situation comes from Table 5.3 above. This shows average labour force growth of 1.1 per cent a year in 1973-9, compared with 1 per cent in 1950-73, but labour input rose by 0.3 per cent a year in the earlier period and fell by 0.1 per cent a year in the later one. This suggests a shortfall in labour demand of 0.5 of a percentage point a year.

Since 1973, growth of output per man-hour has averaged about 1.8 percentage points a year below the performance of 1950-73. Some of the decline was an inevitable waning of the special growth opportunities in the 1950s and 1960s, as indicated in Chapter 5. The sudden rise in energy prices created problems of structural adjustment, and there were also cyclical influences: i.e., the reduced growth in capital stock that the recession has induced, and the lower efficiency of resource allocation, which has been deliberately

promoted in some degree by government policies to prevent unemployment.

In the 1970s, policy was aimed primarily at breaking inflationary
momentum and restoring payments equilibrium. Employment and
output considerations did not receive the priority they did in the
1950s and 1960s. There is, of course, awareness of sacrifice in
output, but as its magnitude is not clear and some decline was
inevitable, there has been a tendency to legitimate these losses by
'structuralist' explanations. Thus it may be argued that unemployment is voluntary because unemployment benefits are too high,
because wages are too high; that there is a shortage of the right
kind of capital; that there is no slack in the economies of these
countries. Such structuralist arguments always recur in periods of
depressed activity, and there was obviously a new structural problem
in the 1970s arising out of the huge increase in the relative price of
energy. My own view is that the structural case is exaggerated[24] and
that some of the loss of output and employment in the 1970s could
have been avoided by less cautious macro-policy.

It is not possible to give more than a very rough estimate of how
much better policy might have achieved. Longer-term factors may
have reduced the underlying growth potential to around 4 per cent
after 1973 (compared with near 5 per cent in the 1950-73 period),
and the inevitable cyclical losses in cooling down inflation, meeting
the OPEC shocks, and learning to live with floating exchange
rates may be reckoned at one and a half year's loss of output. Thus
I am talking of GDP growth rate for 1973-9 in the region of 3 per
cent instead of the 2.5 per cent actually achieved, with the additional
growth concentrated heavily but not exclusively on group A countries. This would have been enough to make unemployment decline
in the recovery period, and would probably have meant somewhat
higher inflation and higher payments deficits. But a slower pace of
deceleration of inflation would have been tolerable, and bigger
payments deficits could have been financed.

The degree of policy failure in the 1970s bears no comparison
with that which occurred in the 1930s, either in the international or
domestic area. But there are substantial long-run dangers in letting
these economies drift into a situation of increasing under-utilization
of growth potential. It means that in each recession the weakness of
investment is greater, the pressure for structuralist activism and less
liberal commercial policies will grow, and increasing unemployment will exacerbate social tension.

APPENDIX A

SOURCES AND METHODS USED TO MEASURE OUTPUT LEVELS AND GROWTH

The output figures refer, wherever possible, to gross domestic product. This broad aggregate covers the output of the whole economy, and excludes income received from or paid for foreign investment. For 1950 onwards, unless otherwise specified, the figures are derived from currently collected official estimates based on almost identical concepts, as published by OECD. Most of them conform closely to the OECD/UN standardized system.[1]

For years before 1950, the estimates have nearly all been made retrospectively and the underlying data are less complete, particularly for years before 1913. Nevertheless, most of the historical estimates are based on substantial statistical research by distinguished scholars, and in some cases emanate from the governmental statistical service responsible for making the more recent official estimates. The long-term measures are obviously not as comparable as those for 1950 onwards, and in some cases may well be substantially revised when further research is done. The weakest figures for the pre-1913 period are those for Belgium, Finland, France, the Netherlands, and Switzerland, so the results for these countries should be regarded as tentative.

Many studies of long-term growth simply ignore developments in war years, so there are usually gaps in the series for 1913 to the early 1920s and from 1938 to the late 1940s. However, wartime experience is of considerable relevance to subsequent developments as well as being interesting in itself. These wartime gaps have therefore been filled by rough estimates wherever possible.

The figures on GDP are presented as indices, corrected where necessary to eliminate the effect of territorial change. These changes have generally not been large, but it seemed worthwhile to eliminate them to improve the comparability of the figures. Ignoring the case of Austria after the First World War, which mainly involved the dismantlement of an empire rather than changes in national boundaries, the biggest changes have occurred in Germany. All the adjustments are described in detail in the country notes.

A major problem in long-term comparisons is the correction for price changes. The choice of different periods as a weighting base can affect quantitative developments significantly. Generally, the prices of an earlier year will give a higher increase in output than those of a later year, because of the tendency to consume more of those items whose relative price falls.

Thus, if one of the countries had used 1870 weights for the whole period 1870-1970 and another country used 1970 weights, the growth rate in the former would have an upward bias relative to the latter. Similarly, one might expect growth to be faster when measured in the prices of a country where growth has been fastest in items that were initially relatively expensive. However, these problems may not be important in practice if the weighting systems are changed every so often so that each series is made up of a number of separate links.[2]

In order to compare levels of output or productivity in the different countries or to add their output together to form an aggregate index, it is useful to find a unit that expresses the comparative value of their currencies more accurately than the official exchange rate. Fortunately, for eight of the countries (Belgium, France, Germany, Italy, Japan, the Netherlands, the UK, and the USA), rather careful estimates of purchasing power are available which make it possible to convert the different countries' output figures into comparable units. The source used was I. B. Kravis, A. Heston, and R. Summers, *International Comparisons of Real Product and Purchasing Power*, Johns Hopkins, 1978, pp. 8 and 175-96. These authors themselves prefer to convert output of different countries in terms of 'international dollars', using a geometric mean of purchasing power parities derived by weighting prices by US quantities and by each country's own quantities. I have not done this but have used the purchasing powers derived by using each country's own quantity weights. When these are applied to adjust the country's GDP expressed in dollars at the official exchange rate, one obtains an estimate of the relative quantities of output valued at 1970 US relative prices.

I prefer to measure output at US relative prices, first, because this is the price structure to which these countries are converging as their productivity and demand patterns approach US levels; and, second, because the concept of US relative prices corresponds to an identifiable reality.[3] The compromise 'international dollar' concept is a device intended for comparisons over the wider income range covered by Kravis and associates (who include Kenya and India in their comparison), but I am not keen on it, because it is difficult to say what it means in real terms in spite of its mathematical charm.

For other countries, earlier careful comparisons are available on Kravis lines for Canada, Denmark, and Norway; but the estimates for Australia, Austria, Finland, Sweden, and Switzerland are much cruder. Canadian estimates were derived from D. Walters, *Canadian Growth Revisited 1950-1967*, Economic Council of Canada, 1970, p. 46, adjusted from a GNP to a GDP basis and extrapolated from 1960 to 1970. Estimates for Denmark and Norway were derived from M. Gilbert and associates, *Comparative National Products and Price Levels*, OEEC, Paris, 1958, p. 23, adjusted from a GNP to a GDP basis and extrapolated from 1955 to 1970 (with a 3.5 per cent downward adjustment for Norway to exclude repairs and maintenance).

Purchasing power ratios for Australia and Finland were derived from I. B. Kravis, 'A Survey of International Comparisons of Productivity', *Economic Journal*, March 1976, pp. 19-20. Australia was linked via the UK, Finland via Denmark. The purchasing power ratio for Austria was supplied by Dr Anton Kausel of the Austrian Statistical Office. Switzerland was adjusted by the German purchasing power ratio, Sweden by the Canadian ratio.

The results of the calculation are shown in Table A1. It should be noted that in all the countries the purchasing power of the currency was higher than the exchange rate relative to the USA in 1970, and all the countries had a lower real GDP per head than the USA.

TABLE A1

A Comparison of Nominal and Real Levels of GDP and the Purchasing Power of Currencies in 1970

	(1) GDP at purchaser's values converted at official exchange rates	(2) Ratio of purchasing power of currency to exchange rate	(3) Real GDP at US relative prices
	(*$ million*)	(*USA = 1.0000*)	(*$ million*)
Australia	35,340	1.3742	48,564
Austria	14,530	1.5525	22,558
Belgium	25,420	1.3870	35,258
Canada	82,800	1.0410	86,195
Denmark	15,880	1.1202	17,789
Finland	10,730	1.4246	15,286
France	141,540	1.3387	189,480
Germany	186,140	1.2574	234,052
Italy	100,270	1.5409	154,506
Japan	207,562	1.5504	321,804
Netherlands	31,680	1.4762	46,766
Norway	10,800	1.2142	13,113
Sweden	32,760	1.0410	34,103
Switzerland	21,030	1.2574	26,443
UK	121,930	1.5014	183,066
USA	988,600	1.0000	988,600

Source: Column (1) is from *National Accounts of O.E.C.D. Countries 1950-79* with Norway adjusted downwards by 3.5 per cent to eliminate repairs and maintenance. Revised US figure supplied by OECD Secretariat. Column (2) derived as described above; column (3) is derived by multiplying the first two columns. In some cases the basic OECD GDP estimates have been revised upwards since the study by Kravis and associates. The significant cases are: Belgium, 1.4 per cent; Italy, 8.5 per cent; and Japan, 3.9 per cent (to which we added 0.92 per cent to include Okinawa).

TABLE A2
Gross Domestic Product at 1970 Prices Adjusted to Exclude the Impact of Frontier Changes[a]
($ million at 1970 US relative prices)

	1820	1870	1913	1950	1979
Australia	(n.a.)	2,257	8,817	19,362	64,382
Austria	(1,293)	2,591	7,216	7,909	31,939
Belgium	1,254	4,715	11,094	16,187	49,103
Canada	(n.a.)	2,285	11,367	32,986	127,002
Denmark	417	1,072	3,308	8,210	22,942
Finland	(n.a.)	674	2,423	5,889	20,423
France	11,852	24,193	48,974	70,816	266,385
Germany	4,770	12,970	42,664	68,688	303,508
Italy	(n.a.)	16,001	29,908	50,724	202,180
Japan	7,285	8,681	24,663	48,044	512,104
Netherlands	938	3,030	7,463	18,136	61,671
Norway	(286)	849	2,093	6,100	19,391
Sweden	(780)	1,726	5,587	15,605	40,718
Switzerland	(609)	2,093	5,068	10,617	28,511
UK	9,052	29,254	65,591	105,471	222,749
USA	3,585	30,557	176,630	488,913	1,335,678

[a] The figures refer throughout to production with 1979 frontiers.

Sources: Estimates derived from table A1 and tables A4 to A8, except for Norway, Sweden and Switzerland in 1820 which were derived by extrapolation of the per capita GDP growth figures shown for 1830-70 by P. Bairoch, 'Europe's Gross National Product: 1800-1975', *The Journal of European Economic History*, Fall 1976, p. 286. I have extrapolated the Austrian estimates of table A4 back from 1830 to 1820, and for Japan, I assumed no change in per capita income from 1820 to 1870. Bairoch also has estimates for Italy and Finland for 1830-70, but the movements seem implausible.

TABLE A3
Gross Domestic Product at 1970 Prices, NOT Adjusted for Territorial Change
($ million at 1970 US relative prices)

	1870	1913	1950	1979
Austria	7,686	19,274	7,909	31,939
Belgium	4,676	11,005	16,187	49,103
Canada	2,255	11,221	32,986	127,002
Denmark	1,026	3,165	8,210	22,942
France	24,113	46,820	70,816	266,385
Germany	20,998	71,838	68,688	303,508
Italy	15,738	29,415	50,724	202,180
Japan	8,659	24,600	47,605	512,104
UK	30,365	68,082	105,471	222,749
USA	30,497	176,278	487,938	1,335,678

N.B.: Countries not included in Table A3 did not undergo geographic change affecting GDP.

Table A2 shows the level of output in 1970 US dollars for selected years 1820-1979 corrected to offset the impact of boundary changes. It was derived by combining the results of the 1970 level estimates of Table A1 with the growth figures of Tables A4 to A8. Table A3 shows output levels within the geographic boundaries of the years cited for those countries where frontiers changed.

SOURCE NOTES FOR TABLES A4-A8: GDP INDICES FOR INDIVIDUAL COUNTRIES

Australia: 1861-1901, GDP from N. G. Butlin, *Australian Domestic Product, Investment and Foreign Borrowing 1861-1938/39*, Cambridge, 1962, pp. 33-4; 1901-51, GDP at 1966/67 prices from M. W. Butlin, *A Preliminary Annual Database 1900/01 to 1973/74*, Discussion Paper 7701, Reserve Bank of Australia, May 1977. All figures adjusted to a calendar year basis.

Austria: 1830-1913, from A. Kausel, 'Osterreichs Volkseinkommen 1830 bis 1913', in *Geschichte und Ergebnisse der zentralen amtlichen Statistik in Osterreich 1829-1979, Beitrage zur osterreichischen Statistik*, Heft 550, Vienna, 1979. 1913-50 gross national product, from A. Kausel, N. Nemeth, and H. Seidel, 'Osterreichs Volkseinkommen, 1913-63', *Monatsberichte des Osterreichischen Institutes fur Wirtschaftsforschung*, 14th Sonderheft, Vienna, August 1965; 1937-45, from F. Butschek, *Die Osterreichische Wirtschaft 1938 bis 1945*, Fischer, Stuttgart, 1979, p. 65. The figures are corrected for territorial change, which has been large. (In 1911-13, present-day Austria represented only 37.4 per cent of the total output of the Austrian part of the Austro-Hungarian Empire.) They refer to the product generated within the present boundaries of Austria.

Belgium: 1846-1913 GDP derived from movements in agricultural and industrial output from J. Gadisseur, 'Contribution à l'étude de la production agricole en Belgique de 1846 à 1913', *Revue Belge d'histoire contemporaine*, vol. IV, 1-2, 1973, and service output which was assumed to move with employment in services (derived for census years from P. Bairoch, *La Population active et sa structure*, Brussels, 1968, pp. 87-8). 1913 weights derived from Carbonnelle: 1913-50 GDP estimates derived from C. Carbonnelle, 'Recherches sur l'évolution de la production en Belgique de 1900 à 1957', *Cahiers Economiques de Bruxelles*, no. 3, April 1959, p. 353. Carbonnelle gives GDP figures for only a few benchmark years but gives a commodity production series for many more years. Interpolations were made for the service sector to arrive at a figure for GDP for all the years for which Carbonnelle shows total commodity production. Figures corrected to exclude the effect of the cession by Germany of Eupen and Malmedy in

1925, which added 0.81 per cent to population and was assumed to have added the same proportion to output.

Canada: Gross national product (expenditure) from O. J. Firestone, *Canada's Economic Development 1867-1953*, London, 1958, p. 276 for 1867-1926; for 1926-50 from *National Income and Expenditure Accounts 1926-1974*, vol. I, Statistics Canada, 1976. Figures adjusted to offset the acquisition of Newfoundland in 1949, which added 1.3 per cent to GNP and 2.6 per cent to population.

Denmark: 1820-1950 GDP at factor cost (1929 prices) from S. A. Hansen, *Økonomisk vaekst i Danmark*, vol. II, Institute of Economic History, Copenhagen, 1974, pp. 229-32 (figures from 1921 onwards adjusted to offset the acquisition of North Schleswig, which added 5.3 per cent to the population, and 4.5 per cent to GDP).

Finland: 1860-1950 GDP from O. E. Niitamo, 'National Accounting and National Statistical Service on the Threshold of the 1980s', *Finnish Journal of Business Economics*, I, 1980.

France: For the eighteenth century J. Marczewski has presented rough estimates of economic growth based partly on the work of his colleague J. C. Toutain, who showed a 60 per cent increase in agricultural output between the first and eighth decade. Toutain's estimates have been criticized by M. Morineau, *Les Faux-semblants d'un démarrage économique*, A. Colin, Paris, 1971, who rejects all evidence of French progress rather in the style of a prosecution attorney. E. Le Roy Ladurie presents a more balanced criticism and also presents an alternative estimate to Toutain which I have used. The sources to 1820 were therefore: 1701-10 to 1820 movement in industry and 1781-90 to 1820 movement in agriculture from J. Marczewski, 'Some Aspects of the Economic Growth of France, 1660-1958', *Economic Development and Cultural Change*, April 1961, p. 375; 1701-10 to 1781-90 agricultural output increase assumed to be 32.5 per cent, the mid-point of the range suggested by E. Le Roy Ladurie, *Le Territoire de l'historien*, vol. I, Gallimard, Paris, 1973, p. 279. 1701-10 to 1781-90 output in services assumed to move parallel with population. 1781-90 to 1820 output in services from J. Marczewski, 'The Take-off Hypothesis and French Experience', in W. W. Rostow (ed.), *The Economics of the Take-Off into Sustained Growth*, Macmillan, New York, 1965, p. 136. 1820-96 GDP derived from separate indicators of industrial, agricultural, building, and service output. Industrial production, agriculture, and building from M. Levy-Leboyer, 'La Croissance économique en France au XIXe siècle', *Annales*, July-August 1968, pp. 802 f. Service output interpolated from Marczewski, 'The Take-off Hypothesis', p. 136. 1896-1950 GDP and 1896 sector weights from J.-J. Carré, P. Dubois, and

E. Malinvaud, *La Croissance française*, Seuil, Paris, 1972, pp. 35 and 637. Interpolation between 1913 and 1920 based on figures for industrial and agricultural output shown in J. Dessirier, 'Indices comparés de la production industrielle et production agricole en divers pays de 1870 à 1928', *Bulletin de la statistique générale de la France, Etudes spéciales*, October-December 1928; service output was assumed stable in this period, and weights for the three sectors were derived from Carré, Dubois, and Malinvaud, op. cit. Interpolation between 1939 and 1946 was based on A. Sauvy's report on national income to the Conseil Economique, *Journal officiel*, 7 April 1954.[4] The figures from 1918 onwards were adjusted downwards by 4.6 per cent to offset the impact of the return of Alsace Lorraine; figures for 1861-70 were multiplied by 95.92 to offset for inclusion of Alsace Lorraine; and for 1860 and earlier by 97.65 to offset both the impact of acquisition of Nice and Savoy in 1861 and the Alsace Lorraine component.

Germany: 1816-50, GDP estimated from Prussian data in R. H. Tilly, 'Capital Formation in Germany in the Nineteenth Century', in P. Mathias and M. M. Postan (eds), *Cambridge Economic History of Europe*, vol. VII, I, 1978, pp. 395, 420, and 441. Using 1850 weights for agriculture, industry, and services from W. G. Hoffmann, F. Grumbach and H. Hesse, *Das Wachstum der deutschen Wirtschaft seit der Mitte des 19 Jahrhunderts*, Springer, Berlin, 1965, p. 454, Prussian per capita output in agriculture and industry were multiplied by population in Germany as a whole. Output in services was assumed to move with population. 1850-1925 net domestic product (value added by industry) at factor cost from Hoffmann, Grumbach and Hesse, op. cit., pp. 454-5. This source gives no figures for 1914-24, but starts again in 1925. The pattern of movement in individual years 1914-24 was derived from annual indices of industrial and agricultural output in Dessirier, op. cit., using Hoffmann's weights for these sectors and adjusting them to fit his sectoral output benchmarks for 1913 and 1925. Service output was interpolated between Hoffmann's 1913 and 1925 figures for this sector. 1925-39 GDP from *Bevölkerung und Wirtschaft 1872-1972*, Statistical Office, Wiesbaden, 1972, p. 250. 1939-44 GNP from E. F. Denison and W. C. Haraldson, 'The Gross National Product of Germany 1936-1944', *Special Paper 1* (mimeographed) in J. K. Galbraith (ed.), *The Effects of Strategic Bombing on the German War Economy*, US Strategic Bombing Survey, 1945. 1946 from *Wirtschaftsproblemen der Besatzungszonen*, D. I. W. Duncker and Humblot, Berlin, 1948, p. 135; 1945 was assumed to lie midway between 1944 and 1946. 1947-50 from *Statistics of National Product and Expenditure No. 2, 1938 and 1947 to 1955*, OEEC, Paris, 1957, p. 63. The estimates are fully corrected for territorial change, which was extremely complicated in Germany. It can be summarized in simplified form as follows (in terms of ratio of old to new territory): 1870, 96.15 per cent; 1918, 108.39 per cent; 1946, 155·35 per cent.[5]

Italy: 1861-1950 GDP at 1938 prices from P. Ercolani, 'Documentazione statistica di base', in G. Fua (ed.), *Lo Sviluppo Economico in Italia*, vol. III, Angeli, Milan, 1975, pp. 410-12. The figures refer to output in the present territory of Italy (*confini attuali*: see p. 388). Figures in an earlier official study, *Annali di Statistica*, serie VIII, vol. 9, Instituto Centrale di Statistica, Rome, 1957, show a gain in output due to territorial change of 3.2 per cent after the First World War and a loss of 1.5 per cent after the Second World War (corresponding population changes were a gain of 4.1 per cent and a loss of 1.4 per cent respectively).

Japan: 1885-1930, GDP at 1934-6 prices from K. Ohkawa, N. Takamatsu, and Y. Yamamoto, *National Income*, vol. I of *Estimates of Long-term Economic Statistics of Japan since 1868*, Toyo Keizai Shinposha, Tokyo, 1974, p. 227. Rough estimate for 1870 was derived by assuming that per capita product rose by 1 per cent a year from 1870 to 1885. This is smaller than the later period, but 1870-85 saw major upheavals in which economic growth was probably slow. 1930-42, gross national product at 1934-6 prices from *National Income White Paper* (in Japanese), 1963 ed., p. 178 adjusted (from 1946) to a calendar year basis. 1952 onwards from *National Accounts of OECD Countries* various editions. In the above sources, Okinawa is included up to 1945, and excluded from 1946 to 1972. An upward adjustment of 0.66 per cent was made for 1946 to offset the impact of territorial change, and 1973 was adjusted down by 0.92 per cent to offset the impact of Okinawa's return.

Netherlands: For 1700 it was assumed that Dutch GDP per head was a little more than 50 per cent higher than that of the UK. This rough assumption is based on comparative evidence of economic structure and relative levels of international trade, investment, and government finance in the two countries as shown mainly in Jan de Vries, *The Dutch Rural Economy in the Golden Age, 1500-1700*, Yale, 1974, and P. Deane and W. A. Cole, *British Economic Growth 1688-1959*, Cambridge, 1964. In 1700 about two-thirds of the UK labour force was in agriculture, and in the Netherlands the proportion was about one-third. I assume that productivity was higher in industry and services than in agriculture in both countries and the evidence suggests strongly that Dutch productivity was higher in each sector than in the UK. Dutch agriculture was more specialized, with a large internal trade carried by canal, exports of dairy products; a quarter of its grain was imported from eastern Europe, and cattle were imported on a large scale from Denmark. Its industry was highly diversified with a great deal of international trade, and the Dutch performed sophisticated finishing processes (bleaching, printing, dyeing) for English woollens and German linens. Activity in international banking, insurance, shipping, and warehousing was on a much larger scale per capita than in the UK. At the end of the seventeenth century the Dutch merchant fleet was about

50 per cent larger than the British but population was a fifth of that in the UK.[6] Gregory King estimated Dutch per capita income as only 4 per cent higher than that of England in 1695 (see G. E. Barnett, *Two Tracts by Gregory King*, Johns Hopkins, Baltimore, 1936, p. 55) but he over-estimated Dutch population by 18 per cent. Assuming that this error was independent of his output estimate (which is not clear), this would raise King's differential to about 23 per cent in favour of the Netherlands as against England. Our own estimates for the UK (see below) imply that UK per capita income in 1700 was about 4.5 per cent lower than that in England and Wales. Adjusting King again for this would produce a differential of 29 per cent in favour of the Netherlands as against the UK. However, King estimates English consumption levels to be one-third higher than the Netherlands (even after adjusting for his population error). This seems implausible. Hence, the evidence of Gregory King, though it points to a lower Dutch advantage than I suggest, is not too persuasive.[7]

In the eighteenth century the Dutch economy stagnated. The process is described in detail without any aggregate quantification by Johan de Vries, *De economische Achteruitgang der Republiek in de Achttiende Eeuw*, Leiden, 1968. From 1700 to 1760 I have assumed that Dutch per capita GDP fell by 10 per cent and then stagnated to 1820, with a fall during the war period 1795-1815. Per capita GNP probably did not decline in the eighteenth century because of the increase in foreign investment and the receipts from it. These receipts, and GDP, were quite adversely affected during the Napoleonic wars and French occupation. I have not made any direct estimate of 1820-70 growth, but this emerges as a by-product from the above and from estimates backcast from 1970 to 1870 from the following sources: 1870-1900 GDP from S. Kuznets, *Economic Growth of Nations*, Harvard, 1971, pp. 12 and 16; 1900-17, 1921-39, and 1948-50 net domestic product, and 1917-20 national income, at constant market prices derived from *1899-1959 Zestig Jaren Statistiek in Tijdreeksen*, Centraal Bureau voor de Statistiek, Zeist, 1959, p. 102; 1939-47 real product in international units interpolated from C. Clark, *Conditions of Economic Progress* (3rd edn), Macmillan, London, 1957, pp. 166-7.

Norway: GDP at market prices. 1865-1950 from *National Accounts 1865-1960*, Central Bureau of Statistics, Oslo, 1965, pp. 348-59 (gross fixed investment was adjusted downwards by a third to eliminate repairs and maintenance).1939-44 movement in national income (excluding shipping and whaling operations carried out from Allied bases 1940-4) from O. Aukrust and P. J. Bjerve, *Hva Krigen Kostet Norge*, Dreyers, Oslo, 1945, p. 45. 1945 assumed to be midway between 1944 and 1946.

Sweden: 1861-1950 GDP from O. Krantz and C. A. Nilsson, *Swedish National Product 1861-1970: New Aspects on Methods and Measurement*, CWK Gleerup, Kristianstad, 1975, p. 171.

Switzerland: 1890-1944 real product in international units from C. Clark, *Conditions of Economic Progress* (3rd edn), Macmillan, London, 1957, pp. 188-9. The link 1938-48 is from *Europe and the World Economy*, OEEC, Paris, 1960. 1948-76 from *Séries Revisées de la Comptabilité Nationale Suisse 1948-1970*, Federal Statistical Office, Berne, 1977, pp. 26-7. The rough estimate for 1870 was derived by backward extrapolation of the 1890-1913 movement in output per head. There is a graphical indication of the growth of Swiss real product in F. Kneschaurek, 'Problemen der langfristigen Marktprognose', *Aussenwirtschaft*, December 1959, p. 336 for 1900-65. This shows faster growth than C. Clark to 1938. On the other hand, U. Zwingli and E. Ducret, 'Das Sozialprodukt als Wertmesser des langfristigen Wirtschaftswachstums', *Schweizerische Zeitschrift fur Volkswirtschaft und Statistik*, March-June 1964, show slower growth for 1910-38 than C. Clark.

UK: 1700-1800 England and Wales from P. Deane and W. A. Cole, *British Economic Growth 1688-1959*, Cambridge, 1964, p. 78 (excluding government) and 1801-31 for Great Britain from p. 282. The Deane and Cole estimates were adjusted to a UK basis, assuming Irish output per head in 1830 to be half of that in Great Britain (as Deane herself hypothesizes in the source mentioned below) and to have been stagnant from 1800 to 1830, assuming that Scottish and Irish output per head in 1800 were three-quarters of that in England and Wales in 1800, and that output per head increased by a quarter in these two areas from 1700 to 1800 (as compared with a growth of 47 per cent in England and Wales). 1830-1855 gross national product at factor cost from P. Deane, 'New Estimates of Gross National Product for the United Kingdom 1830-1914', *The Review of Income and Wealth*, June 1968, p. 106, linked to 1855-1950 GDP at factor cost (compromise estimate) from C. H. Feinstein, *National Income Expenditure and Output of the United Kingdom 1855-1965*, Cambridge, 1972, pp. T18-20. Figures from 1920 onwards are increased by 3.8 per cent to offset the exclusion of output in the area which became the Irish Republic.

USA: GDP, 1820-40 at 1840 prices derived from P. A. David, 'The Growth of Real Product in the United States before 1840: New Evidence, Controlled Conjectures', *Journal of Economic History*, June 1967. The method assumes that 1820-40 agricultural output moved parallel with total population; it derives the agricultural productivity movement from this and further assumes that agricultural and non-agricultural productivity grew at the same pace. Agricultural productivity in 1840 is taken as 51 per cent of non-agricultural. 1840-89 movement of gross national product in 1860 prices[8] derived from R. E. Gallman, 'Gross National Product in the United States 1834-1909', *Output, Employment and Productivity in the United States after 1800*, NBER, New York, 1966, p. 26. Gallman does not actually give figures for 1840, 1850, 1860, 1870, and 1889: these were extra-polated from neighbouring years. The movement in individual years 1870-89 was derived by using the index of output in mining manufacturing and construction in W. A. Lewis, *Growth and Fluctuations 1870-1913*, Allen & Unwin, London, 1978, p. 273; the index of farm production from F. Strauss and L. H. Bean, *Gross Farm Income and Indices of Farm Production and Prices in the United States 1869-1937*, Technical Bulletin 703, US Dept of Agriculture, Washington, 1940, p. 126, Table 61 (Las-peyre's index); and interpolating the movement in services from the residual derived from Gallman. 1889 weights (agriculture 28.1, industry 26.7, other 45.2 per cent) at 1929 prices were derived from *The National Income and Product Accounts of the United States, 1929-1974*, p. 186, and from the 1889-1929 product movement by sector as shown in J. W. Kendrick, *Productivity Trends in the United States*, NBER, Princeton, 1961, pp. 302-3. 1889-1929 GDP from ibid., pp. 298-9. 1929-79 GDP from 'The National Income and Product Accounts of the United States: An Intro-duction to the Revised Estimates for 1929-80', *Survey of Current Business*, December 1980. Figures corrected to exclude the impact of the accession of Alaska and Hawaii in 1960. These two states added 0.5 per cent to total product, but part was already included and the explicit addition was only 0.2 per cent; see *Survey of Current Business*, July 1962, p. 5.

TABLE A4
Movement in GDP, 1700-1849[a]
$(1913 = 100)$

	Austria	Belgium	Denmark	France	Germany	Netherlands	UK	USA
1700				12.51[b]		11.20	3.91	
1760				15.52		10.50	5.52	
1800							9.13	
1810							10.93	
1820		(11.3)	12.6	24.2	(11.2)	12.56	13.8	2.03
1821			13.2	26.1				
1822			13.4	25.1				
1823			13.4	26.5				
1824			13.8	27.6				
1825			13.9	26.6				
1826			14.1	27.2				
1827			14.5	27.8				
1828			14.7	28.0				
1829			14.4	28.7				
1830	21.1		14.5	27.2			18.8	
1831			14.4	27.5	14.6		19.7	
1832			14.8	30.1			19.5	
1833			14.7	30.4			19.7	
1834			15.5	30.0			20.5	
1835			15.4	31.8			21.6	
1836			15.4	31.2			22.4	
1837			15.8	32.6			22.1	
1838			15.9	33.0			23.3	
1839			16.1	30.4			24.4	
1840	24.0		16.6	34.7			23.7	5.07
1841			16.6	35.1			23.2	
1842			16.7	34.9			22.7	
1843			17.6	35.4			23.1	
1844			18.5	37.5			24.5	
1845			19.0	36.0			25.8	
1846		22.5	19.4	35.2			27.5	
1847		23.6	19.3	40.5			27.7	
1848		23.7	20.3	38.4			28.0	
1849		24.4	21.5	39.9			28.5	

[a] Estimates adjusted as far as possible to exclude the impact of frontier changes. Figures in brackets derived by interpolation or extrapolation.
[b] 1701-10.

TABLE A5
Movement in GDP, Annual Data 1850-69[a]
(1913 = 100)

	Australia	Austria	Belgium	Denmark	Finland	France	Germany	Italy	Norway	Sweden	UK	USA
1850		27.8	25.4	22.7		40.0	20.3				28.2	7.8
1851			26.1	21.6		39.4	20.2				29.4	
1852			26.8	22.4		41.5	20.6				29.9	
1853			27.5	22.5		39.1	20.5				31.0	
1854			29.2	22.6		41.2	21.0				31.8	
1855			29.4	25.1		40.7	20.7				32.7	
1856			31.0	23.7		42.6	22.4				34.0	
1857			31.8	24.1		46.1	23.5				34.6	
1858			32.0	23.9		48.5	23.4				34.7	
1859			32.0	25.5		44.8	23.5				35.6	
1860		32.1	33.6	25.3	22.8	47.1	24.9				36.4	12.7
1861	15.2		34.1	25.7		45.4	24.3	48.7		24.1	37.4	
1862	15.0		35.0	26.5		48.3	25.5	49.7		24.9	37.7	
1863	15.5		36.0	28.2		50.7	27.4	48.9		25.6	38.0	
1864	17.2		37.2	27.9		50.3	28.2	50.2		26.1	39.0	
1865	17.1		37.2	28.9		51.8	28.3	52.5	37.6	26.7	40.2	
1866	18.2		38.3	28.9		51.9	28.5	54.7	38.3	27.7	40.8	
1867	20.4		38.5	28.9		48.4	28.6	50.1	39.3	27.9	40.4	
1868	21.4		39.9	29.4		54.4	30.3	51.9	39.1	26.4	41.7	
1869	21.6		41.4	31.1		56.7	30.5	52.9	40.7	27.7	42.0	

[a] Estimates adjusted to exclude the impact of frontier changes.

TABLE A6

Movement in GDP, Annual Data, 1870-1913[a]

(1913 = 100)

	Australia	Austria	Belgium	Canada	Denmark	Finland	France	Germany
1870	25.6	35.9	42.5	20.1	32.4	27.8	49.4	30.4
1871	24.6	38.5	42.6	20.7	32.5		51.2	30.2
1872	27.3	38.8	45.2	17.4	34.3		55.1	32.3
1873	30.2	37.9	45.5	19.1	34.1		51.7	33.7
1874	31.2	39.6	47.0	23.1	35.1		58.5	36.2
1875	34.5	39.8	46.9	22.3	35.7		61.0	36.4
1876	34.5	40.7	47.5	22.5	36.4		58.6	36.2
1877	35.8	42.1	48.1	23.1	35.4		59.9	36.0
1878	39.2	43.5	49.5	22.7	36.8		58.7	37.7
1879	39.9	43.2	50.0	26.6	38.0		56.9	36.8
1880	42.0	43.8	52.5	29.6	38.9	35.5	60.3	36.5
1881	45.0	45.6	53.2	33.6	39.3		62.1	37.4
1882	42.4	45.9	55.0	33.4	40.7		64.4	38.0
1883	48.7	47.8	55.8	32.8	42.1		63.1	40.1
1884	49.1	49.1	56.3	36.1	42.3		61.6	41.1
1885	52.3	48.8	57.0	40.0	42.6		62.1	42.1
1886	52.8	50.4	57.7	36.1	44.3		62.9	42.4
1887	60.4	53.9	59.9	36.1	45.9		63.1	44.1
1888	58.9	53.8	60.3	38.0	46.2		62.7	45.9
1889	63.9	53.3	63.2	37.1	46.8		63.7	47.2
1890	61.7	56.2	64.6	38.0	49.6	44.4	65.5	48.7
1891	66.5	58.2	64.7	44.3	50.6		66.7	48.6
1892	58.3	59.5	66.3	43.3	51.8		68.6	50.6
1893	55.1	59.9	67.3	42.1	52.8		66.9	53.1
1894	57.0	63.4	68.3	41.9	53.9		71.7	54.4
1895	53.7	65.1	69.9	44.1	56.9		70.2	57.0
1896	57.8	66.1	71.3	48.4	59.0		72.4	59.0
1897	54.6	67.5	72.6	42.0	60.4		71.1	60.7
1898	63.1	71.3	73.8	49.8	61.4		75.0	63.3
1899	63.2	72.8	75.3	47.7	64.0		78.9	65.6
1900	66.9	73.4	77.5	49.9	66.2	69.1	80.3	68.4
1901	65.0	73.7	78.2	54.8	69.0	67.4	77.6	66.8
1902	65.9	76.6	79.8	58.8	70.6	65.3	77.6	68.4
1903	67.3	77.3	81.6	60.5	74.8	71.1	80.3	72.2
1904	70.4	78.5	83.7	61.6	76.4	74.1	84.2	75.1
1905	71.3	82.9	86.1	66.3	77.7	75.0	82.9	76.7
1906	78.0	86.1	87.9	70.1	79.9	77.8	84.2	79.0
1907	80.0	91.4	89.2	70.4	82.9	82.6	85.5	82.5
1908	78.3	91.8	90.1	73.4	85.5	82.4	86.8	83.9
1909	82.1	91.5	91.8	81.7	88.8	83.0	88.2	85.6
1910	88.2	92.8	94.2	83.3	91.5	85.3	88.2	88.7
1911	91.3	95.7	96.4	90.5	96.4	88.7	92.1	91.7
1912	95.1	100.5	98.7	92.2	96.4	96.1	100.0	95.7

[a] Estimates adjusted to exclude the impact of frontier changes.

Movement in GDP, Annual Data, 1870-1913[a]
(1913 = 100)

	Italy	Japan	Netherlands	Norway	Sweden	Switzerland	UK	USA
1870	53.5	(35.2)	40.6	40.6	30.9	41.3	44.6	17.3
1871	53.1			41.2	32.0		47.0	18.4
1872	52.6			43.8	34.0		47.1	19.8
1873	54.7			44.7	35.9		48.2	20.1
1874	54.7			46.2	36.3		49.0	20.0
1875	56.2			47.6	35.6		50.2	20.7
1876	55.6			49.0	37.8		50.7	21.6
1877	55.5			49.2	37.8		51.2	23.0
1878	55.7			47.7	37.7		51.4	24.4
1879	56.3			48.3	40.0		51.2	25.8
1880	57.2			49.8	40.3		53.6	27.7
1881	54.4			50.2	40.9		55.5	28.9
1882	57.2			50.0	41.0		57.1	30.1
1883	56.9			49.8	43.2		57.5	30.9
1884	57.6			50.8	43.2		57.6	31.5
1885	58.2	45.6		51.4	43.8		57.3	32.1
1886	59.3	49.4		51.7	44.3		58.2	34.3
1887	59.7	51.7		52.3	43.7		60.5	35.7
1888	59.0	49.4		54.6	45.5		63.2	36.6
1889	57.2	52.0		56.5	46.0		66.6	38.7
1890	61.2	56.6		58.0	47.4	58.0	66.9	41.5
1891	61.8	54.0		58.5	49.3		66.9	43.3
1892	59.4	57.6		59.8	50.0		65.3	47.5
1893	61.4	57.8		61.4	51.4		65.3	45.2
1894	60.7	64.6		61.6	52.8		69.7	43.9
1895	62.0	65.6		62.2	55.9		71.9	49.2
1896	63.0	62.0		64.1	57.8		74.9	48.2
1897	60.5	63.2		67.3	60.2		75.9	52.8
1898	64.4	75.2		67.5	61.8		79.6	53.9
1899	65.3	69.7		69.4	63.0		82.9	58.8
1900	69.8	72.7	74.1	70.6	64.6		82.3	60.4
1901	73.4	75.2	74.3	72.5	63.9		82.3	67.2
1902	73.8	71.4	77.1	74.0	66.3		84.4	67.9
1903	74.8	76.3	78.8	73.7	69.7		83.5	71.2
1904	74.9	77.0	79.4	73.6	71.9		84.0	70.3
1905	77.5	75.7	82.2	74.5	73.3		86.5	75.5
1906	79.1	85.5	81.1	77.2	79.8		89.4	84.2
1907	87.1	88.2	87.1	80.1	83.1		91.1	85.5
1908	87.0	88.8	86.9	82.7	83.4		87.4	78.5
1909	92.4	88.7	89.7	84.9	83.6		89.4	88.1
1910	87.7	90.2	89.3	87.9	88.8		92.2	89.0
1911	93.1	95.0	91.6	90.6	92.6		94.9	91.9
1912	95.3	98.6	98.6	94.7	96.1		96.3	96.2

TABLE A7

Movement in GDP, Annual Data, 1913-49[a]

(1913 = 100)

	Australia	Austria	Belgium	Canada	Denmark	Finland	France	Germany
1914	94.4			93.9	106.3	92.9	94.4	85.2
1915	93.5			96.8	98.9	91.0	86.9	80.9
1916	97.1			101.1	103.1	95.6	83.2	81.7
1917	94.7			103.3	97.0	81.0	80.7	81.8
1918	95.0			104.2	93.8	63.9	76.4	82.0
1919	93.4			109.1	105.9	75.3	75.2	72.3
1920	97.0	66.4	92.5	103.7	110.9	88.7	81.8	78.6
1921	105.9	73.5	94.1	94.3	107.7	92.0	80.5	87.5
1922	110.5	80.1	103.3	101.9	118.6	103.0	93.1	95.2
1923	114.5	79.3	107.0	108.3	131.1	109.1	98.1	79.1
1924	120.5	88.5	110.5	108.1	131.5	115.2	108.2	92.6
1925	122.5	94.5	112.2	112.8	128.5	122.2	109.4	103.0
1926	123.2	96.1	116.0	122.7	136.0	126.7	110.7	105.9
1927	125.7	99.0	120.3	134.3	138.7	137.4	109.4	116.5
1928	123.4	103.6	126.6	146.6	143.4	142.0	115.7	121.6
1929	123.1	105.1	125.5	147.2	153.0	141.2	125.8	121.1
1930	118.1	102.2	124.3	140.9	162.1	138.9	122.0	119.4
1931	113.3	94.0	122.1	123.0	163.9	132.8	117.0	110.3
1932	117.6	84.3	116.6	110.2	159.6	135.2	112.0	102.0
1933	123.3	81.5	119.1	102.9	164.7	144.7	117.0	108.4
1934	127.0	82.2	118.1	115.4	169.7	162.9	117.0	118.3
1935	131.6	83.8	125.4	124.4	173.5	166.8	113.2	127.2
1936	137.1	86.3	126.3	129.9	177.8	178.5	114.5	138.4
1937	143.7	90.9	128.0	142.9	182.1	196.1	120.8	153.4
1938	145.2	102.5	125.1	144.1	186.5	197.5	120.8	169.1
1939	146.2	116.2		154.8	195.4	192.1	125.8	182.7
1940	155.7	113.2		176.6	168.0	169.2	103.8	184.0
1941	173.2	121.3		202.0	151.4	179.5	82.3	195.7
1942	193.1	115.2		239.5	154.8	187.7	73.6	198.4
1943	199.9	118.0		249.2	171.9	204.6	69.8	202.3
1944	193.0	121.0		259.0	189.9	200.8	61.0	207.5
1945	183.4	50.0		253.2	175.6	171.1	66.2	145.3
1946	176.8	58.4		246.4	203.0	193.3	100.6	83.0
1947	181.1	64.4		256.9	214.4	206.1	109.5	101.9
1948	192.8	82.0	132.9	263.3	221.5	219.5	125.8	120.8
1949	205.4	97.5	138.3	269.8	231.5	228.8	134.5	140.7

[a] Estimates adjusted to exclude the impact of frontier changes.

Movement in GDP, Annual Data, 1913-49[a]
(1913 = 100)

	Italy	Japan	Netherlands	Norway	Sweden	Switzerland	UK	USA
1914	99.0	97.0	99.1	102.2	100.2		101.0	92.3
1915	110.8	106.1	100.8	106.6	98.5		109.1	94.9
1916	122.5	122.4	105.3	110.0	104.0		111.5	108.0
1917	126.5	126.7	97.7	100.0	92.5		112.5	105.3
1918	127.5	124.0	92.5	96.3	92.0		113.2	114.8
1919	107.8	140.9	115.7	112.6	96.5		100.9	115.8
1920	100.0	132.2	118.3	119.7	102.8		94.8	114.7
1921	98.0	146.9	122.7	109.8	105.9		87.1	112.1
1922	103.9	146.3	127.5	122.6	111.8		91.6	118.3
1923	109.8	146.3	131.9	125.3	116.9		94.5	133.9
1924	111.8	151.2	136.3	124.7	119.3	119.2	98.4	138.0
1925	119.6	156.7	142.8	132.4	130.4	127.8	103.2	141.2
1926	120.6	158.1	146.2	135.3	138.7	134.2	99.4	150.4
1927	117.6	160.6	154.2	140.5	144.9	141.5	107.4	151.9
1928	126.5	172.8	158.5	145.1	145.3	149.3	108.7	153.6
1929	130.4	178.9	166.5	158.6	156.5	154.5	111.9	163.0
1930	123.5	166.1	168.2	170.3	165.5	153.6	111.1	147.4
1931	122.5	171.6	162.6	157.1	153.9	147.2	105.4	136.1
1932	125.5	173.2	157.0	167.6	150.2	142.2	106.2	117.4
1933	125.5	180.5	152.9	171.6	153.7	149.2	109.3	115.0
1934	125.5	199.9	154.3	177.1	163.3	149.5	116.5	123.9
1935	137.3	204.7	158.3	184.7	172.7	148.9	121.0	134.6
1936	137.3	211.2	161.3	196.0	183.7	149.4	126.5	153.3
1937	146.1	261.2	170.0	203.0	186.6	156.5	130.9	160.7
1938	148.0	270.0	171.6	208.1	192.7	162.6	132.5	153.6
1939	158.8	272.3	178.2	218.0	199.4	162.3	133.8	165.6
1940	159.8	256.0	160.0	198.6	190.7	164.0	147.2	178.4
1941	157.8	260.1	162.8	203.4	190.6	162.9	160.6	207.5
1942	155.9	263.5	148.7	195.5	196.6	158.8	164.6	239.5
1943	141.2	262.8	144.6	191.6	199.9	157.4	168.2	276.0
1944	114.7	254.0	97.7	181.6	207.2	161.2	161.6	295.5
1945	89.8		99.1	203.5	220.6		154.5	291.1
1946	117.6		173.2	225.3	232.1		147.8	247.9
1947	138.2	152.8	200.0	251.1	241.6		145.6	243.5
1948	146.1	171.0	221.4	271.1	251.5	204.1	150.2	253.3
1949	156.9	179.0	235.5	276.4	264.9	196.1	155.8	254.7

TABLE A8
Movement in GDP, Annual Data, 1950-79[a]
(1913 = 100)

	Australia	Austria	Belgium	Canada	Denmark	Finland	France	Germany
1950	219.6	109.6	145.9	290.2	248.2	243.0	144.6	161.0
1951	229.0	117.1	154.2	303.2	246.4	265.6	153.0	177.8
1952	231.1	117.2	153.0	329.6	250.7	274.8	158.2	193.5
1953	238.3	122.3	157.9	345.9	265.2	275.1	162.1	209.5
1954	253.1	134.8	164.4	342.1	274.4	300.0	168.9	225.6
1955	266.9	149.7	172.2	374.7	273.4	322.7	176.8	252.8
1956	276.0	160.0	177.2	406.9	278.9	329.1	187.3	270.9
1957	281.6	169.8	180.5	417.3	291.0	334.1	198.5	286.1
1958	295.1	176.0	180.3	426.2	299.1	333.8	204.3	296.3
1959	313.8	181.0	186.0	443.1	319.7	358.0	210.8	318.2
1960	327.4	195.9	196.0	455.6	338.6	393.6	225.9	346.5
1961	334.8	206.8	205.9	469.5	360.2	423.4	238.3	364.2
1962	348.2	212.2	216.8	501.3	380.7	434.5	254.3	380.2
1963	372.3	221.0	226.3	529.1	383.1	449.2	267.8	391.6
1964	398.8	234.7	242.1	562.9	418.6	472.9	285.3	417.8
1965	416.6	241.5	251.1	601.0	437.7	497.9	298.9	441.4
1966	434.0	255.2	258.7	643.3	449.7	508.4	314.5	452.4
1967	455.7	262.8	269.0	665.4	470.3	520.1	329.3	451.6
1968	485.7	274.6	280.4	702.6	490.3	533.3	343.3	480.0
1969	522.0	291.8	298.9	739.2	524.1	584.6	367.3	517.6
1970	550.8	312.6	317.8	758.3	537.8	630.8	388.3	548.6
1971	577.4	330.2	330.1	811.2	550.9	642.4	409.3	566.3
1972	600.7	350.1	347.7	858.8	580.7	690.9	433.5	587.0
1973	628.0	368.5	369.3	923.2	611.2	736.0	456.8	615.8
1974	648.9	384.3	385.8	955.9	605.8	759.4	471.6	619.1
1975	662.9	377.8	378.4	966.6	602.1	763.8	472.4	607.7
1976	682.1	399.6	398.4	1022.7	649.9	765.7	496.9	639.0
1977	693.8	417.0	401.5	1047.6	661.6	768.5	510.8	658.4
1978	708.6	421.3	413.4	1085.6	670.0	786.0	529.2	680.2
1979	730.2	442.6	423.2	1117.3	693.6	842.8	545.9	711.4

[a] Estimates adjusted to exclude the impact of frontier changes.

Movement in GDP, Annual Data, 1950-79[a]
(1913 = 100)

	Italy	Japan	Netherlands	Norway	Sweden	Switzerland	UK	USA
1950	169.6	194.8	243.0	291.5	279.3	209.5	160.8	276.8
1951	182.5	219.1	247.3	305.0	287.7	226.5	166.6	299.6
1952	190.6	244.5	252.1	315.9	292.6	228.4	166.2	310.6
1953	204.9	262.5	272.8	331.7	302.1	236.5	173.8	322.6
1954	212.4	277.4	291.1	344.5	320.1	249.7	180.5	318.6
1955	226.5	301.1	311.5	351.8	329.8	266.6	186.5	339.8
1956	237.1	323.8	325.4	369.8	340.7	284.2	189.4	346.9
1957	249.7	347.5	335.1	378.3	348.8	295.5	193.1	353.0
1958	261.8	367.8	331.8	383.3	357.0	289.2	193.4	352.0
1959	278.9	401.3	347.4	394.4	375.6	307.5	201.1	373.0
1960	296.5	453.9	378.8	413.0	389.9	329.0	211.6	380.1
1961	320.8	520.0	390.4	433.9	412.2	355.7	218.6	390.0
1962	340.7	556.7	405.9	454.3	429.9	372.7	220.7	412.3
1963	359.9	615.2	420.6	471.5	452.3	390.9	229.3	428.8
1964	369.9	696.4	455.4	495.1	483.6	411.4	241.3	451.3
1965	382.0	732.2	479.3	521.3	503.5	424.5	246.9	478.5
1966	404.9	811.8	492.5	541.0	514.7	435.0	251.9	507.7
1967	433.9	912.8	518.5	574.9	533.1	448.3	258.4	521.5
1968	462.3	1041.2	551.8	587.9	552.5	464.3	269.1	545.4
1969	490.5	1167.9	587.2	614.4	578.8	490.5	273.1	560.8
1970	516.6	1304.8	626.6	626.6	610.4	521.8	279.1	559.7
1971	525.1	1371.4	653.4	655.3	616.5	543.1	286.7	578.0
1972	541.9	1499.5	675.7	689.2	629.2	560.4	292.9	610.3
1973	580.0	1633.7	714.2	717.5	653.3	577.5	314.9	644.0
1974	604.0	1628.1	739.5	744.9	680.0	585.9	311.2	639.2
1975	582.1	1650.4	731.8	786.2	697.0	543.2	308.8	633.6
1976	616.2	1757.1	770.8	839.8	708.1	535.6	321.6	667.4
1977	627.9	1851.9	789.1	869.8	691.2	548.6	324.8	703.6
1978	644.1	1960.7	808.6	898.3	700.6	550.4	336.5	735.9
1979	676.0	2076.4	826.3	926.6	728.8	562.6	339.6	756.2

APPENDIX B

POPULATION

All figures are adjusted to refer to mid-year, and breaks in the series due to territorial change are indicated in the tables. The figures include all nationals present in the country, armed forces stationed abroad, and merchant seamen at sea. Aliens are included only if they are permanently settled. Unless otherwise specified, the figures for 1950 onwards are from OECD, *Labour Force Statistics*.

Australia: Bureau of Census and Statistics, *Demography Bulletin Yearbooks*, to 1957.

Austria: 1960 onwards, OECD, *Labour Force Statistics*; earlier years from *Statistisches Handbuch fur die Republik Osterreich*, 1975, p. 9; *Statistisches Handbuch fur den Bundesstaat Osterreich*, Vienna, 1936, p. 21; and A. Kausel, *Oesterreichs Volkseinkommen 1830 bis 1913*, Statistical Office, Vienna, 1979. The figures refer throughout to the present territory of Austria.

Belgium: Interpolated from *Annuaire Statistique de la Belgique et du Congo Belge, 1955*.

Canada: M. C. Urquhart and K. A. H. Buckley, *Historical Statistics of Canada*, Cambridge, 1965, p. 14. Years before 1870 from E. Kirsten, E. W. Buchholz, and W. Kollmann, *Raum und Bevölkerung in der Weltgeschichte*, Ploetz, Wurzburg, 1956, and information supplied by R. Marvin McInnis.

Denmark: S. A. Hansen, *Økonomisk vaekst i Danmark*, vol. II, Institute of Economic History, Copenhagen, 1974, pp. 201-4.

Finland: O. Turpeinen, *Ikaryhmittainen Kuolleisuus Suomessa vv. 1751-1970*, Helsinki, 1973.

France: 1861-1950, from *Annuaire statistique de la France*, 1966, pp. 66-72; 1700-1860 from L. Henry and Y. Blayo, 'La Population de la France de 1740 à 1860', *Population*, November 1975, pp. 97-9. This source gives figures for five-year intervals which we have interpolated. They referred to the 1861 territory and were therefore multiplied throughout by 98.235 to exclude Savoy and Nice.

Germany: 1946 onwards, from *Statistisches Jahrbuch 1975 für die Bundesrepublik Deutschland*, p. 49 (1950 adjusted to mid-year). Figures refer to Federal Republic including the Saar throughout and also West Berlin.

1817-1913, W. G. Hoffman, F. Grumbach, and H. Hesse, *Das Wachstum der deutschen Wintschaft seit der Mitte des 19 Jahrhunderts*, Springer, Berlin, 1965, pp. 172-5 (for 1870-93 these figures differ a little from those in *Bevölkerung und Wirtschaft 1872-1972*, Statistisches Bundesamt, Wiesbaden 1972, pp. 101-2). 1913-46 information from above sources, *Statistisches Handbuch von Deutschland 1928-1944*, Munich, 1949, p. 18, and I. Svennilson, *Growth and Stagnation in the European Economy*, ECE, Geneva, 1954, p. 236.

Italy: 1861-1949, from *Annuario Statistico Italiano*, 1955 edn, p. 369, and 1944-48 edn, p. 21, adjusted to mid-year. 1950-61, from OECD, *Manpower Statistics 1950-62*. All figures refer to the whole 'present in area' population. 1962 onwards, from OECD *Labour Force Statistics*, with an upward adjustment to include the institutional population. The institutional population was 747,000 in 1961 and 605,000 in 1971. Estimates of the institutional population for other years were made by calculating the rate of decline between 1961 and 1971 and assuming it to be constant.

Japan: 1873-1950, from *Japan Statistical Yearbook 1975*, pp. 9, 10, and 13 adjusted to mid-year. Figures for 1935-46 include armed forces overseas. Data on armed forces and geographic change taken from I. B. Taeuber, *The Population of Japan*, Princeton, 1958, Chapter XVI. It was assumed that in 1946 only half of the overseas forces had been repatriated to Japan. Estimates for earlier years derived from Taeuber, op. cit., pp. 20-7.

Netherlands: 1900-50, from *Seventig Jaren Statistiek in Tijdreeksen*, CBS, The Hague, 1970, p. 14, adjusted to a mid-year basis. 1870-1900, interpolated from census results from *Jaacijfers voor Nederland 1939*, The Hague, 1940, p. 4. Earlier years from J. A. Faber *et al.*, 'Population Changes and Economic Developments in the Netherlands: A Historical Survey', *A.A.G. Bijdragen*, vol. 12, 1965, p. 110.

Norway: *Historical Statistics 1968*, CBS, Oslo, pp. 44-6.

Sweden: O. Johansson. *The Gross Domestic Product of Sweden and its Composition 1861-1955*, Stockholm, 1967, pp. 156-7, and *Historical Statistics of Sweden*, Central Statistical Office, Stockholm, 1955, pp. 2-3.

Switzerland: 1950 onwards (average for year including part of seasonal worker population), from OECD, *Labour Force Statistics*, and OECD Statistics Division. Earlier years from *Annuaire Statistique de la Suisse 1952*, pp. 42-3, and K. B. Mayer, *The Population of Switzerland*, Columbia, 1952, pp. 19 and 29.

United Kingdom: 1855-1949 from C. H. Feinstein, *National Income Expenditure and Output of the United Kingdom 1855-1965*, Cambridge, 1972, pp. T120-1, home population except 1915-20 and 1939 onwards when armed forces overseas are included; 1800-55 from B. R. Mitchell, *Abstract of British Historical Statistics*, Cambridge, 1962, pp. 8-9, linked to 1700-1800 from P. Deane and W. A. Cole, *British Economic Growth 1688-1959*, Cambridge, 1964, p. 6.

United States: *Historical Statistics of the United States, Colonial Times to 1970*, US Department of Commerce, 1975, pp. 8 and 1168, resident population except for 1917-19, and 1930 onwards when armed forces overseas are included.

TABLE B1

Population, 1500-1860

	1500	1600	1700	1760	1820	1830	1840	1850	1860
	('000)	('000)	('000)	('000)	('000)	('000)	('000)	('000)	('00
Australia[a]	0	0	0	0	33	66	360	389	1,12
Austria	1,420	1,800	2,100	2,778	3,189	3,538	3,716	3,950	4,23
Belgium	1,500	1,400	2,000	2,530	3,518	(3,722)	(4,049)	4,413	4,64
Canada[a]	0	0	15	65	640	1,034	1,523	2,404	3,18
Denmark	600	650	700	820	1,097	1,209	1,289	1,424	1,61
Finland	150	200	250	490	1,169	1,364	1,441	1,628	1,73
France[b]	16,400	18,200	21,120	25,246	30,698	32,712	34,284	35,708	36,64
Germany	12,000	15,000	15,000	18,310	24,905	28,045	31,126	33,746	36,04
Italy	10,500	13,300	13,300	16,900	19,000	(21,020)	(22,040)	(24,065)	(24,8C
Japan	15,800	18,700	26,800	28,300	28,900				
Netherlands	950	1,500	1,900	1,960	2,344	2,618	2,869	3,057	3,33
Norway	300	400	500	687	970	1,124	1,241	1,392	1,5S
Sweden	550	760	1,260	1,916	2,574	2,876	3,123	3,462	3,82
Switzerland	800	1,000	1,200	1,480	1,829	(2,101)	(2,222)	(2,379)	(2,5(
UK	4,400	6,800	9,273	11,069	20,686	23,815	26,488	27,524	28,77
USA[a]	0	0	251	1,594	9,618	12,901	17,120	23,261	31,5(

[a] Excludes indigenous populations, which were probably as follows before European settlement: Australia, 250; Canad 1,000; USA, 2,500.

[b] Excludes territories acquired in 1861 (Savoie, Haute Savoie, and part of Alpes Maritimes), which represented 660,0(of the 37,390,000 population of 1861).

Sources: As in country notes supplemented by R. J. Mols, 'Population in Europe 1500-1700', in C. M. Cipolla (ed *Fontana Economic History of Europe*, vol. II, 1972; A. Armengaud, 'Population in Europe 1700-1914', from Cipol op. cit., vol. III; M. Gille, 'The Demographic History of Northern European Countries in the Eighteenth Centur *Population Studies*, June 1949; B. T. Urlanis, *Rost Naselenie v Evrope*, Ogiz, Moscow, 1941, pp. 414-15; J. F. Dewhu and associates, *Europe's Needs and Resources*, Twentieth Century Fund, New York, 1961, p. 911; H. E. Driver, *Indic of North America*, Chicago, 1975, p. 63; E. Kirsten, E. W. Buchholz, and W. Kollmann, *Raum und Bevolkerung in c Weltgeschichte*, Ploetz, Wurzburg, 1956; and P. Bairoch, 'Europe's Gross National Product 1800-1875', *Journal European Economic History*, Fall 1976.

TABLE B2

Mid-year Population, Annual Data, 1870-1913

	Australia	Austria[a]	Belgium	Canada	Denmark	Finland	France	Germany
	('000)	('000)	('000)	('000)	('000)	('000)	('000)	('000)
1870	1,620	4,520	5,056	3,641	1,793	1,754	38,440	39,231
1871	1,675	4,562	5,096	3,705	1,807	1,786	36,190[b]	40,997[c]
1872	1,722	4,604	5,137	3,772	1,821	1,819	36,140	41,230
1873	1,769	4,646	5,178	3,843	1,838	1,847	36,340	41,564
1874	1,822	4,688	5,219	3,910	1,856	1,873	36,490	42,004
1875	1,874	4,730	5,261	3,968	1,874	1,899	36,660	42,518
1876	1,929	4,772	5,303	4,023	1,894	1,928	36,830	43,059
1877	1,995	4,815	5,351	4,078	1,917	1,957	37,000	43,610
1878	2,062	4,857	5,399	4,136	1,940	1,983	37,180	44,129
1879	2,127	4,899	5,448	4,203	1,960	2,014	37,320	44,641
1880	2,197	4,941	5,497	4,273	1,976	2,047	37,450	45,095
1881	2,269	4,985	5,562	4,338	1,995	2,072	37,590	45,428
1882	2,348	5,030	5,628	4,389	2,013	2,098	37,730	45,719
1883	2,447	5,075	5,694	4,444	2,029	2,130	37,860	46,016
1884	2,556	5,121	5,761	4,500	2,051	2,164	38,010	46,396
1885	2,650	5,166	5,829	4,548	2,076	2,195	38,110	46,707
1886	2,741	5,212	5,872	4,592	2,102	2,224	38,230	47,134
1887	2,835	5,257	5,915	4,639	2,124	2,259	38,260	47,630
1888	2,932	5,303	5,959	4,691	2,143	2,296	38,290	48,168
1889	3,022	5,348	6,003	4,742	2,161	2,331	38,370	48,717
1890	3,107	5,394	6,048	4,793	2,179	2,364	38,380	49,241
1891	3,196	5,446	6,115	4,846	2,195	2,394	38,350	49,762
1892	3,274	5,504	6,182	4,895	2,210	2,415	38,360	50,266
1893	3,334	5,563	6,250	4,943	2,226	2,430	38,380	50,757
1894	3,395	5,622	6,319	4,991	2,248	2,511	38,420	51,339
1895	3,460	5,680	6,388	5,038	2,276	2,483	38,460	52,001
1896	3,523	5,739	6,442	5,086	2,306	2,515	38,550	52,753
1897	3,586	5,798	6,496	5,135	2,338	2,549	38,700	53,569
1898	3,642	5,856	6,552	5,190	2,371	2,589	38,820	54,406
1899	3,691	5,915	6,609	5,247	2,403	2,624	38,890	55,248
1900	3,741	5,973	6,666	5,319	2,432	2,646	38,940	56,046
1901	3,795	6,035	6,747	5,396	2,463	2,667	38,980	56,874
1902	3,850	6,099	6,848	5,507	2,491	2,686	39,050	57,767
1903	3,896	6,164	6,941	5,666	2,519	2,706	39,120	58,629
1904	3,946	6,228	7,030	5,842	2,546	2,735	39,190	59,475
1905	4,004	6,292	7,118	6,010	2,574	2,762	39,220	60,314
1906	4,062	6,357	7,200	6,123	2,603	2,788	39,270	61,153
1907	4,127	6,421	7,280	6,429	2,635	2,821	39,270	62,013
1908	4,197	6,485	7,352	6,640	2,668	2,861	39,370	62,863
1909	4,278	6,550	7,419	6,816	2,702	2,899	39,430	63,717
1910	4,375	6,614	7,438	7,006	2,737	2,929	39,540	64,568
1911	4,500	6,669	7,457	7,222	2,770	2,962	39,620	65,539
1912	4,661	6,724	7,530	7,409	2,802	2,998	39,670	66,146
1913	4,821	6,767	7,605	7,653	2,833	3,027	39,770	66,978

[a] Refers to present territory of Austria (frontiers fixed after First World War).
[b] 1871 onwards excludes Alsace and Lorraine which had 1,570,000 inhabitants in 1870 (according to French accoun
[c] 1871 onwards includes Alsace and Lorraine which had 1,574,000 inhabitants in 1870 (according to German accou

Mid-year Population, Annual Data, 1870-1913

	Italy	Japan	Netherlands	Norway	Sweden	Switzerland	UK	USA
	('000)	('000)	('000)	('000)	('000)	('000)	('000)	('000)
1870	26,526	34,437	3,607	1,735	4,164	2,664	31,257	39,905
1871	26,709	34,648	3,650	1,745	4,186	2,680	31,556	40,938
1872	26,884	34,859	3,693	1,755	4,227	2,697	31,874	41,972
1873	27,050	35,070	3,735	1,767	4,274	2,715	32,177	43,006
1874	27,216	35,235	3,799	1,783	4,320	2,733	32,501	44,040
1875	27,382	35,436	3,822	1,803	4,362	2,750	32,839	45,073
1876	27,548	35,713	3,866	1,829	4,407	2,768	33,200	46,107
1877	27,713	36,018	3,910	1,852	4,457	2,786	33,576	47,141
1878	27,879	36,315	3,955	1,877	4,508	2,803	33,932	48,174
1879	28,045	36,557	4,000	1,902	4,555	2,821	34,304	49,208
1880	28,211	36,807	4,043	1,919	4,572	2,839	34,623	50,262
1881	28,377	37,112	4,091	1,923	4,569	2,853	34,935	51,542
1882	28,565	37,414	4,140	1,920	4,576	2,863	35,206	52,821
1883	28,775	37,766	4,189	1,919	4,591	2,874	35,450	54,100
1884	28,985	38,138	4,239	1,929	4,624	2,885	35,724	55,379
1885	29,195	38,427	4,289	1,944	4,664	2,896	36,015	56,658
1886	29,405	38,622	4,340	1,958	4,700	2,907	36,313	57,938
1887	29,615	38,866	4,392	1,970	4,726	2,918	36,598	59,217
1888	29,826	39,251	4,444	1,977	4,742	2,929	36,881	60,496
1889	30,036	39,688	4,497	1,984	4,761	2,940	37,178	61,775
1890	30,246	40,077	4,545	1,997	4,780	2,951	37,485	63,056
1891	30,456	40,380	4,601	2,013	4,794	2,965	37,802	64,361
1892	30,667	40,684	4,658	2,026	4,805	3,002	38,134	65,666
1893	30,877	41,001	4,716	2,038	4,816	3,040	38,490	66,970
1894	31,087	41,350	4,774	2,057	4,849	3,077	38,859	68,275
1895	31,297	41,775	4,833	2,083	4,896	3,114	39,221	69,580
1896	31,507	42,196	4,893	2,112	4,941	3,151	39,599	70,885
1897	31,717	42,643	4,954	2,142	4,986	3,188	39,987	72,189
1898	31,927	43,145	5,015	2,174	5,036	3,226	40,381	73,494
1899	32,137	43,626	5,077	2,204	5,080	3,263	40,773	74,799
1900	32,416	44,103	5,142	2,230	5,117	3,300	41,155	76,094
1901	32,533	44,662	5,221	2,255	5,156	3,341	41,538	77,585
1902	32,700	45,255	5,305	2,275	5,187	3,384	41,893	79,160
1903	32,840	45,841	5,389	2,288	5,210	3,428	42,246	80,632
1904	33,016	46,378	5,471	2,297	5,241	3,472	42,611	82,165
1905	33,194	46,829	5,551	2,309	5,278	3,516	42,981	83,820
1906	33,326	47,227	5,632	2,319	5,316	3,560	43,361	85,437
1907	33,515	47,691	5,710	2,329	5,357	3,604	43,737	87,000
1908	33,788	48,260	5,786	2,346	5,404	3,647	44,124	88,709
1909	34,077	48,869	5,842	2,367	5,453	3,691	44,520	90,492
1910	34,377	49,518	5,902	2,384	5,499	3,735	44,916	92,407
1911	34,711	50,215	5,984	2,401	5,542	3,776	45,268	93,868
1912	35,010	50,941	6,068	2,423	5,583	3,819	45,436	95,331
1913	35,192	51,672	6,164	2,447	5,621	3,864	45,649	97,227

TABLE B3
Mid-year Population, Annual Data, 1913-49

	Australia	Austria[a]	Belgium	Canada	Denmark	Finland[e]	France	Germany[g]
	('000)	('000)	('000)	('000)	('000)	('000)	('000)	('000)
1913	4,821	6,767	7,605	7,653	2,833	3,027	39,770	66,978
1914	4,933	6,806	7,662	7,888	2,866	3,053	39,782	67,790
1915	4,971	6,843	7,697	7,983	2,901	3,083	38,828	67,883
1916	4,955	6,825	7,701	8,006	2,936	3,105	38,255	67,715
1917	4,950	6,785	7,668	8,067	2,972	3,124	37,683	67,368
1918	5,032	6,727	7,599	8,162	3,006	3,125	36,968	66,811
1919	5,193	6,420	7,567	8,331	3,041	3,117	38,700[f]	60,547
1920	5,358	6,455	7,492	8,575	3,079	3,133	39,000	60,894
1921	5,461	6,504	7,444	8,799	3,285[d]	3,170	39,240	61,573
1922	5,574	6,528	7,511	8,927	3,322	3,210	39,420	61,900
1923	5,697	6,543	7,574	9,021	3,356	3,243	39,880	62,307
1924	5,819	6,562	7,646	9,156	3,389	3,272	40,310	62,697
1925	5,943	6,582	7,779[b]	9,307	3,425	3,304	40,610	63,166
1926	6,064	6,603	7,844	9,467	3,452	3,339	40,870	63,630
1927	6,188	6,623	7,904	9,654	3,475	3,368	40,940	64,023
1928	6,304	6,643	7,968	9,851	3,497	3,396	41,050	64,393
1929	6,396	6,664	8,032	10,044	3,518	3,424	41,230	64,739
1930	6,469	6,684	8,076	10,222	3,542	3,449	41,610	65,084
1931	6,527	6,705	8,126	10,387	3,569	3,476	41,860	65,423
1932	6,579	6,725	8,186	10,520	3,603	3,503	41,860	65,716
1933	6,631	6,746	8,231	10,642	3,633	3,526	41,890	66,027
1934	6,682	6,760	8,262	10,750	3,666	3,549	41,950	66,409
1935	6,732	6,761	8,288	10,854	3,695	3,576	41,940	66,871
1936	6,783	6,758	8,315	10,958	3,722	3,601	41,910	67,349
1937	6,841	6,755	8,346	11,054	3,749	3,626	41,930	67,831
1938	6,904	6,753	8,374	11,162	3,777	3,656	41,960	68,558
1939	6,971	6,653	8,392	11,277	3,805	3,686	41,900	69,286
1940	7,042	6,705	8,346	11,392	3,832	3,698	41,000	69,838
1941	7,111	6,745	8,276	11,519	3,863	3,702	39,600	70,244
1942	7,173	6,783	8,247	11,666	3,903	3,708	39,400	70,834
1943	7,236	6,808	8,242	11,808	3,949	3,721	39,000	70,411
1944	7,309	6,834	8,291	11,957	3,998	3,735	38,900	69,865
1945	7,389	6,799	8,339	12,090	4,045	3,758	39,700	67,000
1946	7,474	7,000	8,367	12,314	4,101	3,806	40,290	68,000
1947	7,578	6,971	8,450	12,574	4,146	3,859	40,680	46,992
1948	7,715	6,956	8,557	12,846	4,190	3,912	41,110	48,251
1949	7,919	6,943	8,614	13,469[c]	4,230	3,963	41,480	49,198

[a] Refers to present territory of Austria (frontiers fixed after the First World War).

[b] 1925 onwards includes Eupen and Malmedy ceded by Germany (population 63,000 in 1925).

[c] 1949 onwards includes Newfoundland, which added 347,000 in 1949.

[d] 1921 onwards includes North Slesvig ceded by Germany (population 164,000 in 1920).

[e] The 1940 and 1944 treaties which ceded territory to the USSR had no impact on population as all inhabitants were moved to Finland.

[f] Refers to territory including Alsace and Lorraine from 1919 onwards. 1913-18 figures including Alsace-Lorraine were 41,690,000, 41,700,000, 40,700,000, 40,100,000, 39,500,000, 38,750,000.

[g] 1913-18 refers to German Reichsgebiet before postwar losses. Figures for 1919-46 refer to 1937 territory of the Reich; i.e., the Saar is included throughout (though it did not actually return to Germany until 1935). 1947 onwards refer to the territory of the Federal Republic including the Saar throughout (though it was not actually returned until 1959) and also including West Berlin. 1913-18 figures for the 1937 territory of the Reich would be 60,351,000, 61,081,000, 61,166,000, 61,015,000, 60,701,000, 60,200,000 respectively. There were 1,166,000 people living in the Saar in 1934. In 1938 there were 42,576,000 living in the territory which became the postwar Bundesrepublik (including Saar and West Berlin), and about 46,000,000 in 1946.

Mid-year Population, Annual Data, 1913-49

	Italy[ʰ]	Japan	Netherlands	Norway	Sweden	Switzerland	UK	USA
	('000)	('000)	('000)	('000)	('000)	('000)	('000)	('000)
1913	35,192	51,672	6,164	2,447	5,621	3,864	45,649	97,227
1914	35,708	52,396	6,277	2,472	5,659	3,897	46,049	99,118
1915	36,415	53,124	6,395	2,498	5,696	3,883	46,340	100,549
1916	36,445	53,815	6,516	2,522	5,735	3,883	46,514	101,966
1917	36,718	54,437	6,654	2,551	5,779	3,888	46,614	103,414
1918	36,101	54,886	6,752	2,578	5,807	3,880	46,575	104,550
1919	37,438	55,253	6,805	2,603	5,830	3,869	46,534	105,063
1920	37,580	55,818	6,848	2,635	5,876	3,877	43,718[ʲ]	106,466
1921	37,729	56,490	6,921	2,668	5,929	3,876	44,072	108,541
1922	38,197	57,209	7,032	2,695	5,971	3,874	44,372	110,055
1923	38,505	57,937	7,150	2,713	5,997	3,883	44,596	111,950
1924	38,784	58,686	7,264	2,729	6,021	3,896	44,915	114,113
1925	39,113	59,522	7,366	2,747	6,045	3,910	45,059	115,832
1926	39,462	60,490	7,471	2,763	6,064	3,932	45,232	117,399
1927	39,815	61,430	7,576	2,775	6,081	3,956	45,389	119,038
1928	40,197	62,361	7,679	2,785	6,097	3,988	45,578	120,501
1929	40,549	63,244	7,782	2,795	6,113	4,022	45,672	121,770
1930	40,888	64,203	7,884	2,807	6,131	4,051	45,866	123,188
1931	41,295	65,205	7,999	2,824	6,152	4,080	46,074	124,149
1932	41,584	66,189	8,123	2,842	6,176	4,102	46,335	124,949
1933	41,928	67,182	8,237	2,858	6,201	4,122	46,520	125,690
1934	42,277	68,090	8,341	2,874	6,222	4,140	46,666	126,485
1935	42,631	69,238	8,434	2,889	6,242	4,155	46,868	127,362
1936	42,966	70,171	8,516	2,904	6,259	4,168	47,081	128,181
1937	43,270	71,278	8,599	2,919	6,276	4,180	47,289	128,961
1938	43,597	71,879	8,685	2,936	6,298	4,192	47,494	129,969
1939	44,018	72,364	8,782	2,954	6,326	4,206	47,991	131,028
1940	44,467	72,967	8,879	2,973	6,356	4,226	48,226	132,122
1941	44,831	74,005	8,966	2,990	6,389	4,254	48,216	133,402
1942	45,098	75,029	9,042	3,009	6,432	4,286	48,400	134,860
1943	45,300	76,005	9,103	3,032	6,491	4,323	48,789	136,739
1944	45,454	77,178	9,175	3,060	6,560	4,364	49,016	138,397
1945	45,610	76,224	9,262	3,091	6,636	4,412	49,182	139,928
1946	45,914	76,602[ⁱ]	9,424	3,127	6,719	4,467	49,217	141,389
1947	45,664	77,514	9,630	3,165	6,803	4,524	49,519	144,126
1948	46,004	79,527	9,800	3,201	6,884	4,582	50,014	146,631
1949	46,307	81,329	9,956	3,234	6,956	4,640	50,312	149.188

[ʰ] 1919-46 includes territory ceded to Italy after the First World War. Population of the territory gained in 1919 was 1,474,000. 1947 onwards refers to Postwar territory. The population of territory lost in 1947 was 630,000.
[ⁱ] 1946 onwards refers to postwar territory excluding Okinawa, Karafuto, and Kuriles. Most of the population of Okinawa remained there whereas that of Karafuto and the Kuriles was mainly repatriated. The loss of population due to boundary changes was therefore about 600,000.
[ʲ] 1920 onwards excludes Southern Ireland (population 3,103,000 in 1920).

TABLE **B4**

Mid-year Population, Annual Data, 1950-79

	Australia	*Austria*	*Belgium*	*Canada*	*Denmark*	*Finland*	*France*	*Germany*[a]
	('000)	('000)	('000)	('000)	('000)	('000)	('000)	('000)
1950	8,177	6,935	8,640	13,737	4,271	4,009	41,836	49,983
1951	8,418	6,936	8,679	14,047	4,304	4,047	42,156	50,528
1952	8,634	6,928	8,731	14,491	4,334	4,091	42,460	50,859
1953	8,821	6,933	8,778	14,882	4,369	4,139	42,752	51,350
1954	8,996	6,940	8,820	15,321	4,406	4,187	43,057	51,880
1955	9,201	6,947	8,869	15,730	4,439	4,235	43,428	52,382
1956	9,421	6,952	8,924	16,123	4,466	4,282	43,843	53,008
1957	9,640	6,966	8,989	16,677	4,488	4,324	44,311	53,656
1958	9,842	6,987	9,053	17,120	4,515	4,360	44,789	54,292
1959	10,056	7,014	9,104	17,522	4,547	4,395	45,240	54,876
1960	10,275	7,048	9,154	17,909	4,581	4,430	45,684	55,433
1961	10,508	7,074	9,184	18,269	4,610	4,461	46,163	56,175
1962	10,700	7,130	9,218	18,615	4,647	4,491	46,998	56,837
1963	10,907	7,172	9,283	18,965	4,684	4,523	47,816	57,389
1964	11,122	7,215	9,367	19,325	4,720	4,549	48,310	57,971
1965	11,341	7,255	9,448	19,678	4,758	4,564	48,758	58,619
1966	11,599	7,291	9,508	20,048	4,797	4,581	49,164	59,148
1967	11,799	7,323	9,557	20,412	4,839	4,606	49,548	59,286
1968	12,009	7,360	9,590	20,729	4,867	4,626	49,916	59,500
1969	12,263	7,393	9,613	21,028	4,891	4,624	50,318	60,067
1970	12,507	7,426	9,638	21,324	4,929	4,606	50,772	60,651
1971	12,928	7,456	9,673	21,595	4,963	4,612	51,251	61,302
1972	13,172	7,495	9,711	21,848	4,992	4,640	51,701	61,672
1973	13,382	7,525	9,742	22,125	5,022	4,666	52,119	61,976
1974	13,598	7,533	9,772	22,479	5,045	4,691	52,461	62,054
1975	13,774	7,520	9,801	22,831	5,060	4,712	52,705	61,829
1976	13,917	7,513	9,818	23,025	5,073	4,726	52,893	61,531
1977	14,075	7,518	9,830	23,280	5,089	4,740	53,079	61,400
1978	14,248	7,508	9,841	23,499	5,105	4,752	53,278	61,327
1979	14,417	7,506	9,849	23,691	5,117	4,764	53,478	61,359

[a] Includes Saar and West Berlin throughout.
[b] Includes Okinawa prefecture (Ryuku Islands) from 1973 onwards (added 990,000 to population).
[c] Includes Alaska and Hawaii throughout (population 588,000 in 1950).

Mid-year Population, Annual Data, 1950-79

	Italy	Japan	Netherlands	Norway	Sweden	Switzerland	UK	USA [c]
	('000)	('000)	('000)	('000)	('000)	('000)	('000)	('000)
1950	46,769	82,900	10,114	3,265	7,015	4,694	50,363	152,271
1951	47,099	84,300	10,264	3,296	7,071	4,749	50,574	154,878
1952	47,352	85,600	10,382	3,328	7,125	4,815	50,737	157,553
1953	47,607	86,760	10,494	3,362	7,171	4,877	50,880	160,184
1954	47,912	88,030	10,616	3,395	7,213	4,929	51,066	163,026
1955	48,221	89,060	10,751	3,429	7,262	4,980	51,221	165,931
1956	48,490	89,980	10,888	3,462	7,315	5,045	51,430	168,903
1957	48,753	90,760	11,026	3,494	7,367	5,126	51,657	171,984
1958	49,041	91,580	11,187	3,525	7,415	5,199	51,870	174,882
1959	49,356	92,460	11,348	3,556	7,454	5,259	52,157	177,830
1960	49,642	93,260	11,486	3,585	7,480	5,362	52,559	180,671
1961	49,903	94,090	11,639	3,615	7,520	5,512	52,956	183,691
1962	50,175	94,980	11,806	3,639	7,562	5,666	53,414	186,538
1963	50,652	95,940	11,966	3,667	7,604	5,789	53,691	189,242
1964	51,140	96,950	12,127	3,694	7,662	5,887	54,033	191,889
1965	51,526	98,030	12,292	3,723	7,734	5,943	54,377	194,303
1966	51,899	98,920	12,455	3,753	7,807	5,996	54,653	196,560
1967	52,321	99,970	12,597	3,785	7,869	6,063	54,933	198,712
1968	52,690	101,150	12,725	3,819	7,912	6,132	55,157	200,706
1969	53,006	102,320	12,873	3,851	7,962	6,212	55,372	202,677
1970	53,388	103,403	13,032	3,877	8,046	6,267	55,522	204,879
1971	53,729	104,724	13,194	3,903	8,105	6,324	55,712	207,053
1972	54,140	106,202	13,329	3,933	8,127	6,385	55,869	208,846
1973	54,561	108,702[b]	13,439	3,961	8,136	6,431	56,000	210,410
1974	55,109	110,158	13,545	3,985	8,160	6,443	56,011	211,901
1975	55,523	111,520	13,654	4,007	8,196	6,405	55,981	213,559
1976	55,820	112,768	13,770	4,026	8,219	6,346	55,959	215,152
1977	56,108	113,860	13,853	4,043	8,255	6,327	55,919	216,880
1978	56,328	114,920	13,937	4,060	8,278	6,337	55,902	218,717
1979	(56,518)	115,880	14,030	4,074	8,296	6.348	55,952	220,584

TABLE B5

Net Migration, 1870-1978

	Cumulative totals				Average annual flow			
	1870-1913	1914-49	1950-73	1974-8	1870-1913	1914-49	1950-73	1974-8
	('000)	('000)	('000)	('000)	('000)	('000)	('000)	('000)
Australia	702	700	2,067	233	16	19	86	47
Belgium	325	219	287	60	7	6	12	12
Canada	861	228	2,126	414	20	6	88	83
France	890	236	3,630	58	20	7	151	12
Germany	-2,598	-304[a]	7,070	-132	-59	-17[a]	295	-26
Italy	-4,459	-1,771	-2,139	366	-101	-49	-89	73
Japan	(n.a.)	197	-72	65	(n.a.)	5	3	13
Netherlands	(n.a.)	-29	47	177	(n.a.)	1	2	35
Norway	-589	-129	0	22	-13	-4	0	4
Sweden	-895	83	336	83	-20	2	14	17
Switzerland	20	90	755	-151	1	3	31	-30
UK	-6,415	-1,405[b]	-605	-201	-146	-48[b]	-25	-40
USA	15,820	6,221	8,257	1,939	360	173	344	388
Total	3,671	3,684	21,759	2,803	85	82	906	562

[a] 1922-39 only;   [b] Excludes 1939-45.

Source: 1950-78 from OECD *Labour Force Statistics*, Paris, various issues, and for Australia 1950-58 from *Report of The Committee of Economic Inquiry* (Vernon Report), Canberra, 1965, Table 42. Earlier figures from various official national sources as well as W. Woodruff, *Impact of Western Man*, Macmillan, New York, 1966, p. 108 (Australia); O. J. Firestone, *Canada's Economic Development*, pp. 240-1 (Canada); S. Kuznets, *Economic Growth and Structure*, Harvard, 1965, p. 364 (USA); W. G. Hoffman et al., *Das Wachstum der deutschen Wirtschaft seit der Mitte des 19 Jahrhunderts*, Springer, Berlin, 1965, pp. 173-4 (Germany).

TABLE B6

Vital Statistics, 1820-1978

	Births per 100 population			Years of life expectancy at birth[f]		
	1820	1900	1978	1820	1900	1975
Australia	(n.a.)	2.82	1.57			70.9
Austria	4.30	3.50	1.13		40.1	70.2
Belgium	3.23[a]	2.89	1.24		47.1	71.0
Canada	5.69[b]	2.72	1.52			73.4
Denmark	3.15	2.97	1.21		54.6	73.7
Finland	3.66	3.26	1.35		46.7	71.2
France	3.17	2.13	1.38	39.6	47.0	72.5
Germany	3.99	3.56	0.94		46.6	70.6
Italy	(n.a.)	3.30	1.27		44.5	72.3
Japan	(n.a.)	3.24	1.50			72.0
Netherlands	3.50[c]	3.16	1.26	32.2	52.2	74.6
Norway	3.33	2.97	1.28	43.7	56.3	75.0
Sweden	3.30	2.70	1.12	35.2	55.7	75.0
Switzerland	3.29[d]	2.86	1.14	34.5	50.8	74.5
UK	3.03[e]	2.87[g]	1.23	38.7	50.5[g]	71.8
USA	5.52	3.23	1.52		47.3	72.1
Average	3.78	3.01	1.29	37.3	49.2	72.6

[a] 1830; [b] 1820-30 Quebec; [c] 1840; [d] 1831-40; [e] 1839; [f] average for both sexes;
[g] England and Wales.

Source: Birth rates 1978 from OECD *Labour Force Statistics*, Paris, 1980; life expectancy 1975 from OECD, *Demographic Trends 1950-1990*, Paris, 1979. 1820 and 1900 from B. R. Mitchell, *European Historical Statistics 1750-1970*, Macmillan, London, 1975, for most European countries, Canada from M. C. Urquhart and K. A. H. Buckley (eds), *Historical Statistics of Canada*, Macmillan, Toronto, 1965; Switzerland from K. B. Mayer, *The Population of Switzerland*, Columbia, New York, 1952, p. 75; USA from *Historical Statistics of the United States: Colonial Times to 1970*, US Dept of Commerce, Washington DC, 1975. Estimates of life expectation for years about 1820 are from various national sources and from D. V. Glass and E. Grebenik, 'World Population, 1800-1950', in H. J. Habakkuk and M. Postan, *Cambridge Economic History of Europe*, Cambridge, 1966, p. 73, and for 1900 from B. Mueller, *A Statistical Handbook of the North Atlantic Area*, Twentieth Century Fund, New York 1965, p. 22.

APPENDIX C

LABOUR INPUT AND
LABOUR PRODUCTIVITY

The basic factors determining growth of the labour supply are:
1. growth in population (as affected by the pattern of births, deaths, and migration);
2. changes in demographic structure;
3. changes in activity rates (i.e., the willingness of potential workers to seek employment);
4. changes in annual working hours per person (which is not usually a matter on which individuals have much choice, as weekly hours, holidays and vacations are now generally fixed by collective agreements or legislation).

Actual labour input will differ from potential because of variations in the level of demand. The potential labour supply may not be fully used. The variations in demand are most clearly reflected by changes in the level of unemployment, but this is not the only form of labour slack. Weak demand in labour markets may also cause working hours, activity rates, migration, or productivity to fall below trend levels.

This annex indicates the ways in which the above components have influenced the growth of labour input since 1870.

DEMOGRAPHIC FACTORS

Population growth experience has varied a good deal in the past century. The fastest growing country, Australia, increased its population more than eight-fold, whereas France, the slowest growing country, experienced a rise of just over a third.

By contrast with the variety in population growth experience, changes in demographic structure have been strikingly similar over the long term.
1. The child population (below fifteen years of age) decreased proportionately in all the countries, and in virtually all cases the decline was very substantial. In 1870 the average child population was more than a third of the total, and in 1976 it was less than a quarter.
2. The proportion of old people (sixty-five and over) rose substantially in all the countries, with the sixteen-country average rising from 5 to 12 per cent of the population.
3. The proportion of people of 'working age' (fifteen to sixty-four years) has generally increased, though Austria and France are exceptions to this.

These changes have not been steady. There was, for instance, some temporary decline in the proportion of working age as a result of the postwar baby boom; but the long-run changes have been remarkably clear and similar (see Table C1).

TABLE C1

A Comparison of Demographic Structures in 1870 and 1976
(*Percentages of total population*)

	Population aged 0-14		Population aged 65 and over		Population aged 15-64			
	1870	1976	1870	1976	1870	1913	1950	1976
Australia	42.3	27.1	1.8	8.9	55.9	63.9	65.3	64.0
Austria	33.8	22.8	3.9	15.1	62.2	62.4	66.8	62.0
Belgium	31.9	21.8	6.4	14.0	61.7	64.7	68.1	64.2
Canada	41.6	25.6	3.7	8.7	54.7	62.0	62.6	65.6
Denmark	33.4	22.4	5.8	13.6	60.8	60.2	64.7	64.0
Finland	34.7	21.7	4.7	10.9	60.6	59.2	63.4	67.4
France	27.1	23.6	7.4	13.6	65.5	65.8	65.9	62.9
Germany	34.0	20.9	4.6	14.7	61.4	63.1	67.1	64.3
Italy	32.5	24.2	5.1	11.6	62.4	60.3	65.5	64.2
Japan	33.7	24.3	5.3	8.1	61.0	59.9	59.4	67.6
Netherlands	33.6	24.8	5.5	10.9	60.9	60.1	63.0	64.3
Norway	35.3	23.5	6.2	13.9	58.5	57.9	66.0	62.6
Sweden	34.1	20.6	5.4	15.3	60.5	60.6	66.3	64.0
Switzerland	31.5	21.8	5.5	12.9	63.0	64.0	66.8	65.2
UK	36.1	22.9	5.0	14.2	58.9	64.1	66.9	62.9
USA	39.2	24.4	3.0	10.7	57.8	63.7	65.0	64.9
Average	34.7	23.3	5.0	12.3	60.4	62.0	65.2	64.4

ACTIVITY RATES

The hard core of the labour force has always consisted of adult males, and their activity rates have changed least over time, but activity rates for other categories have changed substantially (see Tables C3 and C4).

The most drastic fall has been for the child population. In 1870 it was still quite common for children to work. Schooling was by no means universal or even compulsory. In most countries before the First World War, the age cut-off point used in censuses for inclusion in the working population was ten years. Germany was somewhat exceptional in having fourteen as the cut-off point as early as 1895.[1] Between the two wars the cut-off point was generally raised to fourteen, and since 1960 the cut-off has generally been raised to fifteen or sixteen. By 1976 only Belgium and Italy included fourteen-year-olds in their official labour force statistics and the numbers involved were negligible. In the USA the official labour force statistics now exclude people under sixteen, but as fourteen- and

TABLE C2

Females as a Proportion of the Labour Force, 1910-76

	Percentage share in total labour force			Percentage share in agricultural employment	
	1910 census round	1950	1976	1910 census round	1976
Australia	23.4[a]	22.4	34.7	2.2[a]	18.8
Austria	35.9	38.5	38.5	39.9	46.4
Belgium	30.9	27.9	34.9	27.0	21.2
Canada	13.4[b]	21.4	37.2	1.6[b]	21.0
Denmark	31.3[b]	33.7	41.5	21.5[b]	27.2
Finland	36.5	40.7	45.6	36.7	41.8
France	35.6[a]	36.0	38.5	31.9[a]	(n.a.)
Germany	30.7[c]	35.1	37.4	46.5[c]	52.5
Italy	31.3[b]	25.5	28.6	32.7[b]	33.1
Japan	38.9[a]	38.5	37.4	43.0[a]	49.1
Netherlands	23.9[d]	23.4	28.3	17.5[d]	15.9[e]
Norway	30.1	27.1	39.2	14.2	32.1
Sweden	27.8	26.4	43.0	24.4	25.2
Switzerland	33.9	29.7	34.2	21.3	25.1
UK	29.0[b]	30.8	37.8	8.7[b]	19.7
USA	21.2	28.8	39.7	14.6	17.5
Average	29.6	30.4	37.2	24.0	29.8

[a] 1913 estimate.   [b] 1911.   [c] 1907.   [d] 1909.   [e] 1975.

fifteen-year-olds are permitted to combine work and education and as figures on their employment are still officially collected, they have been included in the estimates below.

Activity rates for older people have also dropped substantially because of greater coverage and higher benefits of pension schemes and social security income guarantees, and the greater influence of regulations that prevent people from continuing at work (particularly as there has been a decline in the proportion of self-employed, who have greater freedom to make their choices in this matter). The fall in activity rates for older people has been very substantial—big enough to offset the growth in the demographic importance of this group in most countries.

Within the age group between fifteen and sixty-four years, from which the vast majority of the labour force is drawn, differing trends have been at work for males and females. For males of this age there has been a gradual but mild decrease in activity rates. They too were affected to some extent by the increased availability of schooling and pensions. These forces have also affected females, but were substantially outweighed by other influences which have generally raised female activity rates, particularly since 1950.[2]

Table C3

Labour Force Participation Rates around 1950

	Year	Persons under 15	Persons 65 and over	Males 15-64	Females 15-64
Australia	1954	0.7	17.4	94.3	29.5
Austria	1951	(n.a.)	21.0	92.6[a]	47.8[a]
Belgium	1947	1.5	14.1	87.7	26.6
Canada	1951	0.2	21.9	89.5	26.5
Denmark	1950	2.4	21.5	94.8	47.3
Finland	1950	0.5	34.5	93.2	57.4
France	1954	1.0	22.6	89.6	43.6
Germany	1950	1.7	17.2	92.1	43.9
Italy	1957	(n.a.)	16.9	89.3[b]	29.7[b]
Japan	1955	(n.a.)	35.9	84.5[b]	51.8[b]
Netherlands	1947	(n.a.)	20.1	90.4[b]	28.9[b]
Norway	1950	0.0	23.6	93.6	28.9
Sweden	1950	0.2	21.0	93.3	33.7
Switzerland	1950	0.3	28.6	93.6	37.2
UK	1951	0.1	16.0	93.9	40.1
USA	1950	0.9	24.7	88.0	36.1
Average		0.8	22.3	91.3	38.1

[a] Numerator and denominator refer to age group 18-64.
[b] Numerator and denominator refer to age group 14-64.

Table C4

Labour Force Participation Rates around 1976

	Year	Persons under 15	Persons 65 and over	Males 15-64	Females 15-64
Australia	1976		8.1	87.9	49.6
Austria	1976		3.1	81.2	47.4
Belgium	1975	0.5	4.1	81.7	39.8
Canada	1975		10.4	85.7	49.6
Denmark	1976		12.4	86.7	63.9
Finland	1976		3.9	78.7	64.0
France	1975		7.7	82.1	48.1
Germany	1975		9.5	83.8	47.3
Italy	1976	0.3[a]	5.7	79.9	30.8
Japan	1976		27.3	85.2	49.9
Netherlands	1976		3.9	80.0	31.9
Norway	1976		16.5	82.0	54.9
Sweden	1976		6.3	86.9	67.7
Switzerland	1970	0.1	18.9	90.7	48.8
UK	1975		8.2	89.0	54.2
USA	1976	1.5[a]	12.5	82.3	52.8
Average		0.2	9.9	84.0	50.0

[a] 1975.

Aggregate information on labour supply is generally available only from decennial population censuses for the period before the Second World War. Statistical practice was not as well defined then as it is now. The concept of labour force was not yet developed, and the vaguer concept of 'active population' was generally used. This referred to the normal rather than the actual occupation of the respondents and therefore did not usually distinguish between the employed and unemployed. A major grey area was the treatment of female employment, particularly in agriculture (see Table C2).

Farming is largely an occupation of the self-employed and their families. The female labour force in agriculture is usually engaged in both household and agricultural activities in most of the countries covered here, but statistical conventions have differed between countries. In the past, very low female participation rates were registered in Australian, British, Canadian, and US agriculture and very high rates in Austria, Denmark, and Japan. These large inter-country variations in female activity rates are due partly to differences in measurement convention. We have not made any direct adjustment to narrow the spread in female activity rates between countries, but we have used adjusted figures for agricultural females in cases where the female/male ratios in agriculture moved erratically between successive censuses in a particular country.[3] The estimates presented for 1913-50 therefore include adjustments of this kind for Austria, Denmark, France, Italy, and the USA.

For years before 1913 the problems of using census material become greater because variations between successive national census practice and between countries were bigger and the agricultural sector on which these problems were concentrated was larger then. For this period, it seemed preferable to assume that activity rates remained stable. Hence, for 1870-1913, we have assumed that the labour force moved in the same proportion as the population of working age.

For the postwar period, the data situation has improved in terms of conceptual clarity, regularity, and quality of the information. All the countries cited here have in theory adopted the conventions recommended by the ILO in 1954 for measuring labour force, employment, and unemployment,[4] and these conventions are also used by OECD. These are based largely on definitions developed in the USA, which has had a regular labour force survey since 1940. All of these countries except Belgium, the Netherlands, Switzerland, and the UK now have labour force sample surveys at least every year. For 1950 onwards we have therefore generally used the OECD labour force estimates, which are based on sample survey material. These estimates in absolute terms were linked to earlier years, using census measures of movements in activity rate (adjusted as described).[5]

The average ratio of labour force to population changed little from 1870 to 1978, but the situation in individual countries varies a good deal. In Australia, Canada, the UK, and the USA appreciable rises in the ratio have taken place; in France and Italy the opposite has occurred. As indicated above, these changes are due to both demographic factors and rather complex changes in activity rates.

Table C5 shows the change in the structure of employment by sector in 1870 and 1979. The main features are the very large decline in the share of agricultural employment and the rise in service share, with the industrial share rising gradually, then falling.[6]

DETAILED SOURCE NOTES FOR LABOUR FORCE ESTIMATES

For *1870-1913*, it was assumed that, except for the UK and USA (1890-1913), labour force moved in step with population of working age (i.e. those aged fifteen to sixty-four). Austria, Belgium, Germany, Italy, Netherlands, Norway, and Switzerland were derived by interpolation of census data as given in *The Aging of Population and Its Economic and Social Implications*, United Nations, New York, 1956. Otherwise the following sources were used:

Australia: *Official Yearbook of Australia*, 1972, Australian Bureau of Statistics, Canberra, p. 137.

Canada: M. C. Urquhart and K. A. H. Buckley, *Historical Statistics of Canada*, Cambridge, 1965, p. 16.

Denmark: from S. A. Hansen, *Økonomisk Vaekst i Danmark*, vol. II, Akademisk Forlag, Copenhagen, 1974, pp. 202-3.

Finland: *Statistical Yearbook of Finland*, 1973, Central Statistical Office, Helsinki.

France: UN, *The Aging of Population*, op. cit., and *Annuaire statistique 1956* (partie rétrospective), p. 2.

Japan: I. B. Taeuber, *The Population of Japan*, Princeton, 1958, p. 46.

Sweden: derived from *Historical Statistics of Sweden*, vol. I, *Population 1720-1950*, Central Bureau of Statistics, Stockholm, 1955, p. 22.

For *1913-50*, estimates of the change in labour force were derived from A. Maddison, *Economic Growth in the West*, Allen & Unwin, 1964, Appendix D for Belgium, Denmark, Netherlands, Sweden, and Switzerland. Otherwise the following sources were used:
Australia: 1913-60 from M. Keating, 'Australian Work Force and Employ-

ment 1910-11 to 1960-61', *Australian Economic History Review*, September 1967, adjusted to a calendar year basis.

Austria: 1913-53 from A. Kausel, *Oesterreichs Volkseinkommen 1913 bis 1963*, O.I.W., Vienna, 1965. I have adjusted Kausel's figure for 1913 downwards by 10 per cent. He apparently used census activity rates and the 1910 census showed more women than men employed in agriculture, whereas the 1920 census had just half as many women as men in agriculture. I have assumed that the 1913 female-male ratio in agriculture was two-thirds.

Canada: derived from Urquhart and Buckley, *Historical Statistics of Canada*, op. cit., pp. 59-61. The 1913 age cut-off point was ten for 1913, fourteen thereafter. Figures are adjusted to offset the impact of the accession of Newfoundland in 1949.

Finland: derived from P. Bairoch, *The Working Population and Its Structure*, Brussels, 1968, p. 94.

France: 1913-50 from J.-J. Carré, P. Dubois, and E. Malinvaud, *La Croissance Française*, Seuil, Paris, 1972, pp. 80 and 676, whose estimates include adjustments to eliminate variations in the proportion of females in agriculture.

Germany: movement derived by applying activity rates (interpolated from census) to population of working age.

Italy: 1913-50 derived from G. Fua, *Lo sviluppo economico in Italia*, Angeli, Milan, 1975, vol. III, p. 422. The figures were adjusted to eliminate variations in the proportion of females in agriculture: see p. 394.

Japan: 1913-53, K. Ohkawa and H. Rosovsky, *Japanese Economic Growth*, Stanford, 1973, pp. 310-11, and 123 (refers to employment).

Norway: *Trends in Norwegian Economy 1865-1960*, CBS, Oslo, 1966, p. 29 (interpolated where necessary).

United Kingdom: 1870-1955 from C. H. Feinstein, *National Income Expenditure and Output of the United Kingdom 1855-1965*, Cambridge, 1972, pp. T125-7.

United States: 1890-1950 derived from *Historical Statistics of the United States, Colonial Times to 1970*, Bureau of the Census, 1975, pp. 127-8, interpolating where necessary between the decadal census figures. Census figures were adjusted upwards to bring female ratio in agriculture up to the 1910 level (14.6 per cent). The 1910 ratio was not too different from that reported in the Current Population Survey for 1950-70, whereas the other censuses reported implausibly low female activity in agriculture. The age cut-off point was ten for 1913-29, and fourteen thereafter. 1870-90 labour force assumed to move proportionally to population of working age (see *Historicial Statistics*, p. 15).

For *1950 onwards*, figures are taken from OECD *Labour Force Statistics* except as noted above for Australia (to 1960), Austria (to 1953), Japan (to 1953), the UK (to 1955) and as follows:
Austria: 1954 onwards from *Statistisches Handbuch für die Bundesrepublik Osterreich*.

Denmark: 1950-70 from Hansen, *Økonomisk Vaekst i Danmark*, pp. 203-4.

Germany: figures adjusted to include Saar and West Berlin throughout.

Italy: The official labour force sample survey has been affected by various problems which have not been satisfactorily settled. A major problem is that wage and working condition requirements, and the high level of social security payments, give both workers and employers an incentive to work without registering or reporting, either by working at home or by not declaring work in other work places. Some authors consider this unreported work to be as high as 20 per cent of the official labour force estimates; see G. Fua, 'Employment and Productive Capacity in Italy', *Banca Nazionale del Lavoro Quarterly Review*, September 1977. We have assumed that labour force activity rates were stable at the 1950 levels, instead of falling sharply from the 1960s onwards as is implied by the official figures.

Japan: figures adjusted to include Okinawa throughout.

Netherlands: estimated from figures supplied by the Dutch Statistical Office.

United Kingdom: from *British Labour Statistics Yearbook 1976*, HMSO, London, 1978, pp. 122-3 to 1976, and thereafter from Department of Employment *Gazette*.

United States: 1950-9 adjusted upwards by 0.41 per cent to include Alaska and Hawaii. Since 1967, the US official figures on labour force exclude persons below age sixteen, but we included fourteen and fifteen-year-olds throughout as the number working is substantial and continued to rise after 1967. Data from *Employment and Earnings*, and *Handbook of Labor Statistics*, BLS, Washington DC.

UNEMPLOYMENT

Virtually all Western countries now publish an official measure of unemployment, but the scope of these different national indicators still varies a good deal, so that international comparison of unemployment rates can be made only with considerable reservation and after careful adjustment.

The same is true of any long-period comparison because concepts and measures of unemployment have changed over time. The historical sequence has tended to be (1) figures for trade union members; (2) figures for those applying for jobs at unemployment offices; (3) figures for those claiming state insurance benefits (under schemes whose coverage has grown steadily and is now pretty universal for wage and salary-earners in most countries); (4) figures derived from census type enquiries or labour force sample surveys.

Sample surveys generally tend to be more comprehensive in coverage than other sources of data, because they cover the whole population, and ask questions from people who may have little incentive to register as unemployed, such as women and students seeking part-time jobs and new entrants to the labour market. However, not all countries treat the temporarily unemployed in the same way, and not all of them apply the same criteria for testing job search or availability for work.

Most of the countries considered here now have regular labour force sample surveys of the kind carried out in the USA since 1940, but the official unemployment indicator is not based on survey data in Belgium, France, Germany, Netherlands, Switzerland, and the UK.

Furthermore, the questions asked in labour force questionnaires differ between countries in ways that affect the count of the unemployed, and the classification of people as employed or unemployed, active or inactive is influenced by differences in national tradition or labour market institutions which may have nothing to do with the degree of labour slack.

In spite of these pitfalls, there are a number of useful comparative studies of unemployment both in terms of international variation and historical trends. The ILO has performed a useful job in publishing unemployment statistics for most of the countries mentioned here since the 1920s (in the ILO *Yearbooks* issued from 1936 onwards), and although its own publications do not carry figures adjusted to ensure comparability, it has helped promote progress in this direction by meetings of the various Conferences of Labour Statisticians,[7] which in 1954 reached agreement on standardized definitions (on US lines) of the labour force, employment, and unemployment. These ILO guidelines left some grey areas where incomparabilities exist, but OECD has recently made recommendations to clarify most of these problems.[8]

A good historical supplement to the ILO material is W. Galenson and A. Zellner, 'International Comparison of Unemployment Rates', in *The Measurement and Behaviour of Unemployment*, NBER, Princeton, 1957. My own earlier work, *Economic Growth in the West*, Appendix E, contains estimates adjusted to improve international comparability of unemployment levels, and more recent estimates of this kind are available in C. Sorrentino, *International Comparisons of Unemployment*, US Bureau of Labor Statistics, Washington DC, 1978.

For years prior to the First World War, the only countries for which there are reasonable series for any length of time are the UK and the USA: for the UK, a series for 1855-1914 in Feinstein, *National Income, Expenditure and Output of the UK*, pp. T125-6; and for the USA annual estimates are presented by S. Lebergott, *Manpower in Economic Growth*, McGraw-Hill, New York, 1964, p. 512. The Feinstein and Lebergott estimates are presented as percentages of the total labour force. We have not shown annual estimates before 1900 as the estimates of Lebergott for non-census years are very shaky.

	UK	USA
1900	2.4	5.0
1901	3.2	4.1
1902	3.9	3.7
1903	4.6	3.9
1904	5.9	5.4
1905	4.9	4.3
1906	3.5	1.7
1907	3.6	2.8
1908	7.7	7.9
1909	7.5	5.1
1910	4.6	5.8
1911	2.9	6.7
1912	3.3	4.6
1913	2.1	4.3

For 1920-38, unemployment ratios for Belgium, Canada, Germany, Italy, Netherlands, Sweden, Switzerland, and the USA from Maddison, *Economic Growth in the West.* The figures for the USA were adjusted to exclude emergency workers which the official statistics treated as unemployed: see M. R. Darby, 'Three and a Half Million U.S. employees have been Mislaid: Or, An Explanation of Unemployment 1934-41', *Journal of Political Economy*, February 1976, p. 7.

Australia: 1920-60, from M. Keating, 'Australian Work Force and Employment 1910-11 to 1960-1', *Australian Economic History Review*, September 1967, adjusted to a calendar year basis.

Austria: A. Kausel, N. Nemeth, and H. Seidel, 'Osterreichs Volkseinkommen, 1913-63', *Monatsberichte des Osterreichischen Institutes fur Wirtschaftsforschung*, 14th Sonderheft, Vienna, August 1965, for years up to 1953. 1954 onwards from *Statistisches Handbuch fur die Republik Osterreich*, 1977, p. 74.

Denmark: 1920-70, Hansen, *Økonomisk Vaekst i Danmark*, pp. 203-4.

Finland: 1920-38 figures supplied by Kaarina Vattula of University of Helsinki. The figures refer to unfilled applications for work at labour exchanges.

France: 1920-50, J.-J. Carré, P. Dubois, and E. Malinvaud, *La Croissance française*, Seuil, Paris, 1972, pp. 80, 676-7.

Norway: O. Aukrust and J. Bjerke, 'Real Capital and Economic Growth in Norway, 1900-50', *Income and Wealth*, Series VIII, Bowes and Bowes, London 1959, p. 116, and *Trends in Norwegian Economy 1865-1960*, CBS, Oslo, 1966, p. 29.

United Kingdom: Feinstein, *National Income, Expenditure and Output of the UK*, p. T126.

Except as specified, for 1950 onwards the figures were derived from OECD, *Labour Force Statistics*. For the Netherlands, Norway, UK, and the USA adjustments were made to ensure greater international comparability of the figures. For the Netherlands for 1950-72 registered unemployed were adjusted upwards in accordance with ratio of the labour force sample survey results for 1973 to registrations in that year. An upward adjustment was also made for Norway to compensate for partial coverage before 1972. Unemployment in the UK from Sorrentino, *International Comparisons of Unemployment*, adjusted to include Northern Ireland. For the USA unemployment among fourteen- and fifteen-year-olds was added to the official figures. For Sweden the 1950-60 figures are from Maddison, *Economic Growth in the West*.

EMPLOYMENT

Employment was assumed to move parallel to labour force for 1870-1913. For 1913 onwards the figures were derived by subtracting unemployment from the labour force.

ANNUAL WORKING HOURS PER PERSON

Working hours data are among the weakest of those used here. Most of the regular estimates presently available cover only part of the labour force (usually industrial workers), and not all of them reflect changes in holidays and vacations. For the period before the First World War, estimates have to be based on very limited material. As there are broad similarities in the long-run trend of working hours, it was assumed for 1870-1913 that weekly hours per person were the same in all the countries; i.e., 60 in 1870 and 53.8 in 1913, with interpolations for intermediate years. The 53.8 figure for 1913 is derived from the *Hours and Earnings Inquiry* for the United Kingdom in 1906 carried out by the Board of Trade. The figure includes overtime; see A. Maddison, 'Output, Employment and Productivity in British Manufacturing in the Last Half Century', *Bulletin of the Oxford University Institute of Statistics*, November 1955. The 1870 figure is derived from M. A. Bienefeld, *Working Hours in British Industry: An Economic History*, Weidenfeld & Nicolson, London, 1972, p. 111. Bienefeld's figures average 57.4 for 'normal' hours which were grossed up for overtime (using the 1906 ratio—Bienefeld shows 1906 normal hours as 51 on p. 283). Differences between countries in my figures for this period reflect only differences in the length of holidays and vacations.[9]

Weekly working hours for most countries were derived from Maddison, *Economic Growth in the West*, p. 228 for 1913-38; for Australia, Finland, and Japan estimates for 1929 and 1938 were from ILO *Yearbooks of Labour Statistics*, 1938 and 1945-46 edns; Germany, from *Statistisches Handbuch von Deutschland 1928-1944*, p. 480; for Austria it was assumed that working hours were the same as in Germany. For the USA 1929 and 1938 were derived from J. W. Kendrick, *Productivity Trends in the United States*, Princeton, 1961, pp. 306-7 and 312-13, adjusted for days worked per year. For 1950 onwards, figures are from ILO *Yearbooks* unless otherwise stated.

Sources for hours per person from 1950 onwards are listed below. In all cases the figures are an average for both sexes. As average female hours are well below those of males, it is important that both be represented in the sample. *In the case of countries marked with an asterisk the source used made no allowance for changes in days worked per year.* In these cases, the figures were adjusted to exclude hours not worked as noted below.

Australia*: Hours worked in agriculture, industry, and services are available from the quarterly labour force survey from 1965. Hours in 1950 and 1960 assumed to be the same as in the USA.

Austria*: Weekly hours actually worked by wage earners in manufacturing are available for 1964 onwards. This series was linked to the 1955-64 movement in weekly hours paid, and the 1950-5 movement in monthly hours paid.

Belgium: Annual hours worked by the whole employed population (including the impact of holidays) for 1950-60 from S. Mendelbaum, 'Evolution de la quantité et de la durée du travail en Belgique de 1948 à 1962', *Cahiers économiques de Bruxelles*, no. 21, 1er trimestre, 1964, p. 87. 1961 onwards (October) figures on weekly hours of wage earners *'ouvriers inscrits'* rather than *'ouvriers présents'* in manufacturing and construction from *Bulletin de statistique*, Institut National de Statistique.

Canada*: Hours paid per week of wage-earners in manufacturing including hours spent on vacation or public holidays, sick leave, and other paid leave.

Denmark: Total annual hours worked by wage-earners in industry, excluding hours lost in industrial disputes, holidays, sick-days, and compensatory leave were supplied by the Danish Statistical Office.

*Finland**: Weekly hours worked by wage-earners in industry. Data are averages for February, May, September, and November.

France and Germany: Estimates taken from A. Maddison, 'Monitoring the Labour Market', *Review of Income and Wealth*, June 1980.

Italy: Monthly hours actually worked by wage-earners in industry and construction multiplied by 12. Ministry of Labour quarterly survey figures were used as given in *Rassegna di Statistiche del Lavoro*. Alternative figures are available for recent years in the labour force sample survey which shows considerably longer hours. However, the latter source covers only four weeks in the year and excludes many 'occasional workers'.

Japan: Monthly hours actually worked in industry multiplied by 12, *Yearbooks of Labour Statistics*, Tokyo, and *50 Years History of Monthly Labour Statistics*, Ministry of Labour, Tokyo, 1974 (in Japanese).

Netherlands: Detailed estimates were made from national sources in the same way as for France and Germany.

Norway: Hours worked per calendar week by wage-earners in manufacturing and mining. This series includes the impact of vacations, holidays, etc. The figures published in ILO *Yearbooks* (and in *Lonnstatistikk*) are shown separately for males and females. These were averaged by weighting males 80 per cent and females 20 per cent (their respective shares in employment in manufacturing and mining as derived from OECD, *Labour Force Statistics*). 1950 estimate made from earlier series on weekly hours, reduced by 9 per cent to eliminate vacations and public holidays.

Sweden: For years since 1960, the national accounts publications show total hours worked by entrepreneurs and employees in the whole economy. See *Statistical Tables*, 1974:48; *Employment*, Supplement to SMN 1974:89; *National Accounts*, Central Bureau of Statistics, Stockholm, 1974, tables 98 and 43 for 1960-9. 1970-9 from *National Accounts 1970-1979* (N 1980:4.4) Stockholm. The figures refer to actual time worked and reflect the impact of sickness absence, public holidays, vacations, strikes, etc., 1950-60 extrapolated backwards by using movement in monthly hours worked in industry (ILO *Yearbooks*).

*Switzerland**: Weekly hours paid in manufacturing per 'production and related worker'. 1973 onwards, figures adjusted downwards by 1.34 per cent to achieve continuity with earlier series. The figures from 1950 onwards were reduced 5 per cent throughout, as they referred only to manual workers.

United Kingdom*: 1970 onwards from *New Earnings Survey* figures for April. These figures cover all industries and all workers, both manual and non-manual, but this survey started only in 1970. Figures for 1950-75 were therefore derived by adjusting the results of the old survey (which is still continued), which covers only manual workers. The figure for full-time manual males (average of April and October 1950-69 and October for 1970-5) was adjusted downwards by about 5 per cent (ratio of April NES figure for 1976 for all males both manual and non-manual to the October 1976 figure for full-time manual males in the old survey). Full-time manual female hours were similarly adjusted downwards about 15 per cent. Weights for males and females were derived from OECD *Labour Force Statistics*. Old survey figures from back issues of *Department of Employment Gazette*, and *British Labour Statistics, Historical Abstract 1886-1968*, Department of Employment, London, 1971, p. 160.

United States*: Average weekly hours of production or non-supervisory workers on private non-agricultural payrolls, *Handbook of Labor Statistics 1977*, US Bureau of Labour Statistics and *1975 Reference Edition*, p. 176.

Adjustment for Holidays and Vacations

In all cases, the hours figures were adjusted to take account of changes in public holidays and vacations, though information on the latter is rather limited. For vacations and public holidays, the sources used were those cited in Maddison, *Economic Growth in the West*, 'Wages Policy at Home and Abroad', *Westminster Bank Review*, November 1962, p. 33; *New Patterns for Working Time*, OECD, 1973; E. F. Denison, *Why Growth Rates Differ*, Brookings Institution, Washington DC, 1962, p. 363, and A. A. Evans, *Hours of Work in Industrialised Countries*, ILO, Geneva, 1975, interpolated where necessary.

Adjustment for Sickness

It is important to adjust labour input to exclude time lost through sickness. In 1978 time lost from this cause amounted to 13.6 days in France (6.1 per cent of potential working days), 12.5 in Germany (5.6 per cent), and 18.7 in the UK (8.1 per cent): see Maddison, 'Monitoring the Labour Market'. For these countries this source was used for 1960-78; 1950 absence was assumed to be the same as 1960. For the Netherlands, where the loss was bigger, working time was reduced by 4.5 per cent in 1950, 5.2 per cent in 1960, 7.7 per cent in 1970, and 10 per cent in 1978 for this reason. For the USA, the time loss was lower than in Europe, and for 1950-78 was assumed to be 3.5 per cent: see J. N. Hedges, 'Absence from Work—Measuring the Hours Lost', *Monthly Labor Review*, October 1977. For Belgium, Denmark, Italy, Japan, Norway, and Sweden the basic estimate of hours worked for the postwar period seemed to exclude time lost on sickness. For

Canada the loss was assumed to be the same as in the USA (3.5 per cent). In Australia, Austria, Finland, and Switzerland, a 5 per cent working time loss was assumed from this cause for 1950-78. For all countries it was assumed that the time loss from this cause was 2.5 per cent for the period 1870-1938.

PRODUCTIVITY LEVELS

Table C10 is derived by dividing the estimates of GDP in Appendix A by the estimates of total working hours in Appendix C. Both of these are adjusted to exclude the impact of changes in geographic coverage. A comparison of Tables A2 and A3 shows the extent of these geographic changes.

In the case of the UK, the productivity level before 1920 was lower than indicated in Table C10, because Irish productivity was lower than that in the rest of the UK. The estimates in Table C11 show the derivation of the UK productivity levels, including the whole of Ireland, for 1785-1913.

The rough estimates of Dutch productivity (Table C12) are derived by assuming simply that the Dutch employment population ratio in 1700-85 was the same as that of the UK in 1785 and that working hours per person employed were 3,000 per year. The sources for Dutch GDP per head and population estimates are described in Appendices A and B. I have assumed that Dutch GDP per head fell from $440 in 1700 to $400 in 1760 and stagnated at that level until the war period 1795-1815, during which it fell further.

TABLE C5
Structure of Employment in 1870 and 1979

	Agriculture	Industry	Services
	%	%	%
1870			
Australia	30.0	38.0	32.0
Austria	65.0	19.2	15.8
Belgium	43.0	37.6	19.4
Canada	53.0	30.0	17.0
Denmark	51.7	(n.a.)	(n.a.)
Finland	71.2[a]	9.7	19.1
France	49.2	27.8	23.0
Germany	49.5	28.7	21.8
Italy	62.0	23.0	15.0
Japan	72.6[b]	(n.a.)	(n.a.)
Netherlands	37.0	29.0	34.0
Norway	53.0	20.0	27.0
Sweden	53.9[c]	(n.a.)	(n.a.)
Switzerland	49.8	(n.a.)	(n.a.)
UK	22.7	42.3	35.0
USA	50.0	24.4	25.6
Average[d]	48.8	27.5	23.7
1979			
Australia	6.5	30.9	62.6
Austria	10.7	40.5	48.8
Belgium	3.1	34.7	62.2
Canada	5.6	28.7	65.7
Denmark	8.2	29.7	62.1
Finland	11.5	33.7	54.8
France	8.6	35.3	56.1
Germany	6.0	44.0	50.0
Italy	14.6	37.2	48.2
Japan	11.2	34.9	53.9
Netherlands	5.9	31.3	62.8
Norway	8.6	30.1	61.3
Sweden	5.8	32.5	61.7
Switzerland	7.4	39.3	53.3
UK	2.5	38.5	59.0
USA	3.5	30.7	65.8
Average	7.5	34.5	58.0

[a] 1880.
[b] 1872.
[c] Assumes that half of the living-in rural domestic workers were engaged in agriculture.
[d] Excludes Denmark, Japan, Sweden, and Switzerland.

Table C6

(a) Unemployment as a Percentage of the Total Labour Force, 1920-38

	Australia	Austria	Belgium	Canada	Denmark	Finland	France	Germany	Italy	Netherlands	Norway	Sweden	Switzerland	UK	USA
1920	4.6				3.0	1.1		1.7		1.7		1.3		1.9	3.9
1921	5.9		6.1	5.8	10.0	1.8	2.7	1.2		2.6	5.6	6.4		11.0	11.4
1922	5.5		1.9	4.4	9.5	1.4		0.7		3.2	5.2	5.5		9.6	7.2
1923	4.9		0.6	3.2	6.5	1.0		4.5		3.3	1.3	2.9		8.0	3.0
1924	5.5	5.4	0.6	4.5	5.5	1.2		5.8		2.6	0.3	2.4		7.1	5.3
1925	5.6	6.3	0.9	4.4	7.5	2.0		3.0		2.4	3.4	2.6		7.7	3.8
1926	4.6	7.0	0.8	3.0	10.5	1.6	1.2	8.0		2.1	10.4	2.9		8.6	1.9
1927	5.2	6.2	1.1	1.8	11.0	1.5		3.9		2.2	11.3	2.9		6.7	3.9
1928	6.4	5.3	0.6	1.7	9.0	1.5		3.9		1.6	7.6	2.4		7.4	4.3
1929	8.2	5.5	0.8	2.9	8.0	2.8	1.2	5.9	1.7	1.7	5.4	2.4	0.4	7.2	3.1
1930	13.1	7.0	2.2	9.1	7.0	4.0		9.5	2.5	2.3	6.2	3.3	0.7	11.1	8.7
1931	17.9	9.7	6.8	11.6	9.0	4.6	2.2	13.9	4.3	4.3	10.2	4.8	1.2	14.8	15.2
1932	19.1	13.7	11.9	17.6	16.0	5.8		17.2	5.8	8.3	9.5	6.8	2.8	15.3	22.3
1933	17.4	16.3	10.6	19.3	14.5	6.2		14.8	5.9	9.7	9.7	7.3	3.5	13.9	20.5
1934	15.0	16.1	11.8	14.5	11.0	4.4		8.3	5.6	9.8	9.4	6.4	3.3	11.7	15.9
1935	12.5	15.2	11.1	14.2	10.0	3.7		6.5		11.2	8.7	6.2	4.2	10.8	14.2
1936	9.9	15.2	8.4	12.8	9.5	2.7	4.5	4.8		11.9	7.2	5.3	4.7	9.2	9.8
1937	8.1	13.7	7.2	9.1	11.0	2.6		2.7	5.0	10.5	6.0	5.1	3.6	7.7	9.1
1938	8.1	8.1	8.7	11.4	10.5	2.6	3.7	1.3	4.6	9.9	5.8	5.1	3.3	9.2	12.4

TABLE C6

(b) *Unemployment as a Percentage of the Total Labour Force, 1950-79*

	Australia	Austria	Belgium	Canada	Denmark	Finland	France	Germany
1950	1.5	3.9	5.0	3.6	4.0	1.0	2.3	8.2
1951	1.3	3.5	4.4	2.4	4.6	0.3	2.1	7.3
1952	2.2	4.7	5.1	2.9	5.8	0.4	2.1	7.0
1953	2.5	5.5	5.3	2.9	4.4	1.5	2.6	6.2
1954	1.7	5.0	5.0	4.5	3.8	1.0	2.8	5.6
1955	1.4	3.6	3.9	4.3	4.5	0.4	2.4	4.3
1956	1.8	3.4	2.8	3.3	5.1	2.2	1.8	3.4
1957	2.3	3.2	2.3	4.5	4.9	2.2	1.4	2.9
1958	2.7	3.4	3.3	6.9	4.5	2.2	1.6	3.0
1959	2.6	3.1	4.0	5.8	3.1	2.1	1.9	2.0
1960	2.5	2.3	3.3	6.8	2.1	1.4	1.8	1.0
1961	2.3	1.8	2.5	7.0	1.9	1.2	1.5	0.7
1962	2.2	1.9	2.1	5.8	1.6	1.3	1.4	0.6
1963	1.8	2.0	1.7	5.4	2.1	1.5	1.3	0.7
1964	1.6	1.9	1.3	4.3	1.2	1.5	1.1	0.6
1965	1.5	1.9	1.5	3.6	1.0	1.4	1.3	0.5
1966	1.7	1.7	1.6	3.3	1.1	1.5	1.4	0.6
1967	1.8	1.8	2.3	3.8	1.2	2.9	1.8	1.7
1968	1.7	1.9	2.7	4.4	1.6	3.9	2.1	1.2
1969	1.7	1.7	2.1	4.4	1.1	2.8	2.3	0.7
1970	1.6	1.4	1.8	5.6	0.7	1.9	2.4	0.6
1971	1.8	1.2	1.7	6.1	1.1	2.2	2.6	0.7
1972	2.6	1.0	2.2	6.2	0.9	2.5	2.7	0.9
1973	2.4	1.0	2.2	5.4	0.9	2.3	2.6	1.0
1974	2.6	1.1	2.4	5.3	3.5	1.7	2.8	2.2
1975	4.8	1.7	4.2	6.9	4.9	2.2	4.1	4.1
1976	4.7	1.7	5.6	7.1	4.2	4.0	4.4	4.1
1977	5.6	1.5	6.3	8.0	5.1	6.0	4.7	4.0
1978	6.4	1.8	6.8	8.3	6.7	7.4	5.2	3.8
1979	6.1	1.7	7.1	7.4	5.2	6.0	5.9	3.3

(b) *Unemployment as a Percentage of the Total Labour Force, 1950-79*

	Italy	Japan	Netherlands	Norway	Sweden	Switzerland	UK	USA
1950	6.9	1.9	2.8	1.2	1.7	0.0	2.5	5.2
1951	7.3	1.7	3.2	1.5	1.6	0.0	2.2	3.2
1952	7.8	1.9	4.9	1.6	1.7	0.0	3.0	2.9
1953	8.1	1.7	3.5	1.9	1.9	0.0	2.6	2.8
1954	8.3	2.2	2.3	1.8	1.8	0.0	2.3	5.3
1955	7.0	2.5	1.5	1.6	1.8	0.0	2.1	4.2
1956	8.7	2.3	1.0	1.9	1.6	0.0	2.2	4.0
1957	7.0	1.9	1.5	2.1	1.7	0.0	2.4	4.2
1958	6.0	2.0	3.0	3.3	2.0	0.0	3.0	6.6
1959	5.2	2.2	2.1	3.2	1.8	0.0	3.0	5.3
1960	3.9	1.7	1.2	2.3	1.7	0.0	2.2	5.4
1961	3.4	1.4	0.9	1.8	1.5	0.0	2.0	6.5
1962	2.9	1.3	0.9	2.0	1.5	0.0	2.8	5.4
1963	2.5	1.2	0.9	2.4	1.7	0.0	3.4	5.5
1964	3.9	1.2	0.8	2.1	1.6	0.0	2.5	5.0
1965	5.0	1.1	1.0	1.7	1.2	0.0	2.2	4.4
1966	5.4	1.3	1.4	1.6	1.6	0.0	2.3	3.7
1967	5.1	1.3	2.8	1.5	2.1	0.0	3.4	3.8
1968	5.3	1.2	2.5	2.2	2.2	0.0	3.3	3.5
1969	5.2	1.1	1.8	2.1	1.9	0.0	3.0	3.5
1970	4.9	1.1	1.6	1.5	1.5	0.0	3.1	4.9
1971	4.9	1.2	2.3	1.5	2.5	0.0	3.8	5.9
1972	5.7	1.4	3.9	1.7	2.7	0.0	4.1	5.6
1973	5.7	1.3	3.9	1.5	2.5	0.0	2.9	4.8
1974	4.8	1.4	4.4	1.5	2.0	0.0	2.9	5.6
1975	5.3	1.9	5.9	2.3	1.6	0.3	4.1	8.4
1976	6.1	2.0	6.3	1.8	1.6	0.7	5.6	7.6
1977	6.4	2.0	6.0	1.5	1.8	0.3	6.2	7.0
1978	6.6	2.1	6.2	1.8	2.2	0.4	5.5	6.1
1979	7.1	2.1	6.6	2.0	2.1	0.3	5.1	5.8

TABLE C7
Total Labour Force, 1870-1979[a]
(mid-year, '000s)

	1870	1880	1890	1900	1913	1929	1938	1950	1960	1970	1973	1978	1979
Australia	610	861	1,254	1,528	2,076	2,568	2,821	3,510	4,170	5,597	5,974	6,454	6,530
Austria	2,119	2,294	2,479	2,730	3,186	3,474	3,389	3,345	3,364	3,105	3,202	3,312	3,322
Belgium	2,209	2,338	2,602	2,930	3,484	3,665	3,633	3,515	3,573	3,830	3,926	4,079	4,138
Canada	1,305	1,600	1,855	2,109	3,107	4,079	4,722	5,216	6,530	8,483	9,358	10,963	11,287
Denmark	872	949	1,013	1,149	1,358	1,604	1,943	2,060	2,199	2,380	2,447	2,689	2,668
Finland	794	(n.a.)	1,058	(n.a.)	1,338	1,702	1,968	1,978	2,152	2,197	2,245	2,287	2,308
France	19,591	19,782	20,292	20,758	21,225	20,737	19,676	19,676	19,723	20,903	21,574	22,895	23,059
Germany	10,459	11,253	12,276	14,110	17,638	20,231	21,483	23,053	26,351	26,719	26,921	26,174	26,395
Italy	12,980	13,859	14,508	15,173	16,632	18,162	18,844	19,909	21,361	22,428	22,716	23,635	23,829
Japan	(18,028)	(n.a.)	(n.a.)	(n.a.)	26,550	29,736	32,471	36,374	45,426	51,890	53,260	55,320	55,960
Netherlands	1,403	1,523	1,705	1,940	2,365	3,075	3,517	3,728	4,152	4,798	4,925	5,180	5,264
Norway	717	800	795	890	999	1,196	1,345	1,446	1,457	1,557	1,680	1,888	1,909
Sweden	1,945	2,171	2,179	2,339	2,631	3,224	3,329	3,481	3,679	3,913	3,977	4,209	4,268
Switzerland	1,298	1,375	1,431	1,623	1,923	2,004	2,052	2,237	2,706	3,124	3,203	2,951	2,972
UK	12,751	13,676	15,075	16,883	18,964	20,405	22,927	22,965	24,777	25,517	25,743	26,316	26,460
USA	15,280	20,105	25,920	32,106	42,509	52,693	57,240	65,016	73,126	87,432	92,706	104,287	106,618

[a] Estimates have been adjusted to exclude the impact of frontier changes. The figures therefore refer throughout to the 1979 boundaries.

TABLE C8
Total Employment, 1870-1979[a]
(mid-year, '000s)

	1870	1880	1890	1900	1913	1929	1938	1950	1960	1970	1973	1978	1979
Australia	590	833	1,212	1,477	2,006	2,355	2,592	3,459	4,065	5,509	5,832	6,044	6,133
Austria	2,077	2,248	2,429	2,675	3,122	3,282	3,113	3,215	3,285	3,060	3,171	3,253	3,265
Belgium	2,141	2,266	2,521	2,839	3,376	3,636	3,316	3,341	3,456	3,761	3,839	3,800	3,846
Canada	1,266	1,552	1,799	2,047	3,014	3,960	4,183	5,030	6,084	8,007	8,843	10,052	10,449
Denmark	820	892	952	1,080	1,277	1,476	1,739	1,978	2,152	2,364	2,426	2,508	2,529
Finland	785	(n.a.)	1,046	(n.a.)	1,323	1,654	1,917	1,959	2,121	2,156	2,194	2,118	2,169
France	19,395	19,584	20,089	20,550	21,013	20,488	18,948	19,218	19,343	20,393	20,998	21,712	21,704
Germany	10,260	11,039	12,043	13,842	17,303	19,037	21,204	21,164	26,080	26,570	26,648	25,181	25,519
Italy	12,759	13,623	14,261	14,915	16,349	17,853	17,977	18,536	20,528	21,317	21,411	22,064	22,131
Japan	17,685	(n.a.)	21,174	(n.a.)	26,046	29,171	31,855	35,683	44,670	51,296	52,590	54,150	54,790
Netherlands	1,382	1,501	1,680	1,911	2,330	3,023	3,169	3,625	4,101	4,719	4,731	4,857	4,915
Norway	706	788	783	877	984	1,132	1,267	1,428	1,423	1,533	1,654	1,854	1,871
Sweden	1,923	2,147	2,155	2,314	2,602	3,146	3,159	3,422	3,616	3,854	3,879	4,115	4,180
Switzerland	1,285	1,361	1,416	1,607	1,904	1,995	1,984	2,237	2,706	3,124	3,203	2,940	2,962
UK	12,285	12,972	14,764	16,472	18,566	18,936	20,818	22,400	24,225	24,732	24,993	24,870	25,116
USA	14,669	19,301	24,883	30,501	40,681	51,060	50,142	61,651	69,195	83,176	88,213	97,969	100,405

[a] Estimates have been adjusted to exclude the impact of frontier changes. The figures therefore refer throughout to the 1979 boundaries.

TABLE C9
Annual Hours Worked per Person, 1870-1979

	1870	1880	1890	1900	1913	1929	1938	1950	1960	1970	1973	1978	1979
Australia	2,945	2,852	2,770	2,688	2,588	2,139	2,110	1,838	1,767	1,755	1,708	1,579	1,619
Austria	2,935	2,842	2,760	2,679	2,580	2,281	2,312	1,976	1,951	1,848	1,778	1,650	1,660
Belgium	2,964	2,871	2,789	2,707	2,605	2,272	2,267	2,283	2,174	1,986	1,872	1,726	1,747
Canada	2,964	2,871	2,789	2,707	2,605	2,399	2,240	1,967	1,877	1,805	1,788	1,734	1,730
Denmark	2,945	2,852	2,770	2,688	2,588	2,279	2,267	2,283	2,127	1,882	1,742	1,695	1,721
Finland	2,945	2,852	2,770	2,688	2,588	2,123	2,183	2,035	2,041	1,704	1,707	1,684	1,790
France	2,945	2,852	2,770	2,684	2,588	2,297	1,848	1,989	1,983	1,888	1,830	1,727	1,727
Germany	2,941	2,848	2,765	2,684	2,584	2,284	2,316	2,316	2,083	1,907	1,827	1,733	1,719
Italy	2,886	2,795	2,714	2,634	2,536	2,228	1,927	1,997	2,059	1,768	1,612	1,566	
Japan	2,945	2,852	2,770	2,688	2,588	2,364	2,391	2,272	2,432	2,252	2,197	2,116	2,129
Netherlands	2,964	2,871	2,789	2,707	2,605	2,260	2,244	2,208	2,177	1,910	1,825	1,671	1,679
Norway	2,945	2,852	2,770	2,688	2,588	2,283	2,128	2,101	1,997	1,789	1,721	1,577	1,559
Sweden	2,945	2,852	2,770	2,688	2,588	2,283	2,204	1,951	1,823	1,660	1,571	1,461	1,451
Switzerland	2,984	2,890	2,807	2,725	2,624	2,340	2,257	2,144	2,065	1,962	1,930	1,889	1,877
UK	2,984	2,890	2,807	2,725	2,624	2,286	2,267	1,958	1,913	1,735	1,709	1,623	1,617
USA	2,964	2,871	2,789	2,707	2,605	2,342	2,062	1,867	1,795	1,707	1,696	1,620	1,607

TABLE C10

Productivity 1870-1979: GDP Per Man-hour in 1970 US Relative Prices ($)

	1870	1880	1890	1900	1913	1929	1938	1950	1960	1970	1973	1978	1979
Australia	1.30	1.56	1.62	1.49	1.70	2.16	2.34	3.05	4.02	5.02	5.56	6.55	6.48
Austria	0.43	0.50	0.61	0.74	0.90	1.01	1.03	1.25	2.21	3.99	4.72	5.66	5.89
Belgium	0.74	0.89	1.02	1.12	1.26	1.68	1.84	2.11	2.89	4.71	5.70	6.99	7.31
Canada	0.61	0.76	0.86	1.02	1.45	1.76	1.75	3.33	4.54	5.96	6.64	7.08	7.03
Denmark	0.44	0.51	0.62	0.75	1.00	1.51	1.57	1.82	2.45	4.00	4.78	5.21	5.27
Finland	0.29	n.a.	0.37	n.a.	0.71	0.97	1.15	1.48	2.20	4.16	4.76	5.34	5.26
France	0.42	0.53	0.58	0.71	0.90	1.31	1.69	1.85	2.87	4.92	5.80	6.89	7.11
Germany	0.43	0.50	0.62	0.79	0.95	1.19	1.47	1.40	2.72	4.62	5.40	6.65	6.93
Italy	0.44	0.45	0.47	0.53	0.72	0.98	1.28	1.37	2.10	4.10	5.03	5.57	5.83[a]
Japan	0.17	n.a.	(0.24)	n.a.	0.37	0.64	0.87	0.59	1.03	2.79	3.49	4.22	4.39
Netherlands	0.74	n.a.	(0.97)	1.07	1.23	1.82	1.80	2.27	3.17	5.19	6.17	7.44	7.48
Norway	0.40	0.46	0.56	0.63	0.82	1.28	1.62	2.03	3.04	4.78	5.28	6.43	6.65
Sweden	0.31	0.37	0.45	0.59	0.83	1.22	1.55	2.34	3.30	5.33	5.99	6.51	6.71
Switzerland	0.55	n.a.	0.74	n.a.	1.01	1.68	1.84	2.21	2.98	4.31	4.73	5.02	5.12
UK	0.80	0.94	1.06	1.20	1.35	1.70	1.84	2.40	2.99	4.27	4.84	5.47	5.48
USA	0.70	0.88	1.06	1.29	1.67	2.45	2.62	4.25	5.41	6.96	7.60	8.19	8.28

[a] Assumes 1979 hours worked per person to be same as in 1978.

TABLE C11
Derivation of UK Productivity Levels, 1785-1913

	GDP	Population	Employment	Annual hours worked per person	GDP per man-hour	GDP per head of population
	(1970 $ million)	('000)	('000)		(1970 $)	(1970 $)
1913	68,082	45,649	20,310	2,642	1.27	1.491
1900	56,031	41,155	18,020	2,725	1.14	1.361
1890	45,547	37,485	16,150	2,807	1.00	1.215
1880	36,492	34,623	14,190	2,890	0.89	1.054
1870	30,365	31,257	13,440	2,984	0.76	972
1820	9,396	20,686	8,240	3,000	0.38	454
1785	5,147	13,498	5,377	3,000	0.32	381

Sources: As already described in Appendices A and C. UK employment 1855-1913 from C. H. Feinstein, *National Income, Expenditure and Output of the UK, 1855-1965*, Cambridge, 1972, pp. T125-6; earlier years derived from estimates of changes in population of working age as shown in censuses.

TABLE C12
Derivation of Dutch Productivity Levels, 1700-85

	GDP	Population	Employment	Annual hours worked per person	GDP per man-hour	GDP per head of population
	(1970 $ million)	('000)	('000)		(1970 $)	(1970 $)
1700	836	1,900	757	3,000	0.35	440
1785	817	2,043	814	3,000	0.33	400

APPENDIX D

NON-RESIDENTIAL REPRODUCIBLE TANGIBLE FIXED CAPITAL STOCK

In 1964, when I wrote *Economic Growth in the West*, growth analysts had very little comparative information on capital stocks, and the role of capital was handled rather clumsily by use of investment ratios. Now the situation has been transformed, and this appendix links three major new types of information to produce roughly comparable estimates of trends and levels for the seven largest countries: (a) official national estimates for postwar years, based on the perpetual inventory technique pioneered by Raymond Goldsmith, and published regularly as part of the national accounts aggregates; (b) scholarly estimates for prewar years; (c) Irving Kravis's 1970 benchmark comparison of the purchasing power of different currencies over capital goods.

Estimates of capital stock can be made in two ways: (1) by assessments at a given time from wealth surveys, insurance valuations, company book-keeping, or stock exchange values; (2) by cumulating historical series on past investment and deducting investment used up. The second (perpetual inventory) method is preferable because it produces figures whose meaning is clearer, permits analysis of the structure and age distribution of the capital stock, and helps ensure that all relevant assets are included and that non-relevant ones are excluded, which is not the case with survey data. The second method is now generally used in official estimates of capital stock, but for prewar years reliance has usually to be placed on the first.

COVERAGE

The scope we prefer corresponds to those assets (both private and govern-mental) treated as domestic non-residential fixed capital formation in national accounts estimates. We exclude land and natural resources, intangibles like human capital or the stock of knowledge, precious metals, international monetary reserves, foreign assets, inventories, livestock, consumer durables, housing, and military items. All the estimates listed below conform broadly to the desired coverage except those for France, which exclude public capital before 1966, and the pre-1925 US estimates, which include agricultural housing. All the estimates have been adjusted to a mid-year basis, and unless otherwise specified they are adjusted to offset the impact of changes in the territorial boundaries of the countries con-cerned.

Estimates may be on a *net basis*, with allowance made each year for the 'depreciation' of old assets (i.e. for assets that are retired from use and for declines in the use value of existing *assets* that are not retired), or on a *gross basis*,[1] where allowance is made only for retirement and not for the decline in use value. The latter concept is equivalent to assuming that all existing assets are as good as new. The gross concept is generally considered most appropriate for purposes of assessing production potential, because most assets in use are repaired and maintained in such a way that their productive capacity remains near to its original level throughout their life. Net values are useful in measuring profitability or rates of return, because they involve a discount for differences in the expected life of assets. However, Denison feels that the measure most appropriate for assessing the productive potential of the capital stock is an average of the gross and net concept, and Kendrick prefers to use the net stock for this purpose because it comes closer to being a vintaged stock estimate, which takes some account of technical progress and obsolescence.[2]

The level of the net stock will always be lower than the gross, and retirements will be smaller than depreciation, but the relationship between the growth rates of the two measures will depend on the past history of capital formation. The growth rates of gross and net stock are similar when growth has proceeded steadily for long periods, but when growth accelerates, the net stock will rise more rapidly than the gross. The converse is true if growth decelerates.[3]

The most difficult problem arises from the general ignorance about the length of life of assets. Only in Japan does the government try to survey actual business practice in asset retirement; elsewhere retirement is based on hypothetical formulae.[4] Assumptions about asset lives differ between the countries covered here, and this is the most significant non-comparability in the present estimates because they are somewhat sensitive to the lives assumed.[5] The longer the lives assumed, the higher will be the level of the capital stock and (generally speaking) the slower will be its growth.

Table D1 provides summary estimates of the average life expectation of the assets included in official capital stocks for the seven countries covered here.

It is clear that asset lives are assumed to be considerably shorter in France, Japan, and the USA than in the other four countries. Average expectation will of course depend on the mix of assets in the stock as well as on the lives assumed for particular items. Thus, the fall in average lives that is general between 1925 and 1976 presumably is due in most countries to

TABLE D1
Average Life Expectation of Non-residential Fixed
Capital Assets in Official Estimates

	1925	1950	1976
Canada	31.4[a]	31.4	29.2
France	(n.a.)	22.8[b]	20.0
Germany	(n.a.)	40.0	28.6
Italy	43.0	33.3	29.6[e]
Japan	22.5	31.7[c]	19.4[f]
UK	49.1	40.8	33.7
USA	26.8[a]	23.7	22.3[d]
Average	34.6	32.0	26.1

[a] 1926.
[b] Private sector only.
[c] 1956.
[d] 1974.
[e] 1964.
[f] 1975.

Note: Average life expectation calculated by dividing the gross stock of a given year by the depreciation allowance in the same year. If straight-line depreciation is used (as it is for the private sector in all cases except Japan), this will provide a reasonable estimate of average life expectation. (I am indebted to Tom Griffin of the UK Central Statistical Office for pointing out the possibility of estimating life expectation in this way.) The same technique is used by E. F. Denison and W. K. Chung, *How Japan's Economy Grew So Fast*, Brookings Institution, Washington, 1976, p. 223.

a change in the asset mix, with a declining share devoted to long-lived assets.

In some countries, however, official statisticians assume that lives of individual assets have shortened over time. This is the case in Germany and seems to be so in Japan. Some of the pre-1950 estimates are also based on shortening lives. Where asset lives are assumed to decline, the capital stock will increase more slowly than if fixed lives are assumed (see reference to Kirner's study in the Germany source note of this appendix). If technological progress accelerates, assets will be scrapped earlier, but by making only the shortened life adjustment, productive capacity will be understated. If adjustments are made to the scrapping rate for acceleration of technological progress, one should also add a productivity bonus to the later vintages.[6]

RETIREMENT PATTERNS (USED TO CALCULATE GROSS STOCK)

The simplest assumption about asset lives is that they are the same fixed length for each category of capital goods and that all goods of the same kind bought in the same year are scrapped together when their expected life

TABLE D2
*Impact of Variation in Length-of-life Assumption
on Growth Rate of Capital Stock*

		Gross stock		Net stock	
	Annual average compound growth rates in period shown	Longer lives	Shorter lives	Longer lives	Shorter lives
Canada	1946-60	(n.a.)	(n.a.)	5.3	6.0
France	1950-70	4.6	5.0*	5.4	5.7*
Germany	1960-7	7.6*	8.0	(n.a.)	(n.a.)
UK	1947-76	3.5*	3.8	4.2*	4.7
USA	1926-74	2.6	2.6*	2.7	2.8*

* These figures are the ones preferred by their authors, and the alternatives shown are illustrated in the sources cited in the country notes below. The Canadian figures are from Rymes. He provides five variants. Those quoted above are the extremes. His preferred variant has lives 20 per cent shorter than the maximum and shows a growth rate of 5.7 per cent. The variant with lives 20 per cent below the standard shows a growth rate of 6.2 per cent a year—faster than the extreme variant with lives 40 per cent below standard (which shows the 6 per cent growth cited). Rymes considers that his variant with shortest lives (40 per cent below his standard) is closest to that used in the USA—he appears to refer to Bulletin F lives. The French longer lives are quoted by Mairesse and involve assumptions 20 per cent higher for equipment and 30 per cent for construction than those in the officially preferred version. The German alternatives are those of Kirner (pp. 56, 96, and 138), with lives 20 per cent below those he prefers. The UK alternative involves lives one-third shorter than the official series and were furnished by the CSO. The US variant is that of the Dept of Commerce (with Bulletin F lives), the official US estimates being 15 per cent shorter.

is reached. This (rectangular) assumption is not too realistic, as it makes no allowance for accidents, fires, etc. A number of alternative dispersion patterns have therefore been developed in an attempt to produce results likely to be closer to reality. These variations in retirement pattern make estimation procedures rather complex, but the resulting estimates of the aggregate capital stock have not proved very sensitive to plausible variations in the retirement pattern in those countries where alternative assumptions have been tested (i.e. France, Germany, UK and USA).[7] The following retirement patterns are currently used by the countries studied here.[8]

Canada: rectangular

France: lognormal

Germany: gamma probability density function from 1950, rectangular for earlier years

Italy: rectangular

Japan: actual business practice as reported in surveys since 1955, rectangular previously

UK: even spread 20 per cent on each side of average life since 1947, rectangular previously

USA: bell-wise spread 55 per cent on each side of average life since 1926, rectangular previously

Generally, the older estimates for prewar years are based on fixed lives. In fact, retirement practice may be varied over time, but no country makes allowance for such changes except Japan, where the retirement estimate is not based on a formula but on regular surveys of corporate and non-corporate practice.

DEPRECIATION FORMULAE (USED TO CALCULATE NET STOCK)

The countries making official estimates of the net capital stock appear to use straight-line depreciation as the standard technique, so no significant incomparability arises on this score.[9] For Japan, the net estimates cited are not officially published and their methodology is not clear.

In 1970 the ratios of depreciation, retirements, and non-residential capital formation to GDP are shown in the table (not all at 1970 prices).

	Depreciation	Retirements	Gross non-residential fixed investment
Canada	8.9	4.1	16.8
France	9.1	5.6	16.7
Germany	8.1	4.4	19.0
Japan	10.2*	(n.a.)	28.4
UK	7.8	3.9	15.4
USA	9.0	5.8	13.7

* Excludes government depreciation.

PRICE DEFLATORS

A major problem in constructing capital stock estimates arises from the fact that price levels and price structures change over time. This makes it difficult to express the value of assets originating at different times in a common set of prices.

Between 1950 and 1970 the relative price of non-residential capital goods rose slightly in the USA and fell in all the other countries (Table D3). All countries, except the UK, experienced a rise in the relative price of construction, and all experienced a relative decline in the price of machinery and equipment. The change in the relative prices of machinery and construction was quite striking. In Italy, the most extreme case, the ratio of machinery and equipment to construction prices fell to about half its 1950 level.

Not all countries have the same degree of disaggregation in their price indices, and they may not all observe the same criteria in measuring quality

TABLE D3

Relative Price Movements of Capital Goods
(National Prices), 1950-70

	Total non-residential fixed investment deflator divided by the GDP deflator	Non-residential construction investment deflator divided by the GDP deflator	Machinery and equipment investment deflator divided by the GDP deflator
France	94.6	108.3	85.7
Germany	97.7	116.3	81.7
Italy	88.7	125.8	69.3
UK	91.9	95.4	89.6
USA	103.0	110.0	97.2

Source: Deflators for 1950-60 from OECD, *Statistics of National Accounts 1950-61*, and 1960-70 from *National Accounts of OECD Countries 1960-71*.

change or in handling the problem of new commodities.[10] However, some idea of the degree to which these national indices measure price changes accurately can be derived from the results of two cross-section studies of international price levels carried out by OEEC for 1950 and by Irving Kravis for 1970. The later study is more or less a replication of the first, so comparison of the two studies provides a reasonable guide to relative price changes over these two decades.

Table D4 shows that, in 1950, the relative price of non-residential capital goods as a whole was considerably lower in the USA than in the other countries. By 1970 the US advantage in this respect was considerably reduced, and indeed for France and Germany was reversed. The improvement in the relative price position of the other countries was true of both major types of asset, though the 1970 relative price of machinery and equipment remained higher than in the USA in all the other countries.

This overall decline in the relative price of capital goods in other countries *vis-à-vis* the USA broadly confirms the direction of the movements shown in Table D3, where these changes are expressed at national prices. However, we can also restate the findings of Table D4 in terms of the implicit change in relative prices from 1950 to 1970, and compare them with the findings of Table D3 rebased, so that the US movement is taken as the point of reference.

Table D5 suggests that the national deflators for all four European countries may exaggerate the price rise for capital assets.[11] Their estimates of capital stock at constant prices will therefore show too low a rise, at least relative to the USA. The discrepancy is not large for the UK, but is big for Germany and Italy, and suggests a downward bias in the capital stock estimates for these countries.

TABLE D4

Price Levels of Capital Goods in 1950 and 1970 Relative to US Prices
(US relative price level in year specified = 100)

	Total non-residential fixed investment		Non-residential construction		Machinery and equipment	
	1950	1970	1950	1970	1950	1970
France	116.2	98.6	91.1	81.2	153.3	116.0
Germany	141.6	97.8	103.1	72.5	173.0	123.1
Italy	166.3	104.7	106.4	81.3	246.5	128.0
UK	137.5	117.7	139.5	108.1	138.3	127.3
USA	100.0	100.0	100.0	100.0	100.0	100.0

Source: 1950 figures derived from M. Gilbert and associates, *Comparative National Products and Price Levels*, OEEC, Paris, 1958, p. 80, with component weights for different kinds of investment from *Statistics of National Accounts 1950-1961*, OECD, Paris, 1964. 1970 from I. B. Kravis and associates, *International Comparisons of Real Product and Purchasing Power*, Johns Hopkins, Baltimore, 1978, pp. 177-95.

TABLE D5

Price Movements of Capital Goods from 1950 to 1970 at
US Relative Prices and at National Prices

	Movements shown in Table D3 expressed relative to USA at national prices			Implicit movement in relative price structure derivable from Table D4 at US relative prices		
	Total non-residential fixed investment	Non-residential construction	Machinery and equipment	Total non-residential fixed investment	Non-residential construction	Machinery and equipment
France	91.8	98.5	88.2	84.9	89.1	75.7
Germany	94.9	105.7	84.1	69.1	70.3	71.2
Italy	86.1	114.4	71.3	63.0	76.4	51.9
UK	89.2	86.7	92.2	85.6	77.5	92.0
USA	100.0	100.0	100.0	100.0	100.0	100.0

AN INTERNATIONALLY COMPARABLE BENCHMARK FOR 1976

Official time series estimates of capital stock are now prepared regularly in Canada, France, Germany, Italy, Japan, the UK, and the USA, and are described in the following country-specific notes, together with unofficial estimates for earlier years to which they are linked. These estimates are useful for intertemporal comparison and growth analysis within each country, but the absolute levels of these national estimates are difficult to use for international comparisons because of different assumptions about the lives of assets, retirement patterns, and differences in the relative price of assets.

TABLE D6

Derivation of Internationally Comparable Estimates of Non-residential Fixed Capital Stock in 1976 at 1970 US Prices

	Ratio of non-residential gross fixed capital stock to GDP estimated by standard perpetual inventory method (assuming 30-year lives for all assets)[a]	Price of investment goods relative to price in the USA in 1970			Ratio of gross non-residential fixed capital stock to GDP in 1976 US prices at 1970 US prices	1976 GDP at 1970 US prices	1976 gross non-residential fixed capital stock at 1970 US prices
		Non-residential construction	Machinery and equipment	Total non-residential fixed capital			
	(1)	(2)	(3)	(4)	(5)	(6)	(7)
						($ million)	($ million)
Canada	2.77	103.2	106.1	104.65	2.647	116,249	307,711
France	2.34	81.2	116.0	98.60	2.373	242,474	575,391
Germany	2.90	72.5	123.1	97.80	2.965	272,620	808,318
Italy	2.34	81.3	128.0	104.65	2.236	184,295	412,083
Japan	2.86	117.2	140.3	128.75	2.221	433,355	962,481
UK	2.74	108.1	127.3	117.70	2.328	210,942	491,073
USA	2.50	100.0	100.0	100.0	2.500	1,178,831	2,947,077

[a] These ratios can be compared with those from the national estimates in tables D7 to D13 as follows: Canada, 2.8; France, 2.1; Germany, 2.8; Italy, 2.1; UK, 3.1; and USA, 2.1.

Sources: First column estimated by cumulating non-residential fixed capital investment at constant prices from mid-1946 to mid-1976 and expressing the cumulated stock as a ratio to 1976 GDP. All data from official sources except Germany, 1946-60, from W. Kirner, *Zeitreihen für das Anlagevermögen der Wirtschaftsbereiche in der Bundesrepublik Deutschland*, DIW, Berlin, 1968; Italy, 1946-51, from G. Fua, *Lo Sviluppo Economico in Italia*, Vol. 3, Milan, 1969, Japan 1946-52 from K. Ohkawa and H. Rosovsky, *Japanese Economic Growth*, Oxford, 1973. Columns (2) and (3) taken from I. B. Kravis and associates, *International Comparisons of Real Product and Purchasing Power*, Johns Hopkins, Baltimore, 1978, pp. 177-95, and (for Canada) D. Walters, *Canadian Income Levels and Growth: An International Perspective*, Economic Council of Canada, 1968, p. 260. We adjusted the Canadian figures for 1966-70 with the aid of the deflators for national accounts components as given by OECD. The ratios show the purchasing power parity for each item relative to the purchasing power parity for GDP; e.g., for France the purchasing power parity in 1970 was 4.79 francs to the dollar for machinery and equipment (given French expenditure patterns), whereas for GDP it was 4.13 francs, the ratio of the former to the latter being 116:100. Column (4) represents the average of columns (2) and (3). The appropriate weight for the construction and the machinery and equipment price relatives in a figure for the total capital stock will depend on the proportionate importance of construction and machinery and equipment in the total stock. This varies between countries, partly because national definitions of these components vary, so we took the average importance of construction and machinery and equipment. For the six countries where data were available, the average was 50 per cent for each. Column (5) is column (1) divided by column (4). Column (7) is derived by multiplying column (6) by column (5).

In order to improve international comparability, rough benchmark estimates were made for 1976 which correct for some of these measurement problems. The gross capital stock estimate for 1976 was made by the standard perpetual inventory method in terms of 1970 national prices, with thirty-year lives assumed for all assets in each country. The estimates were then converted into 1970 dollars at US relative prices using the Kravis purchasing power ratios of Table D4. The results are presented in Table D6. These benchmark estimates for mid-1976 were then linked to the time series in Tables D7 to D13 in order to calculate Table 3.5 and Graph 3.2 in the text.

Canada

Official mid-year estimates of gross and net non-residential capital stock have been made by Statistics Canada for 1926 onwards (Table D7). The capital stock series are derived by perpetual inventory method. For an account of the methodology see T. K. Rymes, *Fixed Capital Flows and Stocks, Manufacturing, Canada 1926-60, Methodology*, Dominion Bureau of Statistics, February 1967. Retirements are assumed to take place exactly at the end of the average life. Different service lives are assumed for different industries, including government. Service lives of buildings range from twenty to seventy-five years, engineering construction from twenty-five to seventy-five years. Machinery and equipment ranges from three to thirty-five years and lives of capital items charged to operating expenses are assumed to be five years (see Table 2 of *Fixed Capital Flows and Stocks 1926-73* and subsequent editions). Depreciation is assumed on a straight-line basis. Figures for 1926-48 were raised to offset the impact of the Newfoundland accession in 1949, machinery and equipment estimates being raised by 1.3 per cent and construction by 1.4 per cent.

France

J.-J. Carré, P. Dubois, and E. Malinvaud, *La Croissance française*, Seuil, Paris, 1972, p. 204, give figures for 1913 and 1954 for fixed reproducible non-residential capital, based on a mixture of sources including wealth estimates and insurance values, cross-checked against other indicators. For 1950 onwards, estimates are available from INSEE, which exclude governmental assets for 1950-65. They assume lives of sixteen to twenty years for equipment, and thirty to forty years for buildings, straight-line depreciation and a lognormal retirement pattern (see Table D8). The most substantial INSEE publication on capital stocks is J. Mairesse, *L'Evaluation du capitale fixe productif, les collections de l'INSEE*, 18-19C, November 1972, which discusses alternative ways of measuring capital stock.[12]

TABLE D7
Gross and Net Tangible Non-residential Fixed Capital Stock
Canada, 1926-80
(Mid-year estimates, adjusted to offset territorial change, 1950 = 100)

	Gross non-residential fixed tangible capital stock	Gross machinery and equipment capital stock	Gross non-residential construction capital stock	Net non-residential fixed tangible capital stock	Net machinery and equipment capital stock	Net non-residential construction capital stock
1926	62.01	69.32	58.86	62.83	55.01	66.46
1929	67.97	73.06	65.77	69.33	59.75	73.78
1938	73.01	62.76	77.41	69.31	48.24	79.09
1950	100.0	100.0	100.0	100.0	100.0	100.0
1960	172.0	193.7	164.7	187.0	189.9	185.6
1973	321.4	384.1	294.9	362.7	369.3	360.3
1974	338.7	411.1	308.9	381.7	397.9	376.2
1975	357.2	438.8	324.3	402.3	427.0	394.3
1976	375.8	467.1	340.2	422.5	455.5	412.7
1977	394.1	494.5	355.0	441.3	481.8	428.7
1978	411.9	521.0	369.5	459.6	506.8	444.4
1979	430.1	548.0	384.4	478.6	533.4	460.6
1980	449.5	577.7	399.8	498.6	562.1	477.3

TABLE D8
Gross and Net Tangible Non-residential Fixed Capital Stock,
France 1913-78[a]
(Mid-year estimates, adjusted to offset territorial change, 1950 = 100)

	Gross non-residential fixed tangible capital stock	Net non-residential fixed tangible capital stock
1913	(n.a.)	68.5
1950	100.0	100.0
1960	130.8	138.1
1973	249.8	302.5
1974	263.7	319.6
1975	276.7	334.2
1976	289.4	347.9
1977	302.3	361.6
1978	314.5	373.7

[a] Figures for 1950-65 exclude governmental assets.

Germany

Estimates of net capital stock for 1870-1950 at constant prices were taken from W. G. Hoffmann, F. Grumbach, and H. Hesse, *Das Wachstum der deutschen Wirtschaft seit der Mitte des 19. Jahrhunderts*, Springer, Berlin, 1965, pp. 229-54. The methodology and derivation are described from

p. 215 onwards. The figures are based on a mixture of fire insurance, tax data, and long-range series on investment in different types of assets. Straight-line depreciation was used. We raised the figure for 1870 by 4 per cent to include Alsace and Lorraine, the 1918-39 figures by 10.98 to offset territorial losses in the First World War (the 1918-33 figures were raised an additional 1.2 per cent to include the Saar). The figures for 1948-50 were raised by 95.5 per cent to offset losses in the two wars. The coefficients used are those for population. We also adjusted the Hoffmann series from an end-year to a mid-year basis. Agricultural capital (excluding livestock) from pp. 229-30. Agricultural building was reduced 50 per cent to eliminate agricultural housing. Business capital from pp. 244-5. Business inventories prior to 1923 had to be eliminated. This was done by assuming that the inventory to total business equipment and inventory ratio for 1870-1922 was the same as the average prevailing for 1923-39. Estimates of net railway capital stock and net public building and construction capital stock are given pp. 253-4; we assumed that 50 per cent of railway capital represented construction and 50 per cent machinery and equipment.

Official estimates of gross and net capital stocks are available for 1950 onwards and are described in three articles by H. Lützel: 'Das reproduzierbare Anlagevermögen in Preisen von 1962', *Wirtschaft und Statistik*, October 1971, pp. 593-604; 'Das reproduzierbare Sachvermögen zu Anschaffungs—und zu Wiederbeschaffungspreisen', *Wirtschaft und Statistik*, November 1972, pp. 611-24 and 688-94; and 'Estimates of Capital Stock by Industries in the Federal Republic of Germany', *Review of Income and Wealth*, March 1977.

The official estimates are built up on a perpetual inventory basis, and the coverage is similar to that in national accounting estimates of investment, consumer durables and military items being excluded. Lives assumed for assets are not shown but are stated to be somewhat longer than is assumed for fiscal purposes. The Federal Statistical Office assumes that the average length of life of assets has declined over time. It is assumed that retirements are spread around average life in a bell-shaped curve which is slightly left-modal. Some assets are assumed to drop out of use by accidents very early and some to last more than twice as long as average. Depreciation is on a straight-line basis. Public infrastructure (roads, dams, etc.) is neither retired or depreciated. Figures for 1950-60 at 1962 prices are from *Wirtschaft und Statistik*, October 1971, pp. 607-10, and for 1960 onwards at 1970 prices from *Volkswirtschaftliche Gesamtrechnungen*, Federal Statistical Office, Wiesbaden. We have taken gross stocks including public infrastructure, and also included public infrastructure in our net stock estimates. We have adjusted all figures from beginning of the year to a mid-year basis. We corrected for geographic change by raising the 1950-60 estimates (which excluded the Saar and West Berlin) by the 1960 coverage coefficient for each series that is shown in *Wirtschaft und Statistik*, October 1971. The adjusted series for 1950 onwards were then linked to the 1870-1950 estimates.

For alternative estimates of capital stock for 1950-67, see W. Kirner, *Zeitreihen für das Anlagevermögen der Wirtschaftsbereiche in der Bundesrepublik Deutschland*, DIW, Duncker und Humblot, Berlin, 1968. Kirner assumes that individual asset lives are fixed at eighty to a hundred years for public works, forty to seventy years for non-residential construction, and ten to thirty years for equipment. Because of changes in asset composition the average life expectation of assets was 38.5 years in 1960 and 33.7 years in 1967. Kirner gives alternative estimates based on three types of survival function, but the 1950-67 growth of gross and net stock is virtually insensitive to these variations. However, his figures (version with the quasi-logistic retirement function) show somewhat faster growth of capital stock for 1950-67 than do the official estimates based on declining lives: i.e., gross stock growing 6 per cent as against 5.7 and net stock 7.1 per cent compared with 6.8 (Table D9).

TABLE D9

Gross and Net Tangible Non-residential Fixed Capital Stock,
Germany, 1879-1979

(Mid-year estimates adjusted to offset territorial change, 1950 = 100)

	Gross non-residential fixed tangible capital stock	Gross machinery and equipment capital stock	Gross non-residential construction capital stock	Net non-residential fixed tangible capital stock	Net machinery and equipment capital stock	Net non-residential construction capital stock
1870				18.58	14.19	21.93
1880				24.40	19.22	28.34
1890				32.20	28.46	35.05
1900				44.80	43.95	45.46
1913				68.71	71.44	66.63
1929				77.85	75.32	79.78
1938				89.68	84.15	93.91
1950	100.0	100.0	100.0	100.0	100.0	100.0
1960	163.6	172.3	157.9	189.3	218.7	176.1
1973	358.6	403.8	333.7	430.1	513.2	394.7
1974	375.9	423.4	349.7	449.2	532.8	413.3
1975	391.5	439.6	365.0	465.5	544.9	430.6
1976	406.9	455.4	380.0	481.3	557.5	447.1
1977	423.6	472.2	396.4	499.4	573.2	465.6
1978	442.1	490.6	414.9	520.7	593.4	486.9
1979	461.8	511.3	434.0	543.9	618.9	505.8

Italy

Gross and net capital stock estimates for 1881 to 1964 are available in G. Fua (ed.), *Lo Sviluppo Economico in Italia*, vol. III, Angeli, Milan, 1969, pp. 417-22, and pp. 478-537. These estimates refer to capital stock in the present-day territory of Italy. We adjusted them from an end-year to mid-year basis.

These estimates use straight-line depreciation and assume that retirements take place exactly at the end of the average life. Fixed lives are assumed for structures—one hundred years for most public works and public utilities, fifty years for other structures for pre-1891 years and thirty years thereafter. For machinery and transport equipment declining lives are assumed of forty years for assets originating before 1891, thirty-five years from 1891 to 1915, twenty-five years from 1916 to 1946, and eighteen years after 1947. In the four periods through 1890, 1891-1905, 1906-1947, and after 1948, the lives of public utility and structural repairs are assumed to be fifty, forty-five, thirty-five, and twenty-five years respectively (see p. 519). The figures appear to exclude livestock.

For the years 1951-71 estimates of net capital stock including land are available in *Annali di Statistica: Problemi Relativi Alla Definizione, Stima, Rilevazione ed Utilizzazione del Capitale*, Serie VIII, vol. 28, ISTAT, p. 169. As these are not very comparable with those of Fua, estimates of gross capital stock for 1925 onwards were calculated as follows. All construction was assumed to have a fixed fifty-five year life, equipment a fixed life of eighteen years. The investment series to 1952 were from Fua, pp. 511-17, thereafter from *Annuario di Contabilita Nazionale*. War damage was assumed to amount to 7 per cent of the immediate postwar capital stock. It was assumed that all previous vintages of investment were equally affected by war damage (Table D10).

TABLE D10

*Gross and Net Tangible Non-residential Fixed Capital Stock,
Italy, 1882-1978*

(Mid-year estimates adjusted to offset territorial change, 1950 = 100)

	Gross non-residential fixed tangible capital stock	Gross machinery and equipment capital stock	Gross non-residential construction capital stock
1882	20.78	11.52	32.86
1890	25.75	15.60	38.95
1900	30.31	20.07	43.54
1913	45.16	39.19	52.30
1929	66.07	62.63	69.64
1938	85.54	85.68	85.39
1950	100.0	100.0	100.0
1960	150.3	141.7	159.3
1973	315.7	327.7	304.6
1974	332.4	348.7	317.6
1975	347.4	366.7	330.0
1976	361.4	382.7	342.1
1977	375.6	399.6	354.0
1978	388.6	414.3	365.7

Japan

K. Ohkawa and associates, *Capital Stock*, vol. 3, *Estimates of Long-Term Economic Statistics of Japan Since 1868*, Toyo Keizai Shinpo Sha, Tokyo, 1966, pp. 148-51, gives figures for 1874-1940 of gross and net stock of domestic reproducible tangible fixed assets, and p. 262 gives separate gross stock estimates for 1905-60. Equipment is divided into four categories with lives varying from six to twenty years, averaging seventeen years. Buildings and public works are generally assumed to last fifty years. Lives are assumed to be fixed throughout, and it is assumed that all assets are retired exactly at the end of their average life, with zero scrap value. We disregarded the figures prior to 1879 when there seems to have been a jump in coverage.

Figures for 1955 onwards are from the Japanese Economic Planning Agency's estimates of gross stock movements (excluding 'work in progress'); see *Private Enterprise Gross Capital Stock* (in Japanese), EPA, 1977, for the private sector and rough unpublished EPA estimates for the public sector. These figures are based on quinquennial wealth surveys, current business reports, and surveys of capital formation and scrapping rates. Unpublished EPA estimates of private net stocks are available from 1952 onwards, and Denison[13] has also made estimates of net stocks for 1952-71. For 1940 onwards no breakdown seems to be available by type of asset (Table D11).

TABLE D11

*Gross and Net Tangible Non-residential Fixed Capital Stock,
Japan, 1880-1979
(Mid-year estimates, without territorial adjustment)*

	Gross non-residential fixed tangible capital stock (1913 = 100)	Net non-residential fixed tangible capital stock (1913 = 100)		Gross non-residential fixed tangible capital stock (1950 = 100)	Net non-residential fixed tangible capital stock[a] (1950 = 100)
1880	42.55	39.47	1950	100.0	100.0
1890	49.15	46.28	1960	164.8	(183.4)
1900	63.42	61.49			
1913	100.0	100.0	1973	727.0	(800.4)
1929	201.4	198.6	1978	1,061.8	(1,027.0)
1938	275.6	267.0	1979	1,130.1	
1940	302.2	308.1			
1950	334.0	(n.a.)			

[a] 1950 onwards refers to private stock only.

United Kingdom

Figures for 1760-1860 are from C. H. Feinstein, 'Capital Formation in Great Britain', in P. Mathias and M. M. Postan (eds), *The Cambridge Economic History of Europe*, vol. VII, pt I, Cambridge 1978, pp. 42 and 84, with adjustment to a UK basis. These estimates are linked to Feinstein's earlier estimates for 1860-1948 without adjustment, in spite of the fact that they do not match very well (see Feinstein, p. 79).

Figures for 1860-1948 are from C. H. Feinstein, *National Income, Expenditure and Output of the U.K., 1855-1965*, Cambridge, 1972, pp. 196-205 and T96-8. He assumes all assets retired exactly at the end of their average lives; depreciation is mainly straight-line. The figures are a mixture of perpetual inventory and benchmark estimates. Different asset lives are assumed for 1860-1913, 1920-38, and 1948-65 (see p. 201): for railways, he assumes 125 years for the early period and 100 thereafter; for industrial and commercial buildings, 100 for the early period, seventy-three for the middle period and eighty for 1948-65; for other buildings and works the corresponding lengths of life are 125, sixty-seven, and sixty-three years. For plant and machinery, lives are forty, twenty-eight, and thirty years respectively. 1939-47 lives are interpolations between the 1938 and 1948 estimates.

Official gross and net estimates were used for 1948 onwards.[14] In these, average service life is eighty years for industrial and commercial buildings, ten years for road vehicles. For manufacturing, construction, distribution and other services, lives of machinery and equipment are assumed to be one-seventh greater than those used by the tax authorities.[15] In manufacturing, 60 per cent of machinery and equipment has a life of thirty-four years. For coal-mining, gas, electricity, railways, and the Post Office the lives assumed are generally those employed by the undertakings concerned in evaluating depreciation for their own accounts. A life of 100 years is used for railway track and some other assets for which no depreciation is normally allowed for accounting purposes. Retirements are assumed to be evenly distributed from minus 20 per cent to plus 20 per cent of the mean expected life of the relevant asset group (Table D12).

United States

Figures for 1869-1925 mid-year net stock are from J. W. Kendrick, *Productivity Trends in the United States*, Princeton, 1961, pp. 320-5 (procedures described on pp. 34-6, 51-4, and 268-84). We excluded land, non-agricultural housing, inventories, foreign assets, monetary gold and silver from his total, but were not able to exclude agricultural housing. Kendrick's 1896-1949 estimates are derived mainly from R. Goldsmith, *A Study of Saving in the United States,* Princeton, 1956, vol. III. Goldsmith used the same lengths of life as those recommended for calculating depreciation by

TABLE D12

Gross and Net Tangible Non-residential Fixed Capital Stock,
UK, 1760-1979
(Mid-year estimates, adjusted to offset territorial change; 1950 = 100)

	Gross non-residential fixed tangible capital stock	Gross machinery and equipment capital stock	Gross non-residential construction capital stock	Net non-residential fixed tangible capital stock	Net machinery and equipment capital stock	Net non-residential construction capital stock
1760	6.94					
1785	(9.36)					
1800	11.30					
1820	14.33					
1830	16.13					
1860	31.95					
1870	36.16	26.36	40.46	49.55	32.24	60.58
1880	42.15	31.18	46.94	55.20	35.12	67.95
1890	47.68	35.58	52.68	58.37	35.44	72.88
1900	56.74	44.15	61.57	68.03	43.74	83.48
1913	72.04	59.94	75.73	84.03	59.38	99.95
1929	81.01	71.63	86.42	86.76	73.70	96.48
1938	90.15	81.65	94.61	91.86	84.65	98.54
1950	100.0	100.0	100.0	100.0	100.0	100.0
1960	128.5	145.9	118.4	140.8	157.4	130.3
1973	214.8	260.4	188.5	259.8	283.0	245.1
1974	223.0	271.5	195.1	270.1	294.1	254.9
1975	230.8	281.8	201.4	279.5	303.6	264.3
1976	238.2	290.8	207.8	288.0	311.4	273.1
1977	245.4	300.2	213.7	295.8	318.9	281.1
1978	252.5	309.9	219.3	303.2	326.6	288.3
1979	259.5	319.8	224.7	310.3	335.1	294.6

the US Treasury department in 1942 (i.e. Bulletin F lives). Before 1896 Kendrick extended the Goldsmith estimates using S. Kuznets, *Capital in the American Economy*, Princeton, 1961, estimates of capital formation. We used the net-gross stock relation shown by Kuznets to provide crude gross stock estimates.

Figures for 1929-79 end-year gross and net stocks of fixed non-residential business capital and 1959-79 government capital are from J. C. Musgrave, 'Fixed Capital Stocks in the United States: Revised Estimates', *Survey of Current Business*, February 1981; government non-military gross and net fixed non-residential capital for 1929-58 from J. C. Musgrave, 'Government-Owned Fixed Capital in the United States, 1925-79', *Survey of Current Business*, March 1980. The official estimates assume a symmetric bell-shaped retirement distribution. Asset lives for equipment are 15 per cent less than those of Bulletin F[16] and the net series is based on straight-line depreciation. All estimates were converted from an end-year to a mid-year basis and all residential capital was excluded. No correction was made for the incorporation of Alaska and Hawaii (Table D13).

TABLE D13

Gross and Net Tangible Non-residential Fixed Capital Stock,
USA, 1870-1979

(Mid-year estimates; 1950 = 100)

	Gross non-residential fixed tangible capital stock	*Gross machinery and equipment capital stock*	*Gross non-residential construction capital stock*	*Net non-residential fixed tangible capital stock*	*Net machinery and equipment capital stock*	*Net non-residential construction capital stock*
1870	6.52			7.27		
1880	10.36			11.72		
1890	14.93			16.92		
1900	26.01			29.45		
1913	46.93			51.76		
1929	74.3	63.6	78.5	76.8	57.4	84.8
1938	79.9	59.7	87.7	77.9	48.1	90.2
1950	100.0	100.0	100.0	100.0	100.0	100.0
1960	141.1	156.7	135.0	147.4	145.9	148.0
1973	234.1	277.5	217.2	257.1	269.4	252.0
1974	243.5	293.9	223.8	267.1	286.3	259.1
1975	251.4	307.9	229.4	274.7	298.5	264.8
1976	258.6	320.1	234.7	280.4	307.3	269.2
1977	266.5	334.3	240.1	286.6	319.2	273.0
1978	275.1	351.4	245.4	294.3	335.2	277.2
1979	284.5	369.6	251.3	303.1	353.1	282.3

APPENDIX E

COST OF LIVING

For the period 1914-50, consumer price indices were generally derived from *Statistical Yearbooks* of the League of Nations and United Nations. For 1950-5, movements were from OECD, *General Statistics*, September 1962, pp. 59, 102, and 105 except for Australia, Finland, and Japan, which are from ILO *Yearbook*, 1956. For 1955 onwards the figures are from OECD, *Main Economic Indicators* (the *Historical Statistics* volume and current issues). Otherwise the following sources were used:

Australia: 1870-1914, GDP deflator derived from N. G. Butlin, *Australian Domestic Product, Investment and Foreign Borrowing 1861-1938/9*, Cambridge, 1962, pp. 10, 11, 460-1.

Austria: 1874-1913 from D. F. Good, 'The Cost of Living in Austria: 1874-1913', *Journal of European Economic History*, Fall 1976; 1914-50 from B. R. Mitchell, *European Historical Statistics, 1750-1970*, Macmillan, London, 1975, pp. 743-5.

Belgium: 1870-1913 from J. Marczewski, 'Le Produit physique de l'économie française de 1789 à 1913', *Histoire quantitative de l'économie française*, INSEE, July 1965, pp. cxxv-cxxvi.

Canada: 1870-1910 from O. J. Firestone, *Canada's Economic Development 1867-1953*, Bowes and Bowes, London, 1958, p. 178; 1910-50 from M. C. Urquhart and K. A. H. Buckley, *Historical Statistics of Canada*, Macmillan, Toronto, 1965, p. 303-4.

Denmark: 1870-1914 consumption deflator derived from K. Bjerke and N. Ussing, *Studier over Danmarks Nationalprodukt 1870-1950,* Gads, Copenhagen, 1958, pp. 148-9.

Finland: for 1870-1913, no consumer price index was available, so wholesale price index was used, from H. Björkqvist, *Guldmyntfotens Införande i Finland aren 1877-1878*, Bank of Finland, Helsinki, 1953, Table 16 (for 1870-7) and H. Björkqvist, *Prisrörelser och Penningvärde in Finland under Gulmyntfotsperioden 1878-1913*, Bank of Finland, Helsinki, 1958, p. 259 (for 1878-1914); 1914-50 from B. R. Mitchell, *European Historial Statistics 1750-1970*, Macmillan, London, 1975, pp. 743-5.

France: 1820-1913, Marczewski, 'Le Produit physique', pp. civ, cxxv-vi; 1913-14 link from *Annuaire statistique de la France 1954*, 2ᵉ partie, p. 70;

1914-50 from *Annuaire statistique de la France 1960*, p. 387; 1914-20 (13 articles), 1921-59 (34 articles).

Germany: 1820-50 from B. R. Mitchell, *European Historical Statistics 1750-1970*, Macmillan, London, 1975; 1850-1913 private consumption deflator from W. C. Hoffmann and associates, *Das Wachstum der deutschen Wirtschaft seit der Mitte des 19 Jahrhunderts*, Springer, Berlin, 1965, pp. 599 and 601; 1913-23 from G. Bry, *Wages in Germany 1871-1945*, NBER, Princeton, 1960, pp. 440 and 445; 1924-50 from *Bevölkerung und Wirtschaft 1872-1972*, Statistisches Bundesamt, Wiesbaden, 1972, p. 250.

Italy: 1870-1950 from G. Fua, *Lo Sviluppo Economico in Italia*, Angeli, Milan, 1975, p. 434.

Japan: 1879-1944 from *Historical Statistics of Japanese Economy*, Bank of Japan, 1962, p. 49; 1944-46 Tokyo retail price index, 1946-50 consumer price index from *Hundred-Year Statistics of the Japanese Economy*, Bank of Japan, 1966, pp. 80-1.

Netherlands: 1900-50 from *Zestig Jaren Statistiek in Tijdreeksen 1899-1959*, CBS, Zeist, 1959, p. 125.

Norway: 1870-1914 consumer price index from *National Accounts 1865-1960*, CBS, Oslo, 1970, pp. 352-4.

Sweden: 1870-1913 from G. Myrdal, *The Cost of Living in Sweden 1830-1930*, Stockholm, 1933; 1820-70 movement from L. Jörberg, *A History of Prices in Sweden 1732-1914*, vol. II, C.W.K., Gleerup, 1972, pp. 185 and 350.

Switzerland: 1892-1917 from E. Notz, *Die säkulare Entwicklung der Kaufkraft des Geldes*, Fischer, Jena, 1925, pp. 91-3 (31 articles).

United Kingdom: 1820-46 Rousseaux price index from B. R. Mitchell, *Abstract of British Historical Statistics*; 1846-1913, Bowley's index as cited by Marcewski, 'Le Produit physique'; 1913-50 from *The British Economy: Key Statistics 1900-1970*, p. 8 (retail prices, all items).

United States: 1820-1950 consumer price index (B.L.S.) from *Historical Statistics of the United States, Colonial Times to 1970*, pp. 210-11.

TABLE E1
Consumer Price Indices, 1820-60
(1913 = 100)

	France	Germany	Sweden	UK	USA
1820	86.0	62.5	55.9	125.8	141.4
1850	73.8	56.8		92.1	84.2
1860	86.4	70.3		110.8	90.9

TABLE E2
Consumer Prices Indices, Annual Data, 1870-1914
(1913 = 100)

	Australia	Austria	Belgium	Canada	Denmark	Finland	France	Germany
1870	89.4		101.0	83.3	110.9	78	94.1	76.5
1871	89.2		103.0		109.7	81	101.9	79.8
1872	96.1		106.8		108.9	87	99.0	85.0
1873	101.1		115.4		113.6	89	98.6	89.5
1874	98.8	97.4	109.7		116.2	101	97.9	90.3
1875	96.5	91.1	105.8		117.2	102	94.9	85.7
1876	95.9	93.1	111.5		117.0	105	98.2	86.1
1877	94.2	93.0	111.5		111.3	101	99.4	84.5
1878	90.1	89.0	106.8		106.2	84	96.3	82.4
1879	90.4	87.7	103.8		104.5	76	95.2	79.8
1880	89.4	88.0	99.1	79.3	108.6	89	98.4	83.7
1881	88.7	86.8	99.1		107.6	94	97.8	81.9
1882	97.7	87.6	98.1		104.0	87	96.3	82.8
1883	95.0	86.7	99.1		102.8	84	99.0	80.2
1884	92.6	84.5	92.3		98.9	83	97.1	79.2
1885	93.0	80.5	89.4		97.1	77	94.7	77.5
1886	90.3	79.0	81.8		93.7	72	93.3	77.0
1887	90.0	76.9	86.6		91.8	70	90.7	76.4
1888	92.0	76.8	84.6		91.1	70	91.7	77.1
1889	93.3	78.3	86.6		92.7	77	91.9	79.8
1890	93.7	78.5	90.4	76.8	95.1	77	91.1	82.3
1891	85.5	80.4	90.4		97.4	82	92.7	83.2
1892	82.3	77.8	86.6		96.1	82	91.9	82.8
1893	77.9	77.5	83.6		93.7	79	90.4	78.1
1894	73.0	77.1	81.8		90.9	73	93.3	77.0
1895	73.4	78.4	79.8		91.8	73	90.9	77.2
1896	77.4	75.3	76.9		88.9	74	89.4	78.7
1897	78.8	77.2	77.9		84.2	77	87.0	80.1
1898	79.2	79.7	77.9		89.2	80	88.2	80.2
1899	80.6	79.7	78.9		87.9	83	89.4	81.9
1900	78.5	78.8	89.4	71.9	93.0	87	89.4	84.4
1901	84.0	77.8	91.4		95.9	85	89.9	84.3
1902	84.6	76.8	89.4		95.1	85	88.8	84.5
1903	82.9	77.0	89.4		94.5	83	88.5	84.5
1904	82.9	79.3	77.9		92.1	83	87.2	85.0
1905	85.4	86.1	79.8	78.2	93.9	82	86.8	87.7
1906	87.3	86.8	87.5		95.5	87	88.2	92.5
1907	89.1	88.1	90.4		94.4	93	89.4	92.0
1908	88.2	91.5	91.4		96.2	91	91.5	91.5
1909	87.8	94.1	90.4		97.0	93	91.2	94.5
1910	89.2	93.8	92.3	91.2	97.5	95	101.6	98.4
1911	93.3	99.5	98.1	92.7	97.3	97	92.5	97.9
1912	97.0	100.5	104.8	98.3	97.9	100	101.3	99.3
1913	100.0	100.0	100.0	100.0	100.0	100	100.0	100.0
1914	108.6			102.0	104.1	103	99.6	103.0

Consumer Prices Indices, Annual Data, 1870-1914
(1913 = 100)

	Italy	Japan	Netherlands	Norway	Sweden	Switzerland	UK	USA
1870	78.6			76.3	81.3		107.9	127.9
1871	80.1			77.2	83.4		110.8	121.2
1872	90.8			83.3	86.7		117.7	121.2
1873	99.5			89.8	93.6		119.6	121.2
1874	96.6			93.5	97.0		112.8	114.5
1875	80.6			90.2	96.3		108.8	111.1
1876	83.0			89.8	96.6		107.9	107.7
1877	92.2			89.8	96.1		107.9	107.7
1878	85.4			80.5	89.8		102.0	97.6
1879	84.0	38.5		75.8	84.2		99.0	94.3
1880	86.9	44.3		81.4	88.6		102.9	97.6
1881	83.5	48.2		82.3	90.8		101.0	97.6
1882	84.0	45.4		82.8	88.3		100.0	97.6
1883	79.6	40.5		81.4	87.9		100.0	94.3
1884	78.6	37.5		78.1	84.7		95.1	90.9
1885	80.6	39.6		73.5	80.7		89.2	90.9
1886	83.0	37.1		72.1	76.8		87.2	90.9
1887	78.6	37.1		70.2	74.0		86.3	90.9
1888	77.7	36.7		71.6	76.7		86.3	90.9
1889	86.4	39.3		74.0	80.1		87.2	90.9
1890	85.4	43.3		74.0	81.8		87.2	90.9
1891	85.4	42.1		77.2	84.3		87.2	90.9
1892	81.1	42.8		75.8	82.9	85.7	88.2	90.9
1893	80.6	43.6		74.4	79.5	83.9	87.2	90.9
1894	79.6	45.3		72.6	75.5	83.4	83.3	87.5
1895	82.5	49.3		72.1	76.8	81.2	81.4	84.2
1896	79.6	53.0		72.6	76.2	80.2	81.4	84.2
1897	80.6	61.6		72.6	78.7	81.4	83.3	84.2
1898	85.0	66.2		77.7	82.5	84.5	86.3	84.2
1899	83.0	61.6		80.0	86.1	81.9	84.3	84.2
1900	83.5	69.5	86.5	83.3	87.0	78.9	89.2	84.2
1901	80.1	68.2	91.0	82.3	84.9	79.9	88.2	84.2
1902	78.6	71.1	88.8	80.5	85.6	80.4	88.2	87.5
1903	84.0	75.0	88.8	79.5	87.1	82.0	89.2	90.9
1904	81.6	77.0	91.0	80.0	86.0	82.0	90.2	90.9
1905	82.5	79.3	91.0	80.9	87.9	84.8	90.2	90.9
1906	86.9	82.5	91.0	83.3	89.7	87.2	91.2	90.9
1907	86.9	88.6	92.1	86.5	94.3	89.7	93.1	94.3
1908	85.9	85.4	95.5	87.4	95.7	90.9	91.2	90.9
1909	88.3	84.0	94.4	87.4	94.9	92.4	92.1	90.9
1910	94.2	84.7	96.6	89.3	94.8	96.3	94.1	94.3
1911	96.1	90.9	97.8	92.1	93.5	98.6	95.1	94.3
1912	99.0	96.7	98.9	96.7	99.7	102.2	98.0	97.6
1913	100.0	100.0	100.0	100.0	100.0	100.0	100.0	100.0
1914	98.5	90.0	100.0	102.3	102.0	101.8	100.0	101.3

TABLE E3
Consumer Price Indices, Annual Data, 1914-50
$(1914 = 100)$

	Australia	Austria	Belgium	Canada	Denmark	Finland	France	Germany
1914	100	100	100	100	100	100	100	100
1915	113	158		103	116	100	120	125
1916	117	337		111	136	133	135	165
1917	116	672		134	155	244	163	246
1918	120	1,163		151	182	633	213	304
1919	133	2,492		166	211	922	268	403
1920	158	5,115		198	261	889	371	990
1921	150	9,981	366	163	232	1,055	333	1,301
1922	141	263,938	340	153	200	1,033	315	14,602
1923	151	76[a]	399	153	206	1,033	344	[b]
1924	149	86	469	149	216	1,055	395	128[a]
1925	153	97	498	152	211	1,100	424	140
1926	158	103	604	155	184	1,078	560	141
1927	157	106	743	153	177	1,089	593	148
1928	158	108	761	153	175	1,122	584	152
1929	161	111	805	155	173	1,111	621	154
1930	152	111	834	154	165	1,022	618	148
1931	137	106	749	138	156	944	609	136
1932	130	108	673	125	155	933	546	121
1933	126	106	665	120	160	890	520	118
1934	128	106	639	121	167	889	491	121
1935	130	106	643	122	172	890	440	123
1936	133	106	677	124	175	890	480	124
1937	137	106	739	128	181	944	611	125
1938	140	104	755	130	183	978	706	126
1939	144	103	748	129	188	989	763	126
1940	150	106	858	134	234	1,189	909	130
1941	158	107		142	272	1,400	1,062	133
1942	170	108		148	282	1,655	1,238	137
1943	177	109		151	286	1,866	1,578	138
1944	177	109		151	289	1,978	2,013	141
1945	177	116		151	293	2,778	2,778	145
1946	179	147	2,462	157	291	4,422	4,553	158
1947	187	288	2,506	170	298	5,744	7,273	169
1948	203	469	2,876	196	307	7,733	11,529	195
1949	222	611	2,785	203	312	7,843	12,830	209
1950	244	763	2,754	209	331	8,948	13,731	196

[a] Linked to base via prices linked to gold.
[b] Figure was 15,437,000 million.

Consumer Price Indices, Annual Data, 1914-50
$(1914 = 100)$

	Italy	Japan	Netherlands	Norway	Sweden	Switzerland	UK	USA
1914	100	100	100	100	100	100	100	100
1915	109	94	115	117	115	115	124	102
1916	155	102	128	146	130	134	143	115
1917	224	122	136	190	159	171	176	138
1918	289	161	162	253	219	204	200	169
1919	331	213	176	275	257	222	219	193
1920	467	224	194	300	269	224	248	194
1921	467	210	169	277	247	200	224	169
1922	467	210	149	231	198	164	181	165
1923	476	206	144	218	178	164	176	168
1924	481	207	145	239	174	169	176	168
1925	580	211	144	243	177	168	176	173
1926	618	203	138	206	173	162	171	171
1927	547	202	138	186	171	160	167	167
1928	511	196	139	173	172	161	167	165
1929	503	192	138	166	170	161	167	165
1930	476	174	133	161	165	158	157	161
1931	421	159	125	153	160	150	148	147
1932	394	160	116	150	156	138	143	131
1933	363	167	115	147	155	131	143	124
1934	370	171	115	148	155	129	143	129
1935	381	174	111	151	156	128	143	132
1936	409	178	106	155	158	130	148	134
1937	454	193	112	166	163	137	152	138
1938	493	214	114	172	167	137	157	136
1939	516	231	115	174	172	138	162	134
1940	636	295	132	203	194	151	181	135
1941	788	347	151	238	219	174	200	142
1942	1,092	458	162	252	238	193	214	157
1943	1,753	544	167	258	240	203	224	167
1944	4,292	688	172	261	243	208	224	169
1945	9,340	1,011	198	266	243	210	233	174
1946	12,739	60,048	216	272	243	208	243	187
1947	22,020	129,104	224	274	253	217	257	216
1948	23,616	235,896	232	272	264	224	271	231
1949	23,665	311,386	246	274	267	222	281	229
1950	24,404	289,944	270	285	271	219	291	231

TABLE E4

Consumer Price Indices, Annual Data, 1950-80

(1950 = 100.0)

	Australia	Austria	Belgium	Canada	Denmark	Finland	France	Germany
1950	100.0	100.0	100.0	100.0	100.0	100.0	100.0	100.0
1951	120.6	127.7	108.9	110.4	112.5	120.5	116.9	107.8
1952	141.2	149.5	110.3	113.2	114.8	125.6	130.7	110.1
1953	147.1	141.4	110.0	112.2	113.6	128.2	129.2	108.1
1954	148.5	146.7	111.2	112.9	114.8	128.2	128.8	108.3
1955	152.9	147.8	110.9	113.1	122.7	124.4	130.2	110.1
1956	162.4	152.5	114.0	114.7	128.9	138.1	132.8	113.0
1957	166.5	156.0	117.5	118.4	129.4	154.2	137.4	115.2
1958	168.8	159.5	119.2	121.4	130.1	163.2	158.1	117.8
1959	172.0	161.1	120.6	122.8	132.5	166.5	167.9	118.9
1960	178.4	164.1	121.0	124.1	134.2	171.3	173.8	120.5
1961	182.9	170.0	122.1	124.7	139.6	174.3	179.5	123.3
1962	182.2	177.5	123.9	126.2	150.1	182.4	188.3	127.1
1963	183.4	182.4	126.5	128.5	158.2	191.9	197.3	130.9
1964	187.7	189.4	131.9	130.7	163.9	210.9	204.1	133.8
1965	195.2	198.7	137.1	134.0	174.4	222.0	209.2	138.4
1966	200.9	203.1	142.9	139.0	186.1	229.8	214.9	143.3
1967	207.3	211.1	147.0	143.8	199.0	242.7	220.6	145.3
1968	212.9	217.2	151.1	149.8	216.1	265.8	230.7	149.1
1969	218.9	223.7	156.6	156.6	225.2	271.4	245.4	151.9
1970	227.5	233.5	162.8	161.8	238.3	278.9	258.3	157.1
1971	241.4	244.5	169.8	166.5	252.1	297.1	272.5	165.4
1972	255.5	259.9	179.1	174.4	268.8	318.0	288.5	174.5
1973	279.6	279.5	191.6	187.7	293.8	351.4	309.7	186.6
1974	321.9	306.1	215.9	208.1	337.9	412.8	352.1	199.6
1975	370.4	332.0	243.4	230.6	375.1	485.3	393.1	211.6
1976	420.4	356.2	265.8	247.9	408.1	553.2	430.8	221.1
1977	472.3	375.8	284.5	267.7	453.9	626.0	471.3	229.8
1978	509.7	389.4	297.2	291.7	498.9	674.6	514.2	235.7
1979	553.0	405.9	311.3	316.5	547.5	725.2	569.5	246.3
1980	609.4	431.6	332.0	348.6	615.0	807.9	647.0	259.9

Consumer Price Indices, Annual Data, 1950-80
($1950 = 100.0$)

	Italy	Japan	Netherlands	Norway	Sweden	Switzerland	UK	USA
1950	100.0	100.0	100.0	100.0	100.0	100.0	100.0	100.0
1951	109.3	115.6	109.0	116.9	115.2	104.9	108.8	107.9
1952	114.0	122.1	109.0	127.3	124.1	107.6	119.2	110.3
1953	116.3	129.9	109.0	129.9	126.6	106.8	122.9	111.2
1954	119.8	137.7	113.3	135.1	127.8	107.6	125.1	111.6
1955	123.3	136.4	115.5	136.4	131.6	108.5	130.7	111.3
1956	127.4	136.9	117.7	141.5	138.2	110.1	137.1	112.9
1957	129.2	141.1	125.3	145.4	144.0	112.3	142.2	116.9
1958	132.8	140.5	127.5	152.4	150.4	114.2	146.6	120.2
1959	132.2	141.8	128.5	155.8	151.6	113.6	147.3	121.0
1960	135.2	147.0	134.9	156.3	157.9	115.2	148.8	122.9
1961	137.9	154.8	136.3	160.4	161.2	117.3	153.9	124.2
1962	144.5	165.4	138.9	168.7	168.9	122.4	160.6	125.7
1963	155.2	179.4	144.3	173.0	173.8	126.6	163.7	127.3
1964	164.5	186.4	152.0	183.0	179.7	130.6	169.0	128.9
1965	171.8	198.9	158.2	190.8	188.6	135.0	177.2	131.1
1966	175.8	209.0	167.2	197.1	200.8	141.4	184.1	134.8
1967	181.6	217.3	173.0	205.8	209.5	147.0	188.7	138.7
1968	183.9	229.0	179.4	212.8	213.5	150.6	197.6	144.5
1969	188.7	240.9	192.8	219.4	219.1	154.4	208.2	152.3
1970	198.2	259.3	199.8	242.7	234.6	160.0	221.5	161.3
1971	207.7	275.1	214.8	257.7	252.0	170.6	242.3	168.2
1972	219.6	287.6	231.6	276.4	267.0	181.9	259.6	173.7
1973	243.4	321.3	250.1	296.1	285.0	197.8	283.5	184.5
1974	290.0	399.9	274.3	325.2	315.6	217.2	328.7	204.8
1975	339.1	447.0	302.3	364.1	344.9	231.7	408.4	223.6
1976	396.0	489.0	328.9	396.9	380.1	235.6	476.0	236.6
1977	468.9	528.8	350.1	433.3	424.2	238.7	551.3	251.8
1978	525.9	551.2	364.3	469.7	465.6	241.8	597.1	271.0
1979	603.5	569.4	379.8	492.0	499.4	249.6	670.2	295.4
1980	731.3	615.1	404.6	546.7	568.3	259.5	790.7	335.3

APPENDIX F

THE VOLUME OF MERCHANDISE EXPORTS

Unless otherwise specified, the estimates for 1870-1950 are from A. Maddison 'Growth and Fluctuation in the World Economy', *Banca Nazionale del Lavoro Quarterly Review*, June 1962, and for 1950 onwards (and in some cases 1946-9) from the UN *Yearbooks of International Trade Statistics* and the UN *Monthly Bulletins of Statistics*.

The figures are on a calendar year basis. Up to 1950 the indices refer to special exports (excluding re-exports of merchandise). They exclude exports of services unless otherwise specified. The value of exports for 1970 is shown in Table F1.

TABLE F1

Value of Exports f.o.b. in 1970 in US Dollars at Official Exchange Rates

	($ million)		($ million)
Australia	4,482	Japan	19,139
Austria	2,856	Netherlands	11,774
Belgium-Luxembourg	11,600	Norway	2,383
Canada	15,717	Sweden	6,588
Denmark	3,230	Switzerland	5,152
Finland	2,237	UK	18,572
France	17,935	USA	42,590
Germany	38,849		
Italy	13,206	Total 16 countries above	212,310
		World total	311,329

Source: UN, *Yearbook of International Trade Statistics 1976*, vol. I, pp. 21-5, adjusted to exclude re-exports wherever possible. These amounted to $139 million in Australia, $402 million in Canada, $126 million in Denmark, $179 million in Japan, and $775 million in the UK. For Finland, Norway, and Sweden figures on re-exports do not seem to be available. In each of these cases I assumed that re-exports were 3 per cent of the total. The total for the sixteen countries excludes re-exports, but the world total includes some re-exports of some countries (other than our sixteen).

For the following countries and periods, the sources used are listed below.

Australia: 1871-1913 export values from N. G. Butlin, *Australian Domestic Product, Investment and Foreign Borrowing 1861-1938/9*, Cambridge, 1962, pp. 410-11, 436, 438, and 441 (excluding gold); export deflator from

C. P. Kindleberger, *The Terms of Trade*, Chapman and Hall, London, 1936, p. 157 (Wilson's index); 1913-27 from League of Nations, *Review of World Trade*, 1927-9 p. 107 and 1927-30 from the 1938 edn, p. 80; 1930-50 from *Yearbook of International Trade Statistics*, 1950 and 1952 editions, UN, New York. 1921 onwards adjusted to a calendar year basis.

Austria: 1870-1913 from P. Bairoch, *Commerce extérieur et développement économique de l'Europe au XIXe siècle*, Mouton, Paris, 1976, p. 76. 1913-37 from A. Kausel, *Osterreichs Volkseinkommen 1913 bis 1963*, p. 4 (includes exports of services); 1937-50 from UN *Yearbook of International Trade Statistics*, 1959. The Austrian figures refer throughout to the present territory, whose 1913 exports were 47.77 per cent of those of actual 1913 Austria (see Kausel, *Osterreichs Volkseinkommen*, p. 25 and Maddison, 'Growth and Fluctuation', p. 56).

Belgium: 1831-70 from S. Capelle, 'Le Volume de commerce extérieure de la Belgique 1830-1913', *Bulletin de l'Institut de Recherches Economiques*, Louvain, 1938, p. 54; 1870-90 values from B. R. Mitchell, *European Historical Statistics 1750-1970*, Macmillan, London, 1975, p. 489, converted into dollars at 1913 exchange rates and deflated by dollar unit value index in Maddison, 'Growth and Fluctuation'; 1890-1950 volume from Maddison, 'Growth and Fluctuation'; 1939-45 roughly estimated from UN *Yearbook of International Trade Statistics* 1959 by deflating dollar value of exports by US export price index and adjusting to fit within the 1938-46 volume movement. From May 1922 to August 1940 and since May 1945 the statistics apply to the Belgium-Luxembourg customs area.

Canada: 1913-50 from M. C. Urquhart and K. A. H. Buckley, *Historical Statistics of Canada*, Cambridge, 1965, p. 178 (for 1913-25 adjusted to a calendar year basis); pp. 183-4 for the 1913-26 link and p. 179 for 1926-50.

Denmark: 1844-74 export values from S. A. Hansen, *Økonomisk Vaekst i Danmark*, vol. II, Akademisk Forlag, Copenhagen, 1974, pp. 254-7, divided by export price deflator, pp. 293-4. Hansen gives figures starting in 1818 but they are incomplete before 1844. Export values 1875-1950 from K. Bjerke and N. Ussing, *Studier over Danmarks Nationalprodukt 1870-1950*, Gads, Copenhagen, 1958. pp. 152-3 divided by export price index for those years in A. Olgaard, *Growth Productivity and Relative Prices*, Copenhagen, 1966, p. 242.

Finland: 1870-1949 from E. Pihkala, *Finland's Foreign Trade 1860-1917*, Bank of Finland, Helsinki, 1969, p. 63 and H. Oksanen and E. Pihkala, *Finland's Foreign Trade 1917-1949*, Bank of Finland, Helsinki, 1975, p. 39, *Studies in Finland's Economic Growth*, Bank of Finland, Helsinki, 1975.

France: 1715-87 from E. Levasseur, *Histoire du commerce de la France, première partie avant 1789*, Rousseau, Paris, 1911, p. 518, deflated by

60 per cent for price changes (see F. Crouzet, 'England and France in the Eighteenth Century: A Comparative Analysis of Two Economic Growths', in R. M. Hartwell (ed.), *The Causes of the Industrial Revolution in England*, Methuen, London, 1967, p. 146); 1800-10 from a chart in Levasseur, *Histoire du Commerce de la France*, vol. II (1912) (it was assumed that exports in 1800 were at the same level as in 1787); 1810-70 from M. Lévy-Leboyer, 'La Croissance économique en France au XIXe siècle', *Annales*, July-August 1968; 1913-50 from *Annuaire statistique de la France 1966 Resumé rétrospectif*, pp. 350, 360-1. The figures for 1913-18 were derived from a volume index of exports and imports combined, based on share of exports in total trade value.

Germany: 1836-1913 and 1926-7 from W. C. Hoffmann and associates, *Das Wachstum der deutschen Wirtschaft seit der Mitte des 19 Jahrhunderts*, Springer, Berlin, 1965, pp. 530-1. For 1914-18 the figures are estimates based on the assumption that exports in the first eight months of 1914 were the same as in 1913, and pro-rating Germany's total wartime exports in what seemed a plausible pattern. The figures on total wartime exports (12 billion gold marks) are from C. Bresciani-Turroni, *The Economics of Inflation*, Allen & Unwin, London, 1968, p. 85; 1919 was estimated relative to 1920 from information given by Bresciani-Turroni, op. cit., pp. 229 and 248; 1920-25 volume movement from *Statistik des Deutschen Reiches* vol. 329 I-*Der Auswärtige Handel Deutschlands im Jahre 1925*, p. 5; 1928-43 from *Statistisches Handbuch von Deutschland 1928-1944*, Länderrat des Amerikanischen Besatzungsgebiets, Munich, 1949, p. 395; 1944-50 derived from UN *Yearbooks of International Trade Statistics*, 1954 and 1959 eds; 1945-8 figures were assessed in dollars and deflated by US export price index. It should be noted that, prior to 1906, the free ports of Hamburg, Cuxhaven, Bremerhaven, and Geestemünde were not included in the German customs area.

Italy: 1870-1950 merchandise export receipts divided by export price index in G. Fua, *Lo Sviluppo Economico in Italia,* Angeli, Milan, 1975, vol. III, pp. 465-6 and 434-5.

Japan: 1870-3 from M. Baba and M. Tatemoto, 'Foreign Trade and Economic Growth in Japan: 1858-1937', in L. Klein and K. Ohkawa, *Economic Growth: The Japanese Experience since the Meiji Era*, Irwin, Homewood, Illinois, 1968, p. 167; 1873-1905 from K. Kojima, 'Japan's Foreign Trade and Economic Growth', *Annals of the Hitotsubashi Academy*, April 1958, pp. 166-7, whose figures exclude trade with colonies. Trade with colonies included by adjusting Kojima with trade ratios derived from *Historical Statistics of Japanese Economy*, Bank of Japan, 1962, pp. 89-90; 1905-50 from K. Ohkawa and H. Rosovsky, *Japanese Economic Growth*, Stanford, 1973, p. 302 (includes trade with colonies); 1945 derived from 1944-5 value movement shown by UN *Yearbook of International Trade Statistics*, divided by 1944-5 change in cost of living index.

Netherlands: 1720-1870, see note on world trade below. Until 1916 most Dutch commodity trade was expressed at 1845 'official' prices, but part was in current prices and part at 1871 prices. For 1870-1910 we have used estimates at current prices by H. C. Bos, 'Economic Growth of the Netherlands', paper presented at the IARIW meeting in Portoroz, 1959, and deflated by the Belgian export price index. For 1910-21 we have used the value figures deflated by the national income deflator (values being taken from Mitchell, *European Historical Statistics*). For 1870-1916 the figures refer to general trade including re-exports and the absolute values are reduced by two-thirds to eliminate these; 1921-50 export volume from *Zeventig Jaren Statistiek in Tijdreeksen*, the Hague, 1970, p. 92; 1940-5 roughly estimated from UN *Yearbook of International Trade Statistics*, 1959, by deflating dollar value of exports by US export price index.

Norway: 1870-1939 and 1946-50 from *National Accounts 1865-1960*, Central Bureau of Statistics, Oslo, 1970, pp. 356-9 (includes exports of services); 1940-5 from UN *Yearbook of International Trade Statistics*, 1959.

Sweden: 1870-1950 from O. Johansson, *The Gross Domestic Product of Sweden and its Composition 1861-1955*, Stockholm, 1967, pp. 140-1.

Switzerland: 1870-1900 from P. Bairoch, *Commerce extérieur et développement économique de l'Europe au XIXe siècle*, Mouton, Paris, 1976; 1939 onwards from UN *Yearbook of International Trade Statistics*. Between 1959 and 1960 there is a break in the series and it was assumed that Swiss export prices rose 1 per cent as in Germany that year.

United Kingdom: 1700-1800 derived from P. Deane and W. A. Cole, *British Economic Growth 1688-1959*, Cambridge, 1964, pp. 319-21; 1800-1913 from A. H. Imlah, *Economic Elements in the Pax Britannica*, Harvard, 1958, pp. 94-8; 1913-70 from *The British Economy: Key Statistics 1900-1970*, London and Cambridge Economic Service, London, p. 14.

United States: 1790-1860 from D. C. North, *The Economic Growth of the United States 1790-1860*, Prentice-Hall, Englewood Cliffs, NJ, 1961, pp. 221 and 241; 1860-78 estimated by converting the dollar value of exports into gold (the dollar was floating against gold until 1879) and then deflating by UK import price index. Gold price from G. F. Warren and F. A. Pearson, *Gold and Prices*, John Wiley, New York, 1935, p. 154; exports of US merchandise from *Historical Statistics of the U.S., Colonial Times to 1957*, US Dept of Commerce, p. 538, adjusted to a calendar year basis; UK import price index back to 1870 from A. Maddison, 'Growth and Fluctuation' and 1860-70 from A. H. Imlah, *Economic Elements in the Pax*

Britannica, Harvard, 1958, pp. 96-8; 1879-1950 from R. E. Lipsey, *Price and Quantity Trends in the Foreign Trade of the United States*, NBER, Princeton, 1963, Table A2.

ESTIMATES OF WORLD TRADE

There are several estimates of the volume of world trade. My estimates for 1870-1960 appeared in 'Growth and Fluctuation in the World Economy, 1870-1960', *Banca Nazionale del Lavoro Quarterly Review*, June 1962. Since then some new estimates for individual countries have become available as indicated in the country notes above, and I have revised my world series to take account of these for 1870-1950. For 1950 onwards I have used UN estimates adjusted to fit my definitions, i.e. to include trade of all countries, including the communist countries excluded by the UN, and to exclude reexports.

For earlier periods the data are a good deal weaker. The basic source for most estimates is M. G. Mulhall, *The Dictionary of Statistics*, Routledge, London, 1899 (4th edn), p. 128, who gives estimates of world trade (imports plus exports) at current prices back to 1720 with specification of the amounts for the main countries. Mulhall does not give sources, but his aggregate was used by eminent contemporaries of his such as G. Schmoller, *Grundiss der allgemeinen Volkswirtschaftslehre,* Duncker and Humblot, Leipzig, 1904, and O. P. Austin, 'A Century of International Commerce', *North American Review*, November 1900 (Schmoller being the doyen of German economic historians and Austin chief of the US Bureau of Statistics). For 1851 there are estimates by L. Levi, 'On Commercial Statistics and An Attempt at a Universal Commercial Code', *Journal of the Royal Staistical Society*, 1852, which are not too different from Mulhall. A major puzzle with Mulhall is his low estimate of Dutch trade. For 1720 he gives a figure of £13 million for British trade and only £4 million for Holland and Belgium combined, whereas Sir William Petty had estimated Dutch trade to be £21 million and British £10 million in his book *Political Arithmetick* published in 1689. Mulhall's low figure for Dutch trade may be due to exclusion of re-exports, which were about three-quarters of Dutch trade, but even so his estimate is too low, and the rapid growth in Dutch trade that Mulhall shows (a six-fold increase in value terms from 1720 to 1820) does not correspond at all with more recent findings. For an estimate of the volume of Dutch trade from 1624-5 to 1790, see Johan de Vries, *De Economische Achteruitgang der Republiek in de Achttiende Eeuw,* Amsterdam, 1959, p. 27, who shows a decline in trade volume of the Netherlands over the eighteenth century.

S. Kuznets uses Mulhall's estimates for 1720-1880 (deflated by the Rousseaux-Schumpeter-Gilboy price indices) in *Modern Economic Growth,*

TABLE F2

Volume of Exports, 1720-1860

(1913 = 100)

	Austria	Belgium	Denmark	France	Germany	Italy	Netherlands	Switzerland	UK	USA
1720				1.536[f]					0.386	
1760				n.a.			7.35		0.92	
1790				3.45[g]					1.19	0.64
1800				3.45					1.94	1.55
1810				3.45					2.53	1.65
1820	2.32			4.31		7.33	5.88	2.57	2.86	1.31
1830		2.19[a]		4.24					4.47	2.13
1840		4.00[b]	12.92[e]	6.51	4.3				7.38	4.08
1850		6.02[c]	13.59	10.56	5.9				13.07	4.07
1860		12.20[d]	11.60	19.55	9.8				22.68	9.61

[a] 1843.   [b] 1851.   [c] 1861.   [d] 1844.   [e] 1831.   [f] 1715.   [g] 1787.

Source: As described in country notes, except for Austria, Italy, and Switzerland 1820-70, which are derived from value figures of M. G. Mulhall, *The Dictionary of Statistics*, Routledge, London, 1899, p. 128, deflated by the Rousseaux wholesale price index for the UK (see B. R. Mitchell, *Abstract of British Historical Statistics*, Cambridge, 1962, pp. 471-2).

TABLE F3

Volume of Exports, Annual Data, 1870-1913[a]

(1913 = 100)

	Australia	Austria	Belgium	Canada	Denmark	Finland	France	Germany
1870		(23.1)	16.9	17.9	21.0	19.4	31.1	17.7
1871	16.5		21.0	18.4	19.8	22.4	31.6	20.3
1872	21.6		24.0	20.5	23.5	n.a.	40.5	18.7
1873	17.0		25.8	21.6	21.6	n.a.	42.3	17.7
1874	21.3		25.4	19.8	23.6	27.4	43.4	19.0
1875	20.9		25.8	18.6	25.3	24.6	47.3	20.8
1876	23.6		25.3	19.0	27.3	27.9	43.7	21.2
1877	23.5		26.3	19.2	29.2	29.9	42.3	23.9
1878	24.5		27.5	19.0	21.9	25.6	41.6	26.1
1879	23.3		30.0	20.6	32.7	28.4	41.2	24.9
1880	31.3		31.2	22.9	35.0	36.8	43.5	22.4
1881	25.4		33.7	24.4	31.6	30.6	45.0	23.0
1882	28.3		35.0	23.6	29.3	35.3	45.6	23.9
1883	32.0		36.1	22.0	33.0	32.8	46.5	25.0
1884	30.7		37.9	21.8	31.2	34.1	46.1	26.4
1885	29.4		35.2	22.4	29.2	33.6	45.8	25.9
1886	25.7		37.4	23.1	32.3	29.1	48.7	28.1
1887	31.0		38.9	23.0	35.2	29.1	50.7	29.4
1888	34.8		38.9	22.4	34.4	32.6	48.2	29.6
1889	35.2		45.2	22.8	36.5	35.1	53.8	28.3
1890	35.1		45.0	23.6	42.2	34.1	53.0	29.8
1891	56.9		48.1	25.5	44.6	37.3	54.6	29.7
1892	46.0		44.4	28.1	42.7	33.6	56.5	29.4
1893	59.0		44.5	29.2	42.8	40.8	50.0	30.9
1894	60.6		41.8	29.6	51.5	47.3	53.9	31.7
1895	63.6		43.3	31.7	52.7	48.8	58.4	35.8
1896	61.5		44.9	35.7	53.1	52.2	59.6	37.1
1897	55.7		48.6	40.3	51.4	53.0	61.5	38.4
1898	58.0		51.7	41.2	52.2	52.2	56.7	39.6
1899	60.3		54.7	44.0	58.4	53.5	63.5	42.2
1900	58.2		53.9	48.0	56.4	52.0	61.6	44.7
1901	59.4		51.8	50.8	56.3	51.7	65.5	45.2
1902	45.8		54.6	54.3	62.1	55.0	68.7	48.9
1903	43.1		59.2	53.5	69.6	57.5	66.5	52.3
1904	66.0		60.0	51.2	73.7	61.9	68.1	53.6
1905	63.5		62.8	55.0	74.5	67.4	72.2	58.2
1906	70.8		73.7	58.0	71.7	73.4	75.0	64.9
1907	81.3		74.4	56.3	78.6	68.2	80.5	66.3
1908	73.2		66.8	55.4	83.9	65.9	77.3	65.8
1909	82.2		76.4	61.0	80.8	69.4	82.3	68.7
1910	97.9		92.6	62.3	84.7	75.1	88.0	77.4
1911	100.2		97.3	66.2	93.5	81.3	84.9	83.5
1912	91.1		106.4	78.3	97.6	87.3	93.8	89.7
1913	100.0	100.0	100.0	100.0	100.0	100.0	100.0	100.0

[a] Figures refer to the customs territory of the year specified.

Volume of Exports, Annual Data, 1870-1913 [a]
(1913 = 100)

	Italy	Japan	Netherlands	Norway	Sweden	Switzerland	UK	USA
1870	38.7	3.0	24.5	26.1	26.7	(19.3)	31.1	13.0
1871	53.8	4.0		26.0	25.3		34.9	14.8
1872	52.2	4.0		31.0	26.7		36.2	15.0
1873	46.6	4.7		30.5	26.4		34.8	17.0
1874	41.1	4.8		30.3	26.0		34.6	17.8
1875	49.7	4.8		29.1	26.7		34.4	17.1
1876	59.5	6.6		31.6	30.3		33.5	19.6
1877	41.3	7.0		31.0	29.8		34.6	23.8
1878	47.2	7.7		29.8	29.4		34.8	28.7
1879	52.2	7.4		30.8	33.3		36.7	33.1
1880	51.7	6.9	31.8	34.9	34.4		41.2	35.0
1881	56.3	7.7		34.6	33.4		45.1	31.8
1882	54.7	10.0		35.1	36.5		45.6	28.4
1883	54.0	10.5		34.1	37.2		46.9	31.1
1884	55.1	9.4		36.1	37.9		47.3	30.5
1885	43.5	10.0		36.0	39.3		45.0	30.0
1886	49.4	12.4		36.9	37.7		46.9	33.1
1887	51.9	12.9		38.0	41.9		49.1	33.4
1888	46.1	17.8		41.3	45.1		52.2	30.7
1889	49.4	17.3		44.7	43.8		54.3	38.4
1890	43.2	13.2	44.7	45.6	45.4		55.1	40.4
1891	40.2	20.3		44.7	48.0		52.1	44.2
1892	47.1	20.3		45.8	46.8		50.2	45.8
1893	48.7	18.2		47.5	50.7		48.2	43.3
1894	55.1	22.2		45.0	50.6		50.3	46.5
1895	55.2	24.0		44.6	53.3		54.7	45.7
1896	55.0	21.3		47.1	57.1		57.7	56.4
1897	56.1	28.8		52.1	55.2		56.9	63.4
1898	59.1	27.2		48.3	51.4		56.5	73.2
1899	69.7	34.0		48.1	52.0		61.1	70.3
1900	64.4	29.3	55.6	49.4	54.0	63.3	58.6	72.8
1901	68.8	40.3		51.4	50.8		59.2	74.0
1902	74.2	40.9		56.1	56.2		62.8	66.9
1903	74.0	45.0		56.2	62.7		64.5	68.8
1904	77.7	48.4		59.1	59.9		65.9	67.0
1905	84.2	44.5		61.9	65.4		72.4	78.0
1906	89.4	57.6		66.8	69.5		77.8	80.5
1907	89.1	58.2		66.2	70.3		84.1	81.3
1908	79.2	56.7		68.9	67.6		77.4	78.4
1909	85.4	62.7		73.4	63.2		80.7	73.7
1910	91.7	74.3	89.1	78.2	78.0		88.0	73.1
1911	92.2	77.2	88.6	83.6	87.9		91.2	90.0
1912	95.0	89.4	100.9	89.5	96.3		96.3	101.1
1913	100.0	100.0	100.0	100.0	100.0	100.0	100.0	100.0

TABLE F4

Volume of Exports, Annual Data, 1913-50[a]

(*1913 = 100*)

	Australia	Austria	Belgium	Canada	Denmark	Finland	France	Germany
1914				100.3	123.7	68.2	71.3	(80.0)
1915				139.6	116.1	47.3	43.0	(50.0)
1916				188.5	117.8	48.8	45.0	(20.0)
1917				213.5	88.8	29.1	36.0	(20.0)
1918				154.8	39.9	11.4	28.0	(15.0)
1919				139.1	38.6	51.2	45.0	17.0
1920				118.5	77.9	77.6	86.0	36.7
1921	110.0			110.5	87.2	72.4	83.0	44.4
1922	110.4			143.0	96.6	102.7	86.0	61.3
1923	88.9			175.4	123.2	108.7	103.0	52.9
1924	89.5	75.6		174.1	142.5	124.9	119.0	50.8
1925	106.5	82.1	72.8	192.5	138.4	138.9	124.0	65.3
1926	112.3	76.7	76.4	194.0	147.1	142.4	134.0	72.4
1927	108.9	87.1	96.5	193.4	170.4	160.1	146.0	73.1
1928	112.9	91.7	107.8	221.1	179.3	155.7	148.0	82.5
1929	111.9	86.3	107.2	193.2	181.0	161.4	147.0	91.8
1930	118.1	77.3	92.8	172.7	200.0	140.9	132.0	87.0
1931	137.3	65.3	94.4	141.6	214.6	136.1	112.0	79.1
1932	147.6	48.4	73.5	131.3	217.4	142.2	86.0	54.6
1933	139.4	47.0	76.0	143.3	196.0	168.2	88.0	51.2
1934	138.7	48.2	78.5	164.6	182.8	186.0	91.0	45.8
1935	145.5	50.5	87.5	180.4	171.9	196.2	82.0	49.3
1936	139.4	52.2	97.9	221.1	175.5	218.0	78.0	54.4
1937	142.8	65.5	111.3	201.7	194.3	233.7	84.0	62.9
1938	153.8		102.4	192.0	184.8	201.5	91.0	57.0
1939	162.7		(103.0)	221.4	187.2	200.7	88.0	59.5
1940	153.1		(46.0)	255.2	158.8	62.3	40.0	38.5
1941	151.7		(19.0)	337.3	97.5	84.4	30.0	45.5
1942	140.7		(13.0)	464.2	78.4	85.9	45.0	46.3
1943	126.3		(20.0)	526.1	93.2	98.0	41.9	46.9
1944	131.1		(10.0)	549.6	95.1	68.0	25.5	31.1
1945	135.2		(5.0)	505.5	64.6	34.3	9.1	1.6
1946	150.3		39.1	312.6	120.5	94.9	36.4	4.1
1947	152.4	19.3	75.4	327.2	146.4	132.4	63.7	4.9
1948	156.5	35.7	92.9	332.2	138.4	145.9	74.6	9.4
1949	165.3	44.4	102.4	312.9	179.8	174.6	107.4	16.4
1950	158.7	66.6	111.8	311.0	239.5	199.5	149.2	34.8

[a] Figures refer to the customs territory of the year specified.

Volume of Exports, Annual Data, 1913-50[a]
(1913 = 100)

	Italy	Japan	Netherlands	Norway[b]	Sweden	Switzerland	UK	USA
1914	88.3	98.1	(81.3)	97.8	89.4		80.4	86.6
1915	89.2	130.1	(50.5)	103.7	137.8		56.8	135.7
1916	78.9	164.5	(35.0)	104.5	134.3		57.4	163.3
1917	42.5	194.6	(60.0)	70.4	76.1		44.6	142.2
1918	48.9	211.5	(23.8)	61.1	65.1		37.7	119.7
1919	75.1	168.3	(81.3)	67.1	66.5		54.7	146.6
1920	105.5	145.0	(87.4)	90.5	75.8		70.7	141.8
1921	70.7	128.3	83.0	76.0	59.1	62.6	49.3	113.4
1922	80.8	137.6	93.4	97.8	81.2	70.1	68.0	106.8
1923	93.7	117.6	103.7	104.5	79.7	74.4	74.7	108.2
1924	117.3	153.4	124.6	110.8	95.8	87.3	76.0	121.0
1925	127.4	183.6	134.9	121.8	106.0	89.7	74.7	128.0
1926	122.6	196.2	140.0	130.2	114.3	86.6	66.7	137.3
1927	116.1	218.5	160.8	140.8	136.3	98.2	77.3	147.8
1928	117.9	234.6	166.0	143.3	131.3	101.1	80.0	153.6
1929	122.7	257.9	171.2	167.1	156.1	100.7	81.3	158.2
1930	104.7	256.8	160.8	181.1	144.1	90.1	66.7	130.3
1931	98.3	265.8	150.4	159.4	117.4	77.1	50.7	105.9
1932	71.1	261.5	124.6	171.4	98.3	50.3	50.7	81.4
1933	65.3	346.0	114.1	180.6	110.6	52.6	52.0	82.6
1934	56.1	447.3	119.3	187.6	129.2	62.7	54.7	88.4
1935	49.3	525.0	119.3	194.1	131.7	62.4	60.0	93.1
1936	39.4	536.2	124.6	212.6	150.6	63.4	60.0	97.7
1937	73.9	642.5	150.4	233.2	158.1	70.1	65.3	125.7
1938	69.9	588.3	140.0	233.2	159.7	79.3	57.3	125.7
1939	81.7	526.5	129.7	243.0	176.1	77.8	53.3	131.5
1940	63.3	506.9	(78.8)	143.7	119.0	72.0	41.3	153.6
1941	75.8	549.5	(69.0)	104.5	109.8	70.5	28.0	182.7
1942	68.1	387.5	(53.5)	73.2	100.6	58.7	21.3	239.7
1943	67.4	345.4	(48.7)	73.2	93.9	49.9	16.0	350.3
1944	13.6	255.4	(36.7)	65.3	69.9	32.3	17.3	337.5
1945	4.4	30.9	(5.5)	41.8	108.4	45.5	26.7	229.3
1946	39.9	13.5	26.0	132.9	174.2	81.4	57.3	239.7
1947	73.2	32.7	57.0	179.5	200.6	93.3	62.7	320.0
1948	111.6	47.9	83.0	207.2	221.6	101.3	80.0	249.0
1949	115.7	98.4	124.6	225.1	225.6	101.3	88.0	254.9
1950	126.5	210.1	171.2	269.5	275.9	113.2	100.0	224.6

[b] Includes exports of services.

Table F5
Volume of Exports, Annual Data, 1950-79[a]
(1913 = 100)

	Australia	Austria	Belgium	Canada	Denmark	Finland	France	Germany
1950	158.7	66.6	111.8	311.0	239.5	199.5	149.2	34.8
1951	146.7	77.8	130.5	345.6	276.3	249.4	169.6	50.3
1952	158.7	72.1	118.0	380.1	257.9	216.1	149.2	54.1
1953	177.9	100.0	130.5	368.6	285.5	249.4	156.0	61.9
1954	177.5	122.2	142.8	357.1	313.2	282.6	176.4	73.4
1955	182.7	133.2	167.7	391.7	340.9	307.6	203.4	85.1
1956	204.4	160.9	180.1	426.2	350.0	307.6	183.2	100.6
1957	204.4	183.1	173.9	426.2	377.6	340.8	203.4	112.1
1958	206.8	177.6	180.1	426.2	405.3	324.2	210.2	119.7
1959	228.4	188.8	204.9	437.7	442.2	365.8	257.8	135.4
1960	240.5	216.5	223.6	460.8	469.7	432.3	298.4	154.7
1961	262.1	233.2	236.0	495.3	488.3	448.9	312.0	166.3
1962	276.5	244.2	260.8	518.3	525.0	482.1	318.8	170.2
1963	295.8	277.6	291.9	564.4	580.4	490.4	345.8	185.6
1964	317.4	294.1	329.2	668.1	626.4	523.7	366.2	208.8
1965	317.4	310.8	378.9	691.1	681.7	548.6	407.0	224.3
1966	336.6	333.0	397.5	783.2	690.8	590.2	434.0	259.1
1967	363.1	360.7	410.0	840.8	727.8	623.4	454.4	282.2
1968	387.1	416.3	478.2	979.1	801.5	689.9	508.6	324.8
1969	442.4	505.1	565.2	1,036.7	875.0	806.3	583.2	359.6
1970	502.6	555.0	621.1	1,151.8	921.2	831.3	678.2	386.6
1971	536.3	571.7	683.2	1,220.9	967.3	798.0	732.4	409.9
1972	577.1	638.3	751.6	1,347.6	1,041.0	914.4	834.2	444.7
1973	582.0	710.4	875.7	1,474.3	1,114.7	989.2	922.4	514.3
1974	546.4	777.0	875.7	1,405.2	1,188.4	980.9	1,010.5	579.9
1975	593.9	721.5	826.0	1,301.5	1,142.3	814.7	969.8	518.1
1976	653.3	836.9	941.6	1,457.7	1,188.0	953.2	1,066.8	575.1
1977	659.2	858.6	982.9	1,574.8	1,245.1	1,051.0	1,125.0	606.2
1978	647.3	945.2	1,024.2	1,744.0	1,313.6	1,124.3	1,192.9	632.1
1979	730.5	1,118.3	1,073.8	1,783.1	1,439.2	1,230.2	1,318.9	678.7

[a] Figures refer to the customs territory of the year specified.

Volume of Exports, Annual Data, 1950-79[a]
(*1913 = 100*)

	Italy	Japan	Netherlands	Norway	Sweden	Switzerland	UK	USA
1950	126.5	210.1	171.2	269.5	275.9	113.2	100.0	224.6
1951	139.1	252.1	194.0	301.8	286.2	139.0	98.7	285.9
1952	126.5	252.1	205.7	280.3	255.5	133.1	92.0	299.5
1953	139.1	294.1	239.7	280.3	286.2	147.0	94.7	306.3
1954	151.8	336.2	273.9	323.4	306.6	154.9	98.7	299.5
1955	177.1	462.2	296.8	334.2	327.0	170.8	100.7	299.5
1956	202.4	546.3	308.1	377.3	357.7	188.7	112.0	353.9
1957	240.4	630.3	319.6	377.3	398.5	202.6	114.7	381.1
1958	253.0	672.3	342.4	377.3	388.4	198.6	110.7	326.7
1959	303.6	798.3	388.0	431.2	418.9	222.4	114.7	326.7
1960	366.9	924.4	445.1	463.5	480.3	245.8	120.0	387.9
1961	442.7	1,008.5	456.5	495.9	500.7	257.0	124.0	387.9
1962	493.4	1,176.6	490.8	528.2	541.5	273.7	126.7	408.4
1963	518.6	1,302.6	525.1	582.1	592.6	290.5	133.3	435.6
1964	594.5	1,638.8	593.5	679.1	654.0	312.8	137.3	496.8
1965	733.7	2,101.0	650.5	711.5	684.7	346.4	144.0	496.8
1966	834.9	2,395.1	684.8	776.2	735.8	374.3	149.3	530.9
1967	898.1	2,479.2	741.9	819.3	766.3	407.8	148.0	551.3
1968	1,062.6	3,109.5	867.5	927.1	838.0	463.7	168.0	592.1
1969	1,189.1	3,655.7	1,004.4	1,024.1	929.9	525.1	186.7	558.1
1970	1,265.0	4,202.0	1,141.3	1,078.0	1,021.8	558.6	192.0	680.6
1971	1,353.5	5,042.4	1,278.2	1,088.8	1,052.5	575.4	209.3	673.8
1972	1,543.3	5,378.6	1,403.8	1,239.7	1,113.7	608.9	213.1	735.1
1973	1,619.2	5,672.7	1,632.1	1,369.1	1,297.7	676.0	241.9	912.0
1974	1,720.4	6,555.1	1,666.3	1,358.3	1,338.5	703.8	255.3	1,034.5
1975	1,707.7	6,765.2	1,609.3	1,401.4	1,195.5	648.0	253.5	966.5
1976	1,912.6	8,253.5	1,818.5	1,625.6	1,231.4	725.8	276.3	1,005.2
1977	2,032.2	8,997.7	1,786.3	1,569.6	1,195.5	810.0	301.7	1,005.2
1978	2,271.2	9,065.4	1,834.6	1,933.9	1,279.2	848.9	311.8	1,092.1
1979	2,442.0	8,794.8	1,995.5	2,046.0	1,381.1	868.3	319.4	1,214.5

Yale, 1966, pp. 306-8. More recently W. W. Rostow, *The World Economy*, Macmillan, London, 1978, pp. 663-9, has amended the Mulhall figures with better estimates for UK trade (although he includes re-exports), and discusses the problems of the deflator. Another estimate of world trade volume since 1700 can be found in P. Bairoch, *Commerce extérieur et développement économique de l'Europe au XIXe siècle*, Mouton, Paris, 1976, p. 15. Bairoch gives his sources for Europe in detail, but is cryptic about his world index.

For 1720 to 1870, I used the volume estimates for individual countries cited in the country notes above, i.e. France and the UK from 1720, the USA from 1820, Belgium from 1831 and Germany from 1840. For other countries, except the Netherlands for 1720-1820, I used the movements shown by Mulhall, deflated by the price indices cited by Rostow (i.e. Rousseaux-Schumpeter-Gilboy for 1720-1800, and Rousseaux for 1800-70). Individual countries were weighted by my estimates of their 1870 export position. For the Netherlands, it was assumed that exports were 25 per cent higher in 1720 than in 1820, the movement shown by de Vries, op. cit., over the eighteenth century.

My world volume index is seen in Table F6 (Rostow's estimates are shown for comparison).

TABLE F6
Volume of World Exports, 1720-1970
(1913 = 100)

	Maddison's world export volume index	Rostow's world trade volume index
1720	1.35	1.13
1820	3.23	3.10
1840	6.17	5.40
1870	25.00	23.80
1913	100.00	100.00
1950	151.50	
1970	588.10	

NOTES

INTRODUCTION

[1] See A. Maddison, *Economic Growth in the West,* Allen & Unwin, London; Norton, New York.

CHAPTER 1: Economic Epochs and Their Interpretation

[1] For a critical appraisal of these, see E. Hobsbawm, *Karl Marx: Pre-Capitalist Economic Formations,* Lawrence and Wishart, London, 1964. For a critique of non-Marxist growth 'stages', see B. F. Hoselitz (ed.), *Theories of Economic Growth,* Free Press, New York, 1960. W. W. Rostow, *The Stages of Economic Growth,* Cambridge, 1962, is discussed in Chapter 4 below.

[2] See E. H. Phelps Brown and S. V Hopkins "Seven Centuries of the Prices of Consumables, Compared with Builders' Wage-rates", *Economica,* November 1956, p. 32 for evidence of fluctuations in real wages for a limited group of workers in southern England from 1264 to 1954. These Phelps Brown fluctuations are sometimes cited as if they were likely to have been characteristic of living standard fluctuations for the economy as a whole, but they are much too big to make this even remotely probable.

[3] See S. Kuznets, *Population, Capital and Growth,* Heinemann, London, 1974, pp. 139 and 167 suggests a growth rate of 0.2 per cent a year for per capita income in Europe from 1500 to 1750. D. S. Landes, *The Unbound Prometheus,* Cambridge, 1969, p. 14, suggests that from the year 1000 to the eighteenth century European real income per head may have tripled. Both Kuznets and Landes assume faster growth than I do, but I think they may have attached too much weight to British experience, which was probably more favourable to growth than elsewhere. C. M. Cipolla, *Before the Industrial Revolution: European Society and Economy, 1000-1700,* Norton, New York, 1976 also suggests a slow but rising long run trend.

[4] T. R. Malthus, *First Essay on Population 1798,* Macmillan, London, 1966, p. 139.

[5] See P. Laslett, *The World We Have Lost,* Methuen, London, 1973, Chapters 4 and 5. Laslett also describes the work of the Cambridge Group for the History of Population and Social Structure, which has been strongly influenced by the work of Louis Henry of the Institut National d'Etudes Demographiques in Paris, and French historical demographers of the Annales school.

[6] See G. E. Barnett (ed.), *Two Tracts by Gregory King,* Johns Hopkins, Baltimore, 1936, p. 31.

[7] See E. Boserup, *The Conditions of Agricultural Growth,* Allen and Unwin, London, 1965, for a major contribution to anti-Malthusian analysis.

[8] See L. White, *Medieval Technology and Social Change,* Oxford, 1962; B. H. Slicher van Bath, *The Agrarian History of Western Europe AD 500-1850,* Edward Arnold, London, 1963.

[9] See E. Le Roy Ladurie, *Les Paysans de Languedoc,* Mouton, Paris, 1966.

[10] 'Les Masses profondes: la paysannerie', in F. Braudel and E. Larousse (eds), *Histoire économique et sociale de la France,* pt I, vol. 2, PUF, Paris, 1977.

[11] See 'L'Histoire immobile', *Le Territoire de l'historien,* vol. II, Gallimard, Paris, 1978, pp. 24-7.

[12] See also his brilliant reconstruction of thirteenth-century village life, *Montaillou,* Gallimard, Paris, 1978, which shows a well-fed population continuously infested by lice.

[13] See *Agrarkrisen und Agrarkonjunktur*, Parey, Hamburg, 1978, pp. 285-9.

[14] See F. P. Braudel and F. Spooner, 'Prices in Europe from 1450 to 1750', in E. E. Rich and C. H. Wilson (eds), *Cambridge Economic History of Europe*, Vol. IV, Cambridge, 1967, p. 429. This article also embraces the idea that European economic life has for several centuries been dominated by five types of cyclical rhythm (50-year Kondratieffs, 20-year hypercycles, 15-year Labrousse intercycles, 8-10-year Juglars, and 40-month Kitchins). Braudel here and elsewhere seems to have derived his eclectic ideas from Gaston Imbert, *Des mouvements à longue durée Kondratieff*, La Pensée Universitaire, Aix-en Provence, 1959, which presents both an exhaustive survey of various varieties of Kondratieff-Schumpeter-type views and assembles a good many long-term price series to carry back this type of analysis in time. Braudel is not alone in using these fancy schemas, but a note of skepticism is emerging among French historians. See the criticism of Simiand's monetarist price cycles in M. Morineau, 'La Conjoncture ou les cernes de la croissance', in Braudel and Larousse, op. cit. Morineau also discusses some of the problems of welding regional data into national estimates and even discusses problems of measuring GNP for 1500-1750.

[15] See. F. Braudel, *Capitalism and Material Life 1400-1800*, Harper and Row, New York, 1973, p. x, and F. C. Spooner, *The International Economy and Monetary Movements in France, 1493-1725*, Harvard, 1972.

[16] There has been widespread disagreement among historians on the beginnings of capitalism in the context of stage theories of growth, which are more concerned with forms of property or ideology than I am. Sombart dates the beginning of this 'early capitalism to the mid-fifteenth century. Weber, whose concern with motivating forces and the role of the puritan ethic is similar to Sombart's emphasis on the bourgeois spirit and entrepreneurship, also gave capitalism an early birthday. Those who espouse the monetarist theory tend to place its beginnings in the sixteenth century, when the flow of American silver to Spain was at its peak. Dobb dated capitalism back to the latter half of the sixteenth century, but his fellow Marxists have since engaged in a long and inconclusive argument about the nature and timing of the transition from feudalism to capitalism, with Hobsbawm claiming that the seventeenth century was 'the last phase of the general transition from a feudal to a capitalist economy'. See W. Sombart, *Der moderne Kapitalismus*, Duncker and Humblot, Munich, 1928, vol. II (1), p. 14, and vol. II (1), p. xi and xii; M. Weber, *The Protestant Ethic and the Spirit of Capitalism*, Allen and Unwin, London, 1971; M. Dobb, *Studies in the Development of Capitalism*, Routledge & Kegan Paul, London, 1946, p. 18; R. Hilton, (ed.), *The Transition from Feudalism to Capitalism*, Verso, London, 1978; and E. J. Hobsbawm, 'The crisis of the Seventeenth Century', in T. Ashton, *Crisis in Europe 1560-1660*, Routledge & Kegan Paul, London, 1965.

[17] J. A. Schumpeter's posthumous *History of Economic Analysis*, Oxford, 1954, is an encyclopaedic and subtle review of economic literature revealing his great detachment and generosity as a critic. Marx also left a much less polished manuscript survey, *Theories of Surplus Value* (3 vols), Lawrence and Wishart, London, 1969, written in the opposite style with vituperative fervour.

[18] See P. Sraffa and M. H. Dobb, *The Works and Correspondence of David Ricardo*, (10 vols), Cambridge, 1951. The most succinct presentation of Ricardo's schema is in his 'Essay on Profits', vol. iv, pp. 9-41.

[19] Marx's vision of 'the laws of motion' of the capitalist epoch is fairly fully stated in Chapters 22-4 of vol. I of *Capital*. His cycle theory and analysis of different types of unemployment is contained in Sections 3 and 4 of Chapter 23. For a critical assessment and reader's guide, see M. Blaug, *Economic Theory in Retrospect*, Heinemann, London, 1968, Chapter 7. See also M. Dobb, *Political Economy*

and Capitalism, Routledge & Kegan Paul, London, 1937, Chapter V. My presentation of Marx is rather simplified and presents elements with which I am largely in agreement, ignoring the labour theory of value and the division of capital into circulating and fixed. The problem in interpreting Marx is that his major published work on capitalist development was supplemented after his death by 4,500 pages of his preparatory or unfinished work on the same topic.

[20] Here is what he said about the possibility of diminishing returns on land: 'Technological progress effectively turned the tables on any such tendency, and it is one of the safest predictions that in the calculable future we shall live in an *embarras de richesse* of both foodstuffs and raw materials, giving all the rein to expansion of total output that we shall know what to do with. This applies to mineral resources as well.' See J. A. Schumpeter, *Capitalism, Socialism, and Democracy,* Allen and Unwin, London, 1943, p. 116.

[21] See J. Schumpeter, *Imperialism, Social Classes* (ed. B. Hoselitz), Meridian, New York, 1951.

[22] See J. A. Schumpeter, *The Theory of Economic Development*, Oxford University Press, New York, 1961, p. 116.

[23] The above statement of Schumpeter's views is from *The Theory of Economic Development*, which he wrote before the First World War. In later life, he expressed great detachment about the fate of capitalism and stressed that he had not intended to glorify entrepreneurs. In a note to the English language edition of his book, which appeared in 1934, he even suggested that their economic function could not be distinguished from that of robbers (p. 90). In a later work (see *Business Cycles*, 1939), he described how the entrepreneurial function can be institutionalized in large corporations and also put forward a much more complex cycle theory.

[24] See W. E. G. Salter, *Productivity and Technical Change,* Cambridge, 1960.

[25] See T. W. Schultz, 'Investment in Human Capital', *American Economic Review*, March 1961.

[26] See A. Maddison, 'What is Education For?'', *Lloyds Bank Review,* April 1974, for an attempt to classify the different objectives of education and review the critique of the human capital school.

[27] See E. F. Denison and J. P. Poullier, *Why Growth Rates Differ*, Brookings Institution, Washington, 1967, which deals with the situation in nine advanced capitalist countries from 1950 to 1962. He has also written three studies on US growth from 1929 to 1976, of which the latest is *Accounting for Slower Economic Growth,* Brookings Institution, Washington, 1979 (though this deals only with the private sector of the economy), and (with W. K. Chung) *How Japan's Economy Grew So Fast,* Brookings Institution, Washington, 1976. The 1967 study is the one to which I refer here.

[28] See A. Maddison, 'Explaining Economic Growth', *Banca Nazionale del Lavoro Quarterly Review,* September 1972, which also includes a brief survey of the postwar growth literature.

[29] Some of the shortcomings of the total factor productivity approach in long-term historical analysis are clear in the work of McCloskey, who compares UK and US economic performance in the nineteenth century on this basis. See footnote 19 in Chapter 2 below.

[30] See R. Summers, I. B. Kravis, and A. Heston, 'International Comparison of Real Product and Its Composition: 1950-1977', *Review of Income and Wealth*, March 1980.

CHAPTER 2: **Changes in Economic Leadership, 1700-1980**

[1] In defining productivity leadership, I have ignored the special case of Australia, whose impressive achievements before the First World War were due largely to natural resource advantages rather than to technical achievements and the stock of man-made capital. For similar reasons, I call the US a technical leader in 1978 even though its apparent productivity level was lower than that of Kuwait.

[2] See J. W. de Zeeuw, 'Peat and the Dutch Golden Age. The Historical Meaning of Energy-Attainability', *AAG Bijdragen,* 21, Wageningen, 1978.

[3] Gregory King estimated the Dutch savings rate to have been over 11 per cent of national income in 1688 compared with 4 per cent in England and France.

[4] See 'The Crisis of the Seventeenth Century', in T. Ashton, *Crisis in Europe 1560-1660*, Routledge & Kegan Paul, London, 1965, p. 42.

[5] See C. Cipolla, *Before the Industrial Revolution,* Norton, New York, 1976, pp. 281-3, for city sizes.

[6] See Jan de Vries, 'On the Modernity of the Dutch Republic', *Journal of Economic History,* 1973, pp. 191-202, and *The Dutch Rural Economy in the Golden Age,* Yale, 1974.

[7] See D. S. Landes, *The Unbound Prometheus,* Cambridge, 1969, pp. 15-39, for an excellent analysis of the influence of attitudes to science and technology on capitalist development.

[8] See Jan de Vries, 'Barges and Capitalism. Passenger Transportation in the Dutch Economy, 1632-1839', *AAG Bijdragen,* 21, Wageningen, 1978.

[9] For eighteenth-century Dutch experience see the excellent survey by Johan de Vries, *De Economische Achteruitgang der Republiek in de Achttiende Eeuw,* Leiden, 1968.

[10] See J. C. Riley, *International Government Finance and the Amsterdam Capital Market 1740-1815,* Cambridge, 1980, pp. 16 and 84, who estimates 575 million guilders for loans to foreign governments, to which other loans to the private sector and direct investment (e.g. of the Dutch East India Company) should be added. Other authors have suggested higher investments, but Riley thinks they exaggerate. The estimate of national income is that of Metelerkamp for 1792; see H. C. Bos, 'Economic Growth in the Netherlands', IARIW, Portoroz, 1959, mimeographed.

[11] See J. J. McCusker, *Money and Exchange in Europe and America 1600-1775,* Macmillan, London, 1978, pp. 59-60. This source also shows interest rates.

[12] See Jan de Vries, *The Economy of Europe in an Age of Crisis 1600-1750,* Cambridge, 1976, pp. 251-2.

[13] The de Vries type of argument has also been used by M. Elvin, *The Pattern of the Chinese Past,* Eyre Methuen, London, 1973, in a somewhat more developed form to explain the technical stagnation of China after having made such a brilliant and precocious start. Elvin calls it a 'high level equilibrium trap'. I like the phrase but here again the argument is not fully articulated.

[14] This is very clear in agriculture. The main changes in British practice, sometimes called the agricultural revolution, were largely an adoption of already established Dutch techniques. This included (1) development of new root crops for animal fodder such as turnips, clover, and luzerne, which increased soil fertility and permitted greater intensity of land use; (2) improvements in livestock breeding, selection, and output; (3) greater use of additives to increase soil fertility, including animal manure, marl (clay) on thin soils, and lime on muddy soils. There was also a significant increase in the use of new high-calorie crops—maize and potatoes—originating in the New World. See J. D. Chambers and G. E. Mingay, *The Agricultural Revolution 1750-1880*, Batsford, London 1966; and P. Bairoch, 'Agriculture and the Industrial Revolution 1700-1914', *Fontana Economic History of Europe,* vol. 3, 1973, for an account of these changes. Some of these technical developments,

which permitted an increase in agricultural output per person, also led to increased labour input per person, with less land lying fallow and harder work in hitherto slack seasons, which was necessary with increased livestock holdings. Hence labour productivity did not increase as much as per capita income. See J. D. Chambers, 'Enclosure and the Labour Supply', *Economic History Review*, 1952/3, pp. 319-43; and C. P. Timmer, 'The Turnip, The New Husbandry and the English Agricultural Revolution', *Quarterly Journal of Economics*, 1969, p. 392, who suggest that the changes in British agriculture at this time increased land rather than labour productivity.

[15] In 1820 the new cotton textiles and the iron industry represented less than 12 per cent of British GDP. See P. Deane, *The First Industrial Revolution*, Cambridge, 1965, pp. 88 and 108, who gives figures for Great Britain which I have adjusted to a UK basis.

[16] See A. E. Musson and E. Robinson, *Science and Technology in the Industrial Revolution*, Manchester, 1969.

[17] Between 1785 and 1820 French cotton consumption rose from 4,000 to 19,000 tons, and UK consumption from 8,200 to 54,000; i.e. per capita growth rates of 4.2 per cent a year in both cases. In both years French per capita consumption was about a quarter of that in the UK. See B. R. Mitchell, *European Historical Statistics 1750-1970*, Macmillan, London, 1975, pp. 427-8.

[18] In 1914 UK foreign assets amounted to £3.8 billion. See H. Feis, *Europe The World's Banker 1870-1914,* Kelley, New York, 1961, and GDP at market prices to £2.5 billion.

[19] There is a good deal of literature concerning UK rivalry with Germany before the First World War, because Germany had a bigger population and army. But German overall productivity was a good deal below that in the UK and this was probably true of agriculture, industry, and services taken separately. D. Landes, *The Unbound Prometheus*, Cambridge, 1969, and W. A. Lewis, *Growth and Fluctuations 1870-1913*, Allen & Unwin, London, 1978, are two of many authors stressing the German rivalry. D. N. McCloskey, *Economic Maturity and Entrepreneurial Decline, British Iron and Steel, 1870-1913*, Harvard, 1973, goes to the other extreme by virtually denying that the UK was overtaken by the USA. He has been trapped into this position by measuring performance in terms of total factor productivity, which tends to conceal the fact that a major reason why US labour productivity grew faster than that of the UK was that its investment effort was bigger.

[20] The only comprehensive comparison of productivity levels by sector in the UK and USA is D. Paige and G. Bombach, *A Comparison of National Output and Productivity of the United Kingdom and the United States*, OEEC, Paris, 1959, p. 21, for 1950. These can be backcast to 1890 using C. H. Feinstein op. cit., and J. W. Kendrick, op. cit. This procedure shows UK 1890 output per worker to be 63 per cent of US in agriculture, 54 per cent in industry (including construction) and 133 per cent of the USA in services. These levels are roughly confirmed in other studies. D. N. McCloskey (ed.), *Essays in a Mature Economy: Britain After 1840*, Methuen, London, 1971, pp. 291-5, shows labour productivity in British coal mining in 1907 at about half the US 1909 level; E. H. Phelps Brown, *A Century of Pay*, Macmillan, London, 1968, p. 59, cites further evidence for eight industries for 1907-9, with UK output per man averaging 52 per cent of that in the USA. For agriculture P. Bairoch shows a US lead in output per male worker of about 30 per cent in 1890; see P. Bairoch, 'Niveau de développement économique de 1810 à 1910', *Annales: Economies sociétés civilisations*, November-December 1965.

[21] US foreign assets (excluding exchange reserves) amounted to $329 billion in

1976; see *Survey of Current Business*, October 1977, p. 23. Its GDP at market prices in that year was $1,696 billion.

[22] See R. R. Nelson, M. J. Peck, and E. D. Kalachek, *Technology, Economic Growth and Public Policy*, Brookings Institution, Washington, 1967; and Z. Griliches, 'R and D and the Productivity Slowdown', *American Economic Review*, May 1980, pp. 343-7.

[23] This point is taken up again in Chapters 3 and 5.

CHAPTER 3: **Long-term Characteristics of Capitalist Development**

[1] Earlier writers who have stressed the existence of a turning point at this period are J. A. Schumpeter, A. Spiethoff, and M. von Tugan-Baranowsky. The latter was the first to date capitalist dynamics from the second quarter of the nineteenth century; see his *Studien zur Theorie und Geschichte der Handelskrisen in England*, Jena, 1901, p. 41. Spiethoff endorsed this view in 1923: 'Jedenfalls scheint mir erst mit den 1820er Jahren der recht eigentlich kapitalistische Kreislauf der Wechsellagen zu beginnen', *Handwörterbuch der Staatswissenschaften*, Jena, 1923, p. 47; and Schumpeter also adopted it in his *Business Cycles*, vol. I, McGraw-Hill, New York, 1939, p. 254.

[2] See W. W. Rostow, *The Stages of Economic Growth*, Cambridge, 1962, p. 38, and the critique of Rostow's stages in W. W. Rostow (ed.), *The Economics of Take-Off into Sustained Growth*, Macmillan, London, 1965.

[3] See A. Gerschenkron, *Economic Backwardness in Historical Perspective*, Praeger, New York, 1965, pp. 12-16. Recently Gerschenkron's specific characterizations of backwardness have been challenged even for the Russian case; see P. R. Gregory, 'Russian Living Standards During the Industrialization Era, 1885-1913', *Review of Income and Wealth*, March 1980.

[4] I also feel that the presently available estimates probably understate Italian growth rates in the nineteenth century.

[5] See Y. Hayami and V. W. Ruttan, *Agricultural Development: An International Perspective*, Johns Hopkins, Baltimore, 1971, for an analysis of the response of technology to different resource/population ratios in Japan and the USA.

[6] See W. S. Jevons, *The Coal Question*, Macmillan, London, 1865.

[7] D. H. Meadows *et al.*, *The Limits to Growth*, Universe, New York, 1972.

[8] The development of opinion on hours is described in E. J. Hobsbawm, 'Custom, Wages and Work—Load in Nineteenth Century Industry', *Labouring Men*, Doubleday, New York, 1967, and the evolution of hours in M. A. Bienefeld, *Working Hours in British Industry: An Economic History*, Weidenfeld & Nicolson, London, 1972. For German working hours, see W. H. Schröder, 'Die Entwicklung der Arbeitszeit im sekundären Sektor in Deutschland 1871-1913', *Technikgeschichte*, no. 3, 1980, p. 267, who quotes annual figures for Nuremberg industry for 1811-1913 showing a rise in hours from 61.1 in 1821 to a peak of 66.5 in 1870.

[9] The smoothness of labour input in the graphs is due partly to the fact that the pre-1950 data are not annual but refer only to benchmark years. The capital stock data are annual.

[10] The continuing role of small inventors has been stressed by J. Jewkes, D. Sawers, and R. Stillerman, *The Sources of Invention*, St Martins Press, New York, 1958, who found that over half of 61 significant twentieth-century inventions were produced by individual rather than company research. The primordial role of large corporations was asserted by J. A. Schumpeter, *Business Cycles*, McGraw-Hill, New York, 1939, p. 1044: 'economic "progress" in this country is largely the result of work done within a number of concerns at no time much greater than 300 or 400'.

[11] See *Historical Statistics of the United States, Colonial Times to 1970*, US Dept of Commerce, pt 2, 1975, pp. 957-8.

[12] See S. Kuznets, *Secular Movements in Production and Prices*, Houghton Mifflin, Boston, 1930, and A. F. Burns, *Production Trends in the United States since 1870*, NBER, New York, 1934.

[13] See OECD, *Gaps in Technology: Analytical Report*, Paris, 1970, pp. 222-5, for an illustration of the point and references to the literature.

[14] See S. Kuznets, *Economic Change*, Norton, New York, 1953, p. 281. He made the same point earlier in *Secular Movements in Production and Prices*, op. cit., p. 11 where he quotes Julius Wolf's 'laws of retardation of progress'.

[15] Cited by C. Wilson in *Cambridge Economic History of Europe*, vol. IV, 1967, p. 536.

[16] See F. List, *The National System of Political Economy*, Kelley, New York, 1966 (first published in 1841).

[17] See also A. Maddison, 'Economic Growth and Structural Change in the Advanced Countries', in I. Leveson and J. W. Wheeler, *Western Economies in Transition*, Croom Helm, London, 1980.

CHAPTER 4 : Phases of Development Within the Capitalist Epoch

[1] See M. Bronfenbrenner (ed.), *Is the Business Cycle Obsolete?*, John Wiley, New York, 1969, and the comments of R. M. Solow, *Economic History Review*, December 1970: 'The old notion of a fairly regular self-sustaining "business cycle" is not very interesting any more. Today's graduate students have never heard of Schumpeter's apparatus of Kondratieffs, Juglars, and Kitchins, and they would find it quaint if they had.'

[2] See C. Juglar, *Des crises commerciales et de leur retour périodique en France, en Angleterre et aux Etats Unis*, Kelley (reprint), New York, 1967, p. 256.

[3] See M. von Tugan-Baranowsky, *Studien zur Theorie und Geschichte der Handelskrisen in England*, Fischer, Jena, 1901, which developes under-consumptionist explanations of the business cycle.

[4] See W. L. Thorp, *Business Annals*, NBER, New York, 1926; A. F. Burns and W. C. Mitchell, *Measuring Business Cycles*, NBER, New York, 1947, pp. 78-9. See also W. C. Mitchell, *Business Cycles: The Problem and Its Setting*, NBER, New York, 1930, for an excellent history of cyclical analysis.

[5] See Burns and Mitchell, op. cit., p. 270, who state the reasons for not eliminating trend, with which I entirely agree: 'cyclical fluctuations are so closely interwoven with these secular changes in economic life that important clues to the understanding of the former may be lost by mechanically eliminating the latter. It is primarily for this reason that we take as our basic unit of analysis a business cycle that includes that portion of secular trend falling within its boundaries.'

[6] In the period 1889-1978, the NBER recorded twenty-one reference cycles, the industrial production index showed fifteen recessions, and GDP thirteen. The average amplitude of GDP recessions was a 6.5 per cent fall, and of industrial production, 13.3 per cent. Before 1889 the GDP index for the USA contains too heavy an element of interpolation to be used for cyclical analysis.

[7] Estimates are available for Denmark and France for 1820-70, and UK for 1830-70. During these periods these countries showed maximum peak-trough GDP falls of 5.6, 7.6, and 7.0 per cent respectively, i.e., an average of 6.7 per cent.

[8] See N. D. Kondratieff, 'Die langen Wellen der Konjunktur', *Archiv für Sozialwissenschaft und Sozialpolitik*, December 1926, pp. 573-609.

[9] The most sophisticated discussion of the Kondratieff wave in prices for the 1870-1913 period is contained in W. A. Lewis, *Growth and Fluctuations 1870-1913*, Allen & Unwin, London, 1978, which examines whether prices influenced output movements or output influenced prices. Lewis also discusses the role of gold pro-

duction. His conclusion is that the global price movement in this period was most strongly influenced by US agricultural production. Although Lewis uses personalized nomenclature for various cycles and waves, as Schumpeter also did, he does not in fact endorse the idea of Kondratieff waves as a non-monetary phenomenon on an international scale.

[10] It is rather odd that Kondratieff eliminated the population component in which the Kuznetsians have found the best evidence for their own long-wave analysis.

[11] See Kondratieff, op. cit., pp. 586 (graphs) and 607-9 for the data and trend formulae. Kondratieff's graph for coal should be compared with the minor ripples shown in that of S. S. Kuznets, *Secular Movements in Production and Prices*, Houghton Mifflin, Boston, 1930, p. 124, which shows proportionate deviations from a trend calculated from a different formula. In fact, the end-points in Kondratieff's UK coal graph are wrongly drawn. They are accurately represented in the abridged English translation by Wolfgang Stolper 'Long Waves in Economic Life', *Lloyds Bank Review,* July 1978. This recent reprint contains an error in its graph 3, where the long waves in UK cotton textile workers wages are overstated by a factor of 10, because the scale is incorrect.

[12] See G. Garvy, 'Kondratieff's Theory of Long Cycles', *Review of Economic Statistics,* November 1943, for an excellent review of Kondratieff's work and account of his Soviet critics.

[13] It is sometimes suggested that Kondratieff's approach was no advance on ideas put forward by van Gelderen under the pseudonym J. Fedder 'Springvloed', *De Nieuwe Tijd*, Fortuyn, Amsterdam 1913. In fact, he may not have proved much more than van Gelderen—i.e., that there are long swings in the general price level— but in terms of analytic framework and statistical technique, what Kondratieff offered was distinctly novel.

[14] See S. S. Kuznets, *Secular Movements in Production and Prices*, Kelley (reprint), New York, 1967.

[15] Kuznets presented twenty-three indicators for the USA, of which sixteen were commodities with both price and quantity data and six were financial indicators (including the general price index). For the UK he had nine indicators, France and Germany eight each, Belgium five, Canada and Japan two each, Australia and Argentina one each.

[16] See Burns and Mitchell, op cit., p. 428: 'Kuznets did not draw up a list of dates showing the peaks and troughs of his "secondary secular variations". In attempting to determine such a chronology from his American series, we found their turning points so widely dispersed that we could have little confidence in any list we ourselves might extract.'

[17] See S. Kuznets, *Economic Development and Cultural Change*, October 1956, p. 50. This article was rewritten and published as Chapter 1 of *Economic Growth of Nations*, Harvard, 1971, where Kuznets dropped his aggregate chronology.

[18] 'Long Swings in Population Growth and Related Economic Variables', reprinted in S. Kuznets, *Economic Growth and Structure*, Heinemann, London, 1965. See also S. Kuznets, *Capital in the American Economy,* Princeton, 1961, Chapters 2, 7, 8, and 9.

[19] The others include B. Thomas, *Migration and Economic Growth,* Cambridge, 1954; J. G. Williamson, *American Growth and The Balance of Payments: A Study of the Long Swing,* Duke Up, Chapel Hill, MC, 1964; R. A. Easterlin, *Population, Labor Force, and Long Swings in Economic Growth,* NBER, New York, 1968.

[20] See *Historical and Comparative Rates of Production, Productivity and Prices,* Part 2 of *Hearings on Employment, Growth, and Price Levels,* Joint Economic Committee, US Congress, April 1959, pp.411-66; 'The Nature and Significance of Kuznets' Cycles', *Economic Development and Cultural Change,* April 1961; and 'The Passing of the Kuznets' Cycle', *Economica,* November 1968.

[21] See J. Kitchin, 'Cycles and Trends in Economic Factors', *Review of Economic Statistics,* January 1923, pp. 10-16.

[22] Page references are to J. A. Schumpeter, *Business Cycles,* Mc Graw-Hill, New York, 1939.

[23] See J. A. Schumpeter, *Capitalism, Socialism and Democracy,* Allen & Unwin, London, 1943, p. 64.

[24] In fact, Schumpeter was not too explicit on his chronology, which we owe to Kuznet's exegesis after consultation with Schumpeter; see S. Kuznets, 'Schumpeter's Business Cycles', *American Economic Review,* June 1940, for a highly sceptical assessment.

[25] See J. J. van Duin, *De Lange Golf in de Economie,* van Gorcum, Assen, 1979, who is an eclectic revivalist, rather cavalier with the few empirical facts he presents (e.g., p. 7, where he gets the Dutch growth rate wrong); or J. W. Forrester, 'Growth Cycles', *De Economist,* 1977, pp. 525-43, who produces long waves with no data. There is an excellent series of sceptical essays on recent revivalist writings in W. H. Schröder and R. Spree (eds), *Historische Konjunkturforschung,* KlettCotta, Stuttgart, 1981.

[26] See W. W. Rostow, 'Kondratieff, Schumpeter and Kuznets: Trend Periods Revisited', *Journal of Economic History,* December 1975, which contains the essentials of the approach in his *The World Economy,* Macmillan, London, 1978. See E. Mandel, *Late Capitalism,* New Left Books, London, 1975. In addition to these two authors, there are elements of originality in G. Mensch, *Das technologische Patt,* Frankfurt, 1975, who has a Schumpeterian type approach with a detailed catalogue of different types of innovation. He considers that the clustering of innovations determines the tempo of capitalist performance, and that the 1970s slowdown is due to a shortage of exploitable innovations. Mensch has some interesting ideas about lags in application of inventions, but lapses frequently into apocalyptic sermonizing. He presents almost no evidence on the variations in the pace of macroeconomic performance which he is presumably trying to explain, and nowhere makes the leader-follower dichotomy, which is fundamental in analysis of the diffusion of innovation.

[27] Mandel cites several examples of this type of Marxist revisionism, of which the best example in my view is John Strachey, *Contemporary Capitalism,* Gollancz, London, 1956.

[28] My reaction is in fact quite the reverse of K. Eklund, 'Long Waves in the Development of Capitalism', *Kyklos,* no. 3, 1980, who reviews Mandel's theory unfavourably, but incredibly enough agrees with what Mandel says about the conventional wisdom of economic historians and quotes his tables as evidence!

[29] See S. Kuznets in W. W. Rostow (ed.), *The Economics of Take-Off into Sustained Growth,* Macmillan, London, 1963.

CHAPTER 5 : Phases of Productivity Growth

[1] The underlying opportunities for productivity growth were better in the 1913-50 period because the productivity leader was then the USA, whereas in the first half of the 1870-1913 period it had been the UK, whose performance as a leader was less dynamic than that of the USA (as noted in Chapter 2 above). This improvement in opportunities for followers offset some of the disadvantages brought by two world wars. Here, as in Chapter 2, I have ignored the special case of Australia in defining productivity leadership (see footnote 1 of Chapter 2).

[2] See A. Maddison, *Economic Growth in the West,* Allen & Unwin, London, 1964, pp. 48-56, for a further elaboration of the role of demand.

[3] See E. F. Denison, *Accounting for Slower Economic Growth,* Brookings

Institution, Washington, 1979, pp. 138-42; R. H. Rasche and J. A. Tatom, *Federal Reserve Bank of St Louis Review,* June 1977; and J. A. Tatom, *Federal Reserve Bank of St Louis Review,* January 1981.

[4] See L. Rostas, *Comparative Productivity in British and American Industry,* Cambridge, 1948, pp. 28 and 38; A. Maddison, Productivity in Canada, the United Kingdom and the United States', *Oxford Economic Papers,* October 1952 p. 238; and E. C. West, *Canada-U.S. Price and Productivity Differences in Manufacturing Industries, 1963,* Economic Council of Canada, Ottawa, 1971. The West comparisons need adjustment for hours worked which were, on average, 4.8 per cent higher in Canada in 1963.

[5] See D. Paige and G. Bombach, *A Comparison of National Output and Productivity,* OEEC, Paris, 1959, pp. 21 and 64. US output per worker-year- ranged from six times that of the UK in production of fuels to an 11 per cent lead in shipbuilding. US hours per worker were about 8 per cent shorter than those in the UK at that time.

[6] K. Yukizawa, 'Relative Productivity of Labour in American and Japanese Industry and its Change, 1958-1972', in S. Tsuru, ed., *Growth and Resource Problems Related to Japan,* Asahi, Tokyo, 1978.

[7] See also the contribution of B. Klotz, R. Madoo, and R. Hansen to J. W. Kendrick and B. N. Vaccara, *New Developments in Productivity Measurement and Analysis,* Chicago, 1980, p. 243. This processes the results of the 1967 BLS survey for 102 four-digit industries, and finds that: 'productivity in the typical top quartile group of plants is about 65 per cent greater than the industry average and 200 per cent greater than the average of low quartile establishments'.

[8] See E. Lundberg, 'Productivity and Structural Change—A Policy Issue in Sweden', *Economic Journal,* March 1972, p. 476.

[9] Sometimes, the interfirm productivity spreads are interpreted as if they simply reflected efficiency differences. This is sometimes implied in the productivity team reports such as those cited in H. Leibenstein, 'Allocative Efficiency vs. "X-Efficiency"', *American Economic Review,* June 1966, p. 400.

[10] Schumpeter, in his analysis of business cycles, suggested that innovations come in waves which are the main cause of irregularity in the pace of advance of best-practice productivity. Given the large size and diversity of the US economy and the incremental nature of much innovation, it seems to me that irregularity in the pace of advance is likely to be due to a variety of factors that make the rhythm of investment irregular (variations in the pace of potential technical advance being only one of them). Fogel and the modern cliometricians have done a great deal to de-dramatize the impact of even such a major innovation as the railway. 'No single innovation was vital for economic growth during the nineteenth century... Economic growth was a consequence of knowledge acquired in the course of the scientific revolution in the seventeenth, eighteenth and nineteenth centuries. This knowledge provided the basis for a multiplicity of innovations that was applied to a broad spectrum of economic processes... This view makes growth the consequence not of one or a few lucky discoveries but of a broad supply of opportunity created by the body of knowledge accumulated over all preceding centuries': R. W. Fogel, *Railroads and American Economic Growth*, Johns Hopkins, Baltimore, 1964, pp. 234-6.

[11] J. Schmookler, *Invention and Economic Growth,* Harvard, 1966.

[12] See N. Rosenberg, *Perspectives on Technology,* Cambridge, 1976, Chapter 15.

[13] The problems and opportunities of backwardness are well analysed by K. Ohkawa and H. Rosovsky, *Japanese Economic Growth,* Stanford, 1973, pp. 89-95 and 213-38.

[14] See W. Beckerman and Associates, *The British Economy in 1975,* NIESR, London, 1965, Chapter II, and A Lamfalussy, *The United Kingdom and the Six,* Macmillan, London, 1963. It should also be noted that the discussion of trade as an

'engine of growth' for developing countries is concerned mainly with the demand aspect See R. Nurkse, *Equilibrium and Growth in the World Economy,* Harvard, 1962, Chapter 11; and also I. B. Kravis, 'Trade as a Handmaiden of Growth: Similarities between the Nineteenth and Twentieth Centuries', *Economic Journal,* December 1970.

[15] In the 1870s most of the UK's big trade rivals raised their tariff levels and several launched themselves on the gold standard with deflationary policies. Both tended to reduce the UK's competitive position. See J. A. Schumpeter's comments, *History of Economic Analysis,* Allen & Unwin, London, 1963, p. 770.

[16] See E. F. Denison, *Why Growth Rates Differ,* Brookings Institution, Washington, 1967, and my comments on Denison in 'Explaining Economic Growth', *Banca Nazionale del Lavoro Quarterly Review,* September 1972, for an analysis of the postwar situation. See also T. Scitovsky, *Economic Theory and Western European Integration,* Allen & Unwin, London, 1958, who stresses the importance of competition but downplays the impact of greater specialization and scale economies as a result of postwar trade liberalization.

[17] The only case of a proportion slightly above 50 per cent was Switzerland in the first half of the 1960s.

[18] Output of government services is usually measured by the growth of labour input, and hence shows no productivity change except in so far as labour inputs are weighted by skill or education. Furthermore, no rent or depreciation is imputed for schools, roads, or other public assets, so the level of output and productivity in government appears lower to this extent. In housing services, there is the problem that the flow of output occurs with little or no labour input. These problems are discussed in detail in E. F. Denison, 'The Shift to Services and the Rate of Productivity Change', *Survey of Current Business,* October 1973. Denison avoids the problem by measuring productivity only in the non residential business sector. However, if one uses GDP as the aggregate measure of output, logic requires adherence to the same measurement conventions in sectoral analysis. In any case, the incidence of these particular statistical problems in services is rather similar in each country at a given level of aggregate real product. Apart from the statistical problems, there are conceptual difficulties involved in paritioning productivity gains into those that arise 'insector' and the gains from structural shifts. The 'joint product' of the two influences may be significant, and its partitioning is somewhat arbitrary; see A. Maddison, 'Productivity in An Expanding Economy', *Economic Journal,* September 1952, for a discussion of these conceptual problems.

[19] See E. F. Denison, *Why Growth Rates Differ*, Brookings Institution, Washington 1967, and G. L. Perry, 'Potential Output: Recent Issues and Present Trends', *Brookings Reprint,* 1978.

[20] See A. Maddison, 'Long-run dynamics of Productivity Growth', *Banca Nazionale del Lavoro Quarterly Review,* March 1979.

[21] See E. F. Denison, 'Effects of Selected Changes in the Institutional and Human Environment Upon Output per Unit of Input', *Survey of Current Business,* January 1978.

[22] See F. H. Hahn and R.C.O. Matthews, 'The Theory of Economic Growth: A Survey', *Economic Journal,* December 1964, p. 845.

[23] See N. Kaldor, *Causes of the Slow Rate of Economic Growth of the United Kingdom,* Cambridge, 1966, whose main point was the correlation between employment and productivity growth in manufacturing known as Verdoorn's Law; and 'The Irrelevance of Equilibrium Economics', *Economic Journal,* December 1972, where he adds a new argument about the three dimensional character of space.

CHAPTER 6 : **The Role of Policy in Economic Performance**

[1] See R. G. Lipsey, 'Structural and Demand Deficient Unemployment Reconsidered', in A. M. Ross (ed.), *Employment Policy and the Labor Market,* Berkeley, 1965.

[2] There is evidence that governmental budget activity stabilized output growth in six of the seven countries analysed by B. Hansen and W. W. Snyder, *Fiscal Policy in Seven Countries 1955-1965,* OECD, Paris, March 1969, p. 69, the only exception being the UK.

[3] See R. C. O. Matthews, 'Why has Britain Had Full Employment Since the War?', *Economic Journal,* September 1968.

[4] See H. G. Johnson, *Inflation and the Monetarist Controversy,* North Holland, Amsterdam, 1972, p. 6.

[5] See M. Friedman and A. J. Schwartz, *A Monetary History of the United States 1867-1960,* Princeton, 1963.

[6] See C. P. Kindleberger, *The World Depression 1929-1939,* Allen Lane, London, 1973; and A. Maddison, 'Economic Policy and Performance in Europe 1913-70' in C. M. Cipolla (ed.), *Fontana Economic History of Europe,* vol. 5 (2), Collins, London, 1978, for alternative views of the world crisis and its causes.

[7] See A. Leijonhufvud, *Keynes and the Classics,* Occasional Paper 30, Institute of Economic Affairs, London, 1969, p. 9: 'It is understandable that the infamous "Treasury View" looms large in British accounts of Keynes' efforts in this period, but it may be questioned whether it was held anywhere outside London'; and D. Patinkin's critique of Friedman's revisionist intellectual history, in 'The Chicago Tradition, the Quantity Theory and Friedman', *Journal of Money Credit and Banking,* February 1969.

[8] See W. H. Beveridge, *Full Employmet in a Free Society,* Allen & Unwin, London, 1944; R. Nurkse, *The Course and Control of Inflation,* League of Nations, 1946; and A. J. Brown, *The Great Inflation 1939-1951,* Oxford, 1955.

[9] For an intepretation of the Scandinavian inflationary mechanism under fixed exchange rates, see L. Calmfors, *Swedish Inflation and International Price Influences,* Institute for International Economic Studies, Stockholm, March 1975. In a small country in a fixed exchange rate system, the sector producing tradeables is a price-taker. Both employers and unions accept that wage increases should equal the sum of the world price increase plus domestic productivity growth. Wages in the non-traded sector follow those in the sector producing tradeables. This structuralist explanation of the Scandinavian inflation mechanism was developed simultaneously in Norway and Sweden: see O. Aukrust, 'Inflation in the Open Economy: A Norwegian Model', in L. B. Krause and W. S. Salant (eds), *World-wide Inflation,* Brookings Institution, Washington, 1977; and G. Edgren, K. O. Faxen, and C. E. Ohdner, *Wage Formation and The Economy,* Allen & Unwin, London, 1973.

[10] See C. A. R. Crosland, *The Future of Socialism,* Jonathan Cape, London, 1956, p. 211; J. K. Galbraith, *The Affluent Society,* Hamish Hamilton, London, 1958; G. Myrdal, *Beyond the Welfare State,* Duckworth, 1960; and D. Bell, *The End of Ideology,* Free Press, New York, 1960.

[11] See M. Friedman, 'The Role of Monetary Policy', *American Economic Review,* March 1968, p. 11. E. S. Phelps made essentially the same point about adaptive processes in inflationary expectations at about the same time as Friedman: see 'Phillips Curves, Expectations of Inflation and Optimal Unemployment Over Time', *Economica,* August 1967.

[12] A more optimistic view of the 1970s is reflected in P. McCracken *et al.,* *Towards Full Employment and Price Stability,* OECD, Paris, June 1977, p. 103: 'A key conclusion we draw from this assessment of factors underlying recent experience, is that the most important feature was an unusual bunching of unfortunate events

unlikely to be repeated on the same scale, the impact of which was compounded by some avoidable errors in economic policy... this upheaval is not necessarily a sign of permanent change to an inevitably more unstable and inflationary world'.

[13] See Bank for International Settlements, *Forty-Third Annual Report,* June 1973, pp. 167-71.

[14] See S. E. Rolfe and J. L. Burtle, *The Great Wheel: The World Monetary System,* McGraw-Hill, New York, 1973, for a lively description of US policy in this period.

[15] The official attempts to reform Bretton Woods were concerned mainly with liquidity problems and the change in the nature of reserves. They had minor success in creating special drawing rights (SDRs) which augmented reserves somewhat: see J. Williamson, *The Failure of World Monetary Reform, 1971-74,* Nelson, London, 1977, for an analysis of official attempts to reform the system.

[16] O. Emminger, 'The Exchange Rate as an Instrument of Policy', *Lloyds Bank Review,* July 1979, p. 4.

[17] P. M. Oppenheimer, 'Why Have General Anti-Inflation Policies Not Succeeded?' in E. Lundberg (ed.), *Inflation Theory and Anti-Inflation Policy,* Macmillan, London, 1977.

[18] The 1973 boom did not have the same intensity in all Western countries. The UK was the most extreme case, with a rise in GDP of 8 per cent—almost three times its postwar norm,—whereas in Germany 1973 was a year of normal expansion.

[19] See D. E. Hathaway, 'Food Prices and Inflation', *Brookings Papers on Economic Activity,* no. 1, 1974.

[20] W. D. Nordhaus, 'The Worldwide Wage Explosion', *Brookings Papers on Economic Activity,* no. 2, 1972, for a succinct and sophisticated review and testing of ten different hypothetical causes of what by the standards of those days appeared to be a wage explosion. They included monetarist, naive Phillips Curve, expectations augmented Phillips Curve, real income frustration, critical threshold, trade union militancy, demographic, increased labour reservation price, Scandinavian, and devaluation types of causality. See also M. Scott and R. A. Laslett, *Can We Get Back to Full Employment?* Macmillan, London, 1978, for a more recent analysis of 'marksmen, militants, and mixers' theories. For more sociological explanations of these phenomena, see C. Crouch and A. Pizzórno, *The Resurgence of Class Conflict in Western Europe since 1968,* Macmillan, London, 1978; and F. Hirsch and J. H. Goldthorpe, *The Political Economy of Inflation,* Martin Robertson, London, 1978; A. Glyn and D. Sutcliffe, *British Capitalism, Workers and the Profits Squeeze,* Penguin, Harmondsworth, 1972, is an interesting example of the burgeoning academic Marxist literature of the 1970s, which analyses the possibility that union militancy may squeeze profits and hence destroy capitalism.

[21] Between 1973 and 1980, developing country indebtedness rose from $119 billion to $446 billion: see OECD, *Development Cooperation, 1980 Review,* Paris, 1980, p. 220.

[22] For Friedman's views on policy, see 'The Counter-Revolution in Monetary Theory', and 'Unemployment Versus Inflation?', *Occasional Papers,* IEA, London, nos. 33 and 44 respectively, 1970, and 1975; see also *The Optimum Quantity of Money and Other Essays,* Aldine, Chicago, 1969. For a refutation of monetarist theories of fiscal impotence, see A. S. Blinder and R. M. Solow, 'Analytical Foundations of Fiscal Policy', in A. S. Blinder, *et al., The Economics of Public Finance,* Brookings Institution, Washington, 1974; see also A. T. Peacock and G. K. Shaw; 'Is Fiscal Policy Dead?', in *Banca Nazionale del Lavoro Quarterly Review,* June 1978. For a reply to the monetarist views on the inevitability of hyperinflation, see F. Modigliani, 'The Monetarist Controversy or Should we Forsake Stabilisation Policies?? *American Economic Review,* March 1977, p. 12. Modigliani quotes the Friedman argument: 'An attempt at stabilizing the economy

at full employment is bound to be destabilizing because the full employment or natural rate is not known with certainty and is subject to shifts in time; and if we aim for the incorrect rate, the result must perforce be explosive inflation or deflation. By contrast, with a constant money supply policy, the economy will automatically hunt for and eventually discover, that shifting natural rate, wherever it may be hiding.' He replies thus: 'This argument, I submit, is nothing but a debating ploy. It rests on the preposterous assumption that the only alternative to a constant money growth is the pursuit of a very precise unemployment target which will be adhered to indefinitely no matter what, and that if the target is off in the second decimal place, galloping inflation is round the corner. In reality all that is necessary to pursue stabilization policies is a rough target range that includes the warranted rate, itself a range and not a razor edge.'

[23] See G. C. Watkins and M. A. Walker, *Reaction: The National Energy Program,* Fraser Institute, Vancouver, 1981, for a critique of Canadian policy.

[24] See A. Maddison, 'Monitoring the Labour Market', *Review of Income and Wealth,* June 1980.

APPENDIX A : Sources and Methods Used to Measure Output Levels and Growth

[1] The new standardized system is described in *A System of National Accounts,* UN, New York, 1968. The previous system is described in *A Standardised System of National Accounts,* OEEC, Paris, 1959. For our purposes, the two systems are virtually identical.

[2] See A. Maddison, 'Phases of Capitalist Development', *Banca Nazionale del Lavoro Quarterly Review,* June 1977, pp. 121-4 for a discussion of these problems.

[3] See A. Maddison, 'Comparative Productivity Levels in the Developed Countries, *Banca Nazionale del Lavoro Quarterly Review*, December 1967, for a more detailed exposition of the same point.

[4] Sauvy's estimates for this period seem reasonable when checked against estimates of wartime agricultural and industrial output. See M. Cepède, *Agriculture et alimentation en France durant la IIe guerre mondiale,* Genin, Paris, 1961, and *Annuaire de statistique industrielle 1938-1947,* Ministère de l'Industrie et du Commerce, Paris, 1948.

[5] See A. Maddison, 'Phases of Capitalist Development', *Banca Nazionale del Lavoro Quarterly Review,* June 1977, pp. 133-4, for full details.

[6] See R. Davis, *The Rise of the English Shipping Industry,* Macmillan, London, 1962, p. 27, for the size of British fleets; and W. Vogel, 'Zur Grösse der europaischen Handelsflotten im 15., 16. and 17. Jahrhundert', Festschrift D. Schäfer, *Forschungen und Versuche zur Geschichte des Mittelalters und der Neuzeit,* G. Fischer, Jena, 1915, p. 331, for Dutch shipping.

[7] H. C. Bos, 'Economic Growth of the Netherlands', IARIW, Portoroz, 1959 (mimeographed) presented a rough estimate of Dutch per capita income in 1688 compared with 1910, which is not different from my estimate, though the approach is quite different.

[8] The movement in our estimates for the USA between 1840 and 1889 is very similar to those of T. S. Berry, *Revised Annual Estimates of American Gross National Product: Preliminary Annual Estimates of Four Major Components of Demand,* Bostwick Press, Virginia, 1978, which is not surprising, as they are both benchmarked on Gallman. Before 1840 Berry's estimates show faster growth than David's.

APPENDIX C : **Labour Input and Labour Productivity**

[1] See C. D. Long, *The Labor Force Under Changing Income and Employment,* NBER, Princeton, 1958, pp. 408-32, for details.

[2] The following have been important factors affecting female activity: declines in fertility have meant that they had fewer children to bear and rear; schools have played a growing role as child-minders; household responsibilities have been discharged more productively because of improved equipment in the home and more outside purchases of food and clothing previously provided within the household; shorter work weeks and the greater availability of job opportunities in the service sector have increased possibilities for female employment; women are faced with less discrimination and have better education relative to males than in the past; the reduction in activity by youth and older workers has itself created new job possibilities for women. See Long, op. cit., pp. 268-9 for a discussion of this problem. A more recent discussion of United States trends can be found in W. G. Bowen and T. A. Finegan, *The Economics of Labor Force Participation,* Princeton, 1969.

[3] In making such adjustments, we kept the interests of international comparability in mind. Thus for the USA, where the 1910 census showed higher female activity in agriculture than subsequent censuses, we adjusted the subsequent years upwards to conform to the 1910 ratio. S. Lebergott, *Manpower in Economic Growth,* McGraw-Hill, New York, 1964, makes the reverse adjustment for the United States; i.e., he adjusts the 1910 rate downwards. Similarly, in adjusting for vagaries in the female activity rate in Austria from one census to another, we adjusted the exceptionally high 1910 rate downwards, closer to the lower ratio shown in the 1920 Austrian census.

[4] See ILO, *International Recommendations on Labour Statistics,* Geneva, 1976, p. 28.

[5] In this respect, the following estimates differ from those I presented earlier in *Economic Growth in the West,* Allen & Unwin, 1964, p. 211, where the census concept was the master link, and the OECD/ILO-type data were used simply to show movements from 1950 onwards.

[6] See A. Maddison, 'Economic Growth and Structural Change in the Advanced Countries', in I. Leveson and J. W. Wheeler, *Western Economies in Transition,* Croom Helm, London, 1980, for a more detailed analysis of structural changes.

[7] See *International Recommendations on Labour Statistics,* ILO, Geneva, 1976.

[8] See *Measuring Employment and Unemployment,* OECD, Paris, 1979.

[9] See Maddison, *Economic Growth in the West,* p. 225, for a discussion of the data available on working hours for this period.

APPENDIX D : **Non-residential Reproducible Tangible Fixed Capital Stock**

[1] In 1978 the ratio of net to gross non-residential capital stock was 65.4 per cent in Canada, 59.9 per cent in France, 69.8 per cent in Germany, 63.7 per cent in the UK and 59.1 per cent in the USA, according to the official sources cited in the country notes below.

[2] E. F. Denison, *Why Growth Rates Differ,* Brookings Institution, Washington, DC, 1967, p. 141, and J. W. Kendrick, *Productivity Trends in the United States,* NBER, Princeton, 1961, pp. 35-6.

[3] See R. W. Goldsmith, *The National Wealth of the United States in the Postwar Period,* NBER, 1962, Chapter 3, for a discussion of the algebra of capital stock estimates.

[4] When official capital stock estimates were first made, the lives implicit in the depreciation allowances set by tax authorities were often taken as a guide (present tax

depreciation practice is described in OECD, *International Comparison of Tax Depreciation Practices,* Paris, 1975), but most official statisticians now use longer lives than those in the tax code.

[5] My conclusion on this point is based on Table D2. It is different from that of Denison, *Why Growth Rates Differ,* p. 425, who suggests on the basis of US evidence that differences in length-of-life assumptions do not affect the capital stock estimates very much. However, it is clear even from the evidence he presents that significant differences may arise.

[6] The only official estimate with a vintage bonus is one of the variants presented by Mairesse for France. This produces a very high growth of capital stock, but it would seem that his bonus (5 per cent annual for machinery and equipment and 2 per cent for structures) is unreasonably high, for reasons discussed by Denison, *Why Growth Rates Differ,* p. 149.

[7] This is not true in Canada, where a study by Koumanakos has shown estimates quite sensitive to different assumptions, but some of those used by Koumanakos are quite extreme and have not been used in Canada or elsewhere.

[8] Their impact is illustrated graphically by M. Ward, *The Measurement of Capital,* OECD, Paris, 1976.

[9] However, there are some exceptions. In Germany and Italy no depreciation is made on certain government assets, and in the UK a few assets such as ships and Post Office capital are not subject to straight-line depreciation.

[10] In principle, most countries appear to follow the line laid down by Denison, *Why Growth Rates Differ,* p. 134; i.e., the price deflator is designed to measure changes in the cost of producing capital goods and not their capacity to produce other goods.

[11] The deflators for investment will not be the same as those for the capital stock because the relative weight of individual assets is different; e.g., construction has a greater weight in the capital stock than in investment, because construction investment has a longer life than that of other assets.

[12] Another INSEE study worthy of note is a comparison of French and German capital stocks using French methods: see *Efficacité et rentabilité des systèmes productifs en République Fédérale d'Allemagne et en France,* INSEE, June 1977.

[13] See E. F. Denison and W. K. Chung, *How Japan's Economy Grew so Fast,* Brookings Institution, Washington, DC, 1976, pp. 220-1.

[14] For an account of the official methodology, see *National Account Statistics: Sources and Methods,* CSO, London, pp. 383-7; T. J. Griffin, 'Revised Estimates of the Consumption and Stock of Fixed Capital', *Economic Trends,* October 1975; T. J. Griffin, 'The Stock of Fixed Assets in the United Kingdom: How to Make the Best Use of the Statistics', *Economic Trends,* October 1976.

[15] G. A. Dean, 'The Stock of Fixed Capital in the United Kingdom in 1961', *Journal of the Royal Statistical Society,* series A, 127, 1964.

[16] These lives are longer than those in force for tax purposes since 1962. See *Survey of Current Business* December 1966, p. 35.

INDEX

Abel, W. 7, 12
Abramovitz, M. 73-7
advancing agrarianism 6, 13
agrarianism 4, 5
agricultural land 9-10, 15, 17, 39, 46-7, 257
agricultural policy (US), 135, 140
agricultural productivity 116-21, 259
agricultural technique 10, 34, 47, 258-9
agriculture, British 258-9; Dutch 29, 33
allocation of resources 59, 60, 62, 97, 99, 101-2, 113; 115, 122-4, 156
Arrow, K. J. 105, 123
Aukrust, O. 266

Bairoch, P. 38, 118, 161-2, 180, 196, 243, 245, 254, 258-9
balance of payments 27, 130, 134, 143-4, 147, 149-50, 154, 157
Beckerman, W. 111, 264
Bell, D. 136, 266
best-practice 22, 104-5, 108
Beveridge, W.H. 26, 266
Bienefeld, M. A. 201
Blaug, M. 256
Bombach, G. 103, 259, 264
Bos, H. C. 245, 258, 268
Boserup, E. 255
Braudel, F. P. 12-13, 255-6
Bresciani-Turroni, C. 244
Bretton Woods, see international payments system
Brown, A. J. 266
Burns, A. F. 58, 261-2
business cycles 18-20, 26, 60-1, 64-6, 87, 97-102, 129-30, 133-7, 156

Calmfors, L. 266
capital: foreign 33, 37-40, 128; per worker or man hour 15, 54, 109-10; replacement widening and deeping 15; role in economic growth 18; stock 5, 14, 19, 23-4, 46, 53-6, 95, 100, 109-10, (British) 37, (US) 39; and technical progress 22, 24, 56-7; vintages 15, 22, 105; see also human capital
capitalism 4, 5, 6, 15-16, 43; breakdown

theories 18, 79; interpretations (Marx) 18, 19, (Ricardo) 16, 17, (Schumpeter) 19-21, 'late' 82; merchant 13-15; phases 64-95
Cipolla, C. M. 180, 255, 258, 266
Clark, C. 21, 47, 166-7
Club of Rome 47
conflict: social 2, 28, 135-6, 157; class 5, 17, 18
conjuncture 97, 101, 102
Crosland, C. A. R. 136, 266
Crouzet, F. 244
currency, see exchange rates and international payments system
cycle, see business cycles

Deane, P. 35, 40, 165, 167, 180, 245
deindustrialization 17, 116; see also 'industrialization'
demand management 26, 84, 90, 92, 94, 99-102, 108-9, 111, 115, 124, 127-8, 136, 140, 144-6, 153-7
demography, see fertility, mortality, migration, and population
Denison, E. F. 23-4, 94, 102, 114, 122, 164, 203, 215-16, 257, 263, 265, 269-70
depression, see business cycles
Dobb, M. 256

economic epochs 1, 4-28
economic indicators, see indicators of economic performance
economic policy 14-15, 17, 19, 25-7, 32, 35-8, 78, 82-4, 94-5, 99-100, 111-15, 126-57
economies of scale and specialization 14, 36, 46, 59-62, 114, 123
Edgren, G. 266
education 16, 23, 37, 52, 110-11
Emminger, O. 139, 266
employment: full 95, 268
energy 48, 101-2, 124, 142-4, 149-52; see also oil and OPEC
entrepreneurs and entrepreneurship 19-20, 78-9, 112, 123, 257
exchange rates 33, 38; fixed 113, 133-4,